SOTL RESEARCH METHODOLOGIES

Combining real examples with a roadmap of how to construct studies, analyze results, and share work, this book serves as a primary research methodology text for the field of Scholarship of Teaching and Learning (SoTL).

The volume seeks to explore key aspects of SoTL that are often missing in past frameworks: research-based ontologies, epistemologies, and ethical axiologies. Chapters map out the expansive continuum of SoTL by detailing its history and key work while incorporating Indigenous perspectives on pedagogy and research methodologies. The text also features methods of qualitative and quantitative data generation essential for SoTL such as conducting interviews and focus groups, procuring data through questionnaires and artifact observation, and sharing results for dissemination in traditional and public scholarship.

A comprehensive guide for conducting SoTL research, this book illustrates a broad array of contexts and a spectrum of research methodologies to expand, enrich, and support both novice and experienced SoTL practitioners and researchers in answering the contexts and questions at the heart of teaching and learning.

Michelle Yeo is Professor and Director of the Mokakiiks Centre for the Scholarship of Teaching and Learning at Mount Royal University, Canada.

Janice Miller-Young is Professor of Mechanical Engineering at the University of Alberta, Canada.

Karen Manarin is Professor of English at Mount Royal University, Canada.

SOTL RESEARCH METHODOLOGIES

A Guide to Conceptualizing and Conducting the Scholarship of Teaching and Learning

Michelle Yeo, Janice Miller-Young, and Karen Manarin

Routledge
Taylor & Francis Group
NEW YORK AND LONDON

Designed cover image: © Getty Images

First published 2024
by Routledge
605 Third Avenue, New York, NY 10158

and by Routledge
4 Park Square, Milton Park, Abingdon, Oxon OX14 4RN

Routledge is an imprint of the Taylor & Francis Group, an informa business

Library of Congress Cataloging-in-Publication Data
Names: Yeo, Michelle M. L., author. | Miller-Young, Janice, author. | Manarin, Karen, author.
Title: SoTL research methodologies : a guide to conceptualizing and conducting the scholarship of teaching and learning / Michelle Yeo, Janice Miller-Young, and Karen Manarin.
Description: New York, NY : Routledge, 2024. |
Includes bibliographical references.
Subjects: LCSH: Teaching--Research--Methodology. |
Learning--Research--Methodology. | Learning and scholarship.
Classification: LCC LB1028 .Y45 2024 (print) | LCC LB1028 (ebook) |
DDC 370.721--dc23/eng/20230821
LC record available at https://lccn.loc.gov/2023025747
LC ebook record available at https://lccn.loc.gov/2023025748

ISBN: 978-1-642-67240-4 (hbk)
ISBN: 978-1-642-67241-1 (pbk)
ISBN: 978-1-003-44705-4 (ebk)

DOI: 10.4324/9781003447054

Typeset in Galliard
by Taylor & Francis Books

CONTENTS

ILLUSTRATIONS

Figures

Tables

PREFACE

This book is intended for practitioners of the Scholarship of Teaching and Learning (SoTL), as the first research methodology text of its kind written specifically for the field. In our work with SoTL researchers, both novice and experienced, and indeed in our own research endeavors we have often felt the need for such a book. We finally decided to write it.

As a movement, SoTL is usually traced back to the work of Boyer (1990), who defined four overlapping types of scholarship in the academy—scholarship of discovery, scholarship of application, scholarship of teaching (now termed Scholarship of Teaching and Learning), and scholarship of integration. In the more than thirty intervening years, SoTL has grown to receive more awareness and emphasis at post-secondary institutions, as the importance of high-quality teaching has gained attention. Early work conceptualized SoTL as flowing from the questions and problems that instructors encounter in their everyday work with students, originally conceived of in fairly narrow terms as practitioner research. While this practitioner focus remains at the heart of SoTL, it has expanded, and now includes a broader array of contexts and questions, requiring a spectrum of research methodologies to investigate them.

There are many distinctions to be made—between SoTL, educational research, and discipline-based educational research; between quantitative and qualitative research; and between research paradigms that reflect radically different worldviews. Because SoTL is conducted by researchers from the gamut of academic disciplines, the landscape or what is often referred to as the "big tent" of SoTL (Huber & Hutchings, 2005) represents heterogeneous groups consisting of disciplinary experts in their respective fields, who also are curious about teaching and learning. This tent can be thought of as a meeting place where very different ideas about what research is, how it should be conducted, and how it should be shared all come together in a space that is at once generative and potentially conflicting.

This complex space is really why we wrote this book. We are all SoTL researchers and have facilitated development programs with new SoTL researchers. In seeking information about how to go about conducting SoTL research in the literature, while there are many excellent resources we refer to in this book, we found there was no one resource that combined a high-level map along with concrete information about how to construct a study, how to analyze results, and how to share the work, illustrated with SoTL examples. We hope that this book will be useful to a variety of people across post-secondary institutions and beyond. We have written the book with the novice SoTL researcher at the forefront of our minds, as they try to make sense of a relatively new, diverse, and complex field that is still developing.

Many new SoTL researchers are highly trained researchers in their home discipline, but often moving into the SoTL space asks that they learn new approaches, methodologies, and methods that are unfamiliar, and may even seem to conflict with what they have come to understand about research practice. In a sense, this book is especially designed with these highly accomplished academics—yet novice SoTL researchers—in mind. But we also wrote this book to expand, enrich, and support experienced SoTL researchers as well. In the beginning, the discourse of SoTL was necessarily limited to a relatively small number of people, representing the perspectives of those who had the vision to create the movement in the first place. We think it important that SoTL researchers become familiar with these voices, but also to recognize how the field has developed and evolved. We think it important, as we proceed, that SoTL not allow itself the luxury of an echo chamber, with the same small group of researchers simply citing one another. Thus, we are also writing to researchers in discipline-based educational research and education research more broadly. We think it critical that these fields talk to one another. SoTL, for all that it is a relatively "new" field with a few short decades of work to its name, can benefit greatly from the range and depth of teaching and learning research that has come before. This relationship is bi-directional, however, and we note increasing interest from these longer-standing disciplines. We wrote this book, too, for educational developers and leaders who may be similarly working with novice SoTL researchers. And last, but certainly not least, we hope that SoTL-engaged students may find this book useful and of interest.

How to Use This Book

While new SoTL researchers (we use the terms "SoTL researcher" and "SoTL practitioner" interchangeably throughout) may be keen to progress straight to the pragmatic elements of actually conducting the work, we encourage any reader of this text to begin with the chapters that make up the first section. These foundational ideas will help to make sense of the wide variety of designs and methodologies described in subsequent chapters. Indeed it is our position that some of what has been missing in SoTL is a strong understanding of how various research methodologies rest on a foundation of different world views (ontologies), different understandings of how that world can be known (epistemologies), and different values and ethical considerations (axiologies).

Part I is an introduction to the field and to the spectrum of research methodologies found in SoTL. In Chapter 1, we will introduce the developing movement of SoTL—a bit about its history, and some of the key early work that has shaped the field. In Chapter 2, we will explore where SoTL questions come from, and think about different ways these questions can be framed. Since SoTL work can encompass everything from positivistic to transformative perspectives, with critical realist and interpretive approaches in between, in Chapter 3 we map out this continuum and describe the world-views that underlie the various perspectives. These beliefs about the world and about knowledge shape all subsequent decisions about how the research is carried out. We incorporate, as well, Indigenous perspectives on pedagogy and research methodologies in this and Part III, which while holding elements in common to the paradigms we describe, also sits wholly outside of Western knowledge systems.

Part II explores some of the many ways SoTL researchers can generate data to answer their research questions. Mainly, we can gather data that has been generated for some other purpose (like grades, assignments, or documents); we can ask people to respond to us (whether in written, oral, or pictorial form); we can observe them doing something; or we can reflect. These different types of data can reveal rich and provocative insights about teaching and learning, but they are fundamentally different. Chapter 4 describes generating quantitative data, and one of the most common ways to do this, through questionnaires. Chapter 5 addresses how to design and conduct interviews and focus groups, whereas Chapter 6 explores gathering data through artifacts, observation, and reflection.

Part III is a more detailed exploration of the methodologies introduced in the first part—if Part I answers the question of "why," then Part III addresses the "how" of analysis—what to do once you have your data. Depending upon your research paradigm and your question, you might be approaching this through quantitative and statistical analysis (Chapter 7), through a qualitative empirical lens (Chapter 8), mixed methods (Chapter 9), or you may be using what we will describe as one of the "Big Q" methodologies found in the interpretive (Chapter 10) or transformative (Chapter 11) chapters. It is worth mentioning here that while most SoTL work involves collecting data, other methods such as a philosophical method can be pursued.

Part IV addresses one of the principal tenets of scholarship: that what we learn about teaching and learning must be shared with others. Lee Shulman (1993) boldly called for an end to pedagogical solitude, insisting that we make teaching "community property," by evaluating artifacts beyond student evaluations of instruction or classroom visits. Huber and Hutchings (2005) call for the development of the "teaching commons" and insist on the idea of "going public" with what we have learned about teaching and learning. For a long time, this "going public" has meant participating in traditional academic genres, including scholarly articles, conference presentations, and grant proposals. More recently, scholars like Chick and Friberg (2022) have argued that we need to try to reach a wider public beyond the academy. In Chapter 12 we explore common academic genres of SoTL, while in Chapter 13 we give some advice on how to present quantitative and qualitative data visually. In Chapter 14 we consider ways you might amplify your work, to academic and non-academic audiences, through a variety of channels, and contemplation of SoTL as public scholarship. In "Final Thoughts," we close the book with a summary and some considerations for the future.

Who We Are and What We Bring to This Work

With such a broad and ambitious scope for the book, readers may wonder who we are and what knowledge and experiences inform the writing of this book. We began working together in 2009, as faculty members involved in the inaugural "SoTL Scholars Program" at Mount Royal University. Janice and Karen were participants seeking support for developing SoTL inquiry projects related to their teaching of Engineering and English undergraduate courses, respectively. Michelle, an educational researcher and developer, was recruited to help facilitate. In addition to conducting and publishing these first SoTL studies, we began to collaborate by researching the program itself in terms of the experiences of participants, including our own, and to develop resources and programs to help other faculty conduct SoTL research projects. We each also sought other opportunities to learn about conducting and facilitating SoTL by joining scholarly associations, serving on ethics boards, engaging in multidisciplinary communities of practice and collaborative writing groups, and ultimately taking on formal leadership roles (Figure 0.1). While we each have our own research agendas and disciplinary topics of interest, we continue to collaborate and learn from each other, especially about research methodologies and their associated assumptions, languages, and conventions. This book represents our multi-year effort to expand and elaborate upon what we have found to be a useful framework for conceptualizing and communicating SoTL (Miller-Young & Yeo, 2015) from our previous, commonly cited article into a book.

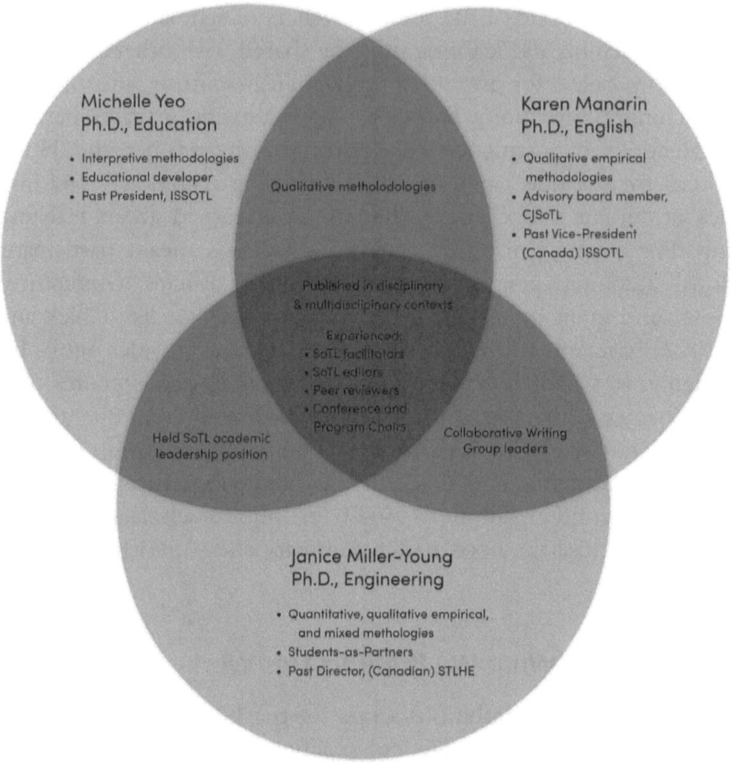

FIGURE 0.1 The authors' overlapping and distinct experiences in SoTL are represented in a Venn diagram.

Once we made the decision to include Indigenous methodologies and pedagogies in the book, we knew that, as white settler scholars, we would need to include the voice of an Indigenous scholar. We are incredibly grateful for the guest author contributions of our colleague Dr. Gabrielle Weasel Head, a member of the Kainaiwa Nation, part of the Blackfoot Confederacy; she comes to this work positioned as an Indigenous scholar deeply embedded in her Blackfoot ancestral ways of knowing. Gabrielle's additions to this book have been critical—we have noted her as an author on the sections specifically regarding Indigenous methodologies, but she also made other invaluable contributions throughout. It is her perspective that helps make our own positionality within Western knowledge systems visible to ourselves.

Advice to Begin

We are excited to join you on some part of your journey in SoTL, whether you have been working in the field for many years, or just starting out. We encourage you to start small. Like any other field, SoTL cannot be mastered overnight. But as you start in a stepwise manner, it's also worth surveying the big picture. As Michelle remembers Tony Angelo once describing at a conference in reference to learning—in order to learn to dance, we need a lot of time on the dance floor, but it's also worth climbing up to the balcony once in a while to get a broader view. We hope that this book provides you with a good balance of the balcony and the ballroom floor. As you travel between them, be open to learning from other disciplines, check in to make sure you are understanding and respecting others using different methodologies and perspectives. We ourselves encountered many of our own disciplinary biases and ways of thinking as we co-authored this book. So we can say from experience: take advantage of as many opportunities to learn as possible and be comfortable with being uncomfortable. SoTL has a reputation as a welcoming place, and we hope that this book can be part of your early or continued welcome.

ACKNOWLEDGMENTS

We would like to thank Dr. Cherie Woolmer, Canada Research Chair in SoTL at Mount Royal University, who provided contributions, feedback, and advice on the sections regarding Students-as-Partners, where she has both expertise and a great deal of experience. She also assisted in conceptualizing the idea of sharing SoTL with students as a form of knowledge mobilization in Chapter 14.

We would like to acknowledge the Office of the Provost at the University of Alberta, and the Mokakiiks Centre for Scholarship of Teaching and Learning for providing the funding to support our undergraduate information design student, Jayden Fandrick, who created the figures for this book. Jayden helped us communicate complex ideas in visual form. We would also like to thank Dr. Nancy Chick for her enthusiastic support of our proposal, and our editor from Stylus Publishing, David Brightman, who shepherded our book through its early stages.

We were supported by our institutions (Mount Royal University and the University of Alberta) in writing this book through the granting of sabbatical leaves, and for this we are grateful. We are also grateful for the many conversations we have had with novice and less novice practitioners of SoTL.

PART I

Thinking About SoTL

1

UNDERSTANDING SOTL

In this chapter, we introduce the reader to the Scholarship of Teaching and Learning (SoTL), highlighting some key moments of its global history. We also distinguish between SoTL and scholarly teaching on the one hand and SoTL and educational research on the other. Recognizing the diversity of methodological approaches and assumptions, we consider how to judge SoTL before identifying common ethical considerations in a wide range of disciplines and professional fields.

What Is the Scholarship of Teaching and Learning (SoTL)?

You might have heard about SoTL through your Teaching and Learning Center, at various conferences, or in publications about teaching and learning. But what is it exactly? Is it the same as scholarly teaching? And how does it differ from educational research conducted by people in Education faculties on the one hand and disciplinary-based educational research (DBER) on the other? Can anyone do it? If people from diverse backgrounds with different concepts of scholarship and methodologies can conduct SoTL research, how can we judge quality?

A Rose by Any Other Name? The Importance of Definitions

Over the past three decades, SoTL has been promoted in higher education as a way for academics across disciplines to improve teaching through evidence-based practices. Of course, educational research both within higher education disciplines and the primary and secondary levels existed long before the term SoTL was coined, and the term itself has been used in

DOI: 10.4324/9781003447054-2

various ways. Gurung and Schwartz (2009) argue for the term "pedagogical research" as "less value-laden" than SoTL (p. 2), a claim that humanities scholars might challenge given assumptions around "research" vs. "scholarship" (Kyd, 2010; Manarin, 2016). Gurung and Schwartz (2009) position pedagogical research as a larger umbrella term that includes SoTL, action or teacher research (terms usually associated with how students learn and teachers teach in K–12 settings), and scholarly teaching. They also recognize the importance of DBER, claiming that "Just as a rose by any another [sic] name is still a rose, so too research on teaching and learning is still essentially pedagogical research, no matter what discipline the research is based in" (p. 3). Norton (2009), on the other hand, sees pedagogical action research by university lecturers as a subset of the broader field of SoTL; she connects it to Bass's (1999) call to rethink teaching "problems" as something worth investigating in a recurring spiral: identify problem, think of ways to tackle problem, do or implement the intervention, evaluate the intervention, modify future practice (pp. 70–71). This is a common, though not the only, way to generate SoTL questions, but first let's explore some of the differences between SoTL, scholarly teaching, and DBER. We believe that practitioners in all of these areas will find useful information in this book; however, our main focus is SoTL.

SoTL and Scholarly Teaching

The term SoTL is relatively new, even though scholarly inquiry into how people teach and learn goes back centuries. Ernest Boyer is often credited with beginning the SoTL movement. In *Scholarship Reconsidered: Priorities of the Professoriate* (1990), he argued for the importance of "the Scholarship of Teaching," or what some might now call scholarly teaching (Potter & Kustra, 2011; Richlin & Cox, 2004). This movement to recognize the intellectual work required to teach well at the post-secondary level sought to transform higher education by transforming reward structures. Proponents began to emphasize the importance of sharing insights and building knowledge beyond individual classrooms (Hutchings & Shulman, 1999). For example, in 2000, *Higher Education Research and Development* published a special issue on the Scholarship of Teaching (Martin & Ramsden, 2000). Following a paradigm shift from teaching to learning (Barr & Tagg, 1995), the movement added the word "learning" to its name, and in 2001, the first international conference on SoTL occurred in London. Since then, SoTL journals, societies, and development programs have developed in many places.

But what is it exactly? SoTL is sometimes described as a "systematic reflection on teaching and learning made public" (McKinney, 2004), but this definition doesn't describe what systematic reflection or going public

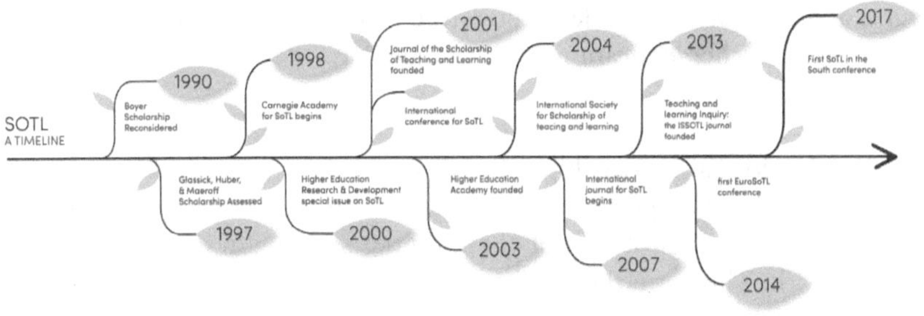

FIGURE 1.1 Key Moments in SoTL: branches of SoTL shaped by local and international contexts.

looks like or how the assumptions that underlie our concepts of teaching and learning influence, not only our methods, but also our findings. Weimer (2006) includes both "wisdom of practice" articles, focusing primarily on the author's experiences, and research articles, involving data beyond the author's reflections, in her typology of scholarly work on teaching and learning. Hutchings, Huber, and Ciccone (2011) note that

> the scholarship of teaching and learning encompasses a broad set of practices that engage teachers in looking closely and critically at student learning in order to improve their own courses and programs, and to share insights with other educators who can evaluate and build on their efforts. (*p. xix*)

This definition provides a few more details in terms of practice and purpose, but still doesn't offer a lot of specific guidance. It also doesn't address the issue of learning theories underpinning our practices in the classroom and our investigations to improve these practices. As McKinney (2004) notes, "Definitions tend to focus on activities or processes" (p. 6), but often they are very general—in part because proponents of SoTL don't want to exclude particular disciplines or approaches and in part because teaching and learning are remarkably complex and context dependent.

SoTL practitioners' desire to be inclusive manifests in metaphors. Proponents of SoTL will talk of the "big tent" approach, an image proposed by Huber and Hutchings (2005). They suggest that all faculty members should be involved in SoTL if SoTL is seen as systematic reflection about teaching and learning. They don't expect all faculty members to publish SoTL articles in peer-reviewed journals, but they want to build the "teaching commons," another influential metaphor for SoTL, where faculty and students share knowledge about teaching and learning in various forms. Dan Bernstein (2010) argues that "the goal of SOTL is to have every teacher treat every course as an opportunity to learn how to create better learning environments and generate richer educational experiences" (p. 4). Lee Shulman (2000) argues that

> We develop a scholarship of teaching when our work as teachers becomes public, peer-reviewed and critiqued. And exchanged with members of our professional communities so they, in turn, can build on our work. These are the qualities of all scholarship.
>
> *(p. 50)*

"Big tent" SoTL, then, encompasses a wide range of activities.

In contrast to "the big tent" approach to SoTL activities, some, like Potter and Kustra (2011) and McKinney (2014), argue that SoTL requires definitional parameters. As McKinney notes, "If SoTL becomes everything, it is nothing." Potter and Kustra distinguish between SoTL, which they define as

> the systematic study of teaching and learning, using established or validated criteria of scholarship, to understand how teaching (beliefs, behaviors, attitudes, and values) can maximize learning, and/or develop a more accurate understanding of learning, resulting in products that are publicly shared for critique and use by an appropriate community,
>
> *(p. 2)*

and scholarly teaching, "teaching grounded in critical reflection using systematically and strategically gathered evidence, related and explained by well-reasoned theory and philosophical understanding, with the goal of maximizing learning through effective teaching" (p. 3). They argue that SoTL and scholarly teaching are distinct constructs (p. 5), but "At the heart of both is critically-reflective practice, behaviors informed by critical reflection on one's beliefs, attitudes, values and practices, and their effects on student learning" (p. 11). Chick (2017) argues for the importance of reading SoTL as a scholarly teacher. In this book, we focus primarily on the principles and practices that underpin SoTL as formal scholarship, even though many of the elements we discuss can also contribute to a robust practice of scholarly teaching. Indeed, SoTL practitioners may find themselves moving back and forth along a continuum from formal studies to scholarly teaching. For this reason, we use the terms SoTL practitioners and SoTL researchers interchangeably in this book.

SoTL and Educational Research, Including DBER

Some may argue that formal research into teaching and learning requires a type of expertise that most faculty do not have. As Geertsema (2016) notes,

"Given that the vast majority of faculty are neither social scientists nor specialists in education, they do not know the methods of the social sciences, nor do they have extensive familiarity with the literature and discourse of education" (p. 123). After all, "Like other fields of study and disciplines, education has research traditions and a culture revolving around ways of knowing, knowledge buildng [sic] and knowledge construction" (Kanuka, 2011, p. 6). SoTL's claims to be something "new" may be both offensive and baffling to educational researchers like Kanuka, as is the claim "that simply by virtue of teaching in the higher education sector makes one a credible researcher in this field" (Kanuka, 2011, p. 9). One type of educational research is more concerned with using theory (either developing, building upon, or testing) to explore how transferable their findings might be to another context; other types of educational research are interested in understanding what is happening in a particular context, and describing it in enough detail that others can decide whether the findings are transferable to their context or not. SoTL inquiries are more commonly grounded in particular contexts, and, like other types of educational research, should not be atheoretical, as we will explore throughout this book.

While learning theories developed through educational research have much to offer SoTL inquiries, faculty members working in the various disciplines also bring value to SoTL. Kanuka (2011) acknowledges that there are "disciplinary differences, with very distinct ways of knowing. These disciplinary differences need to be researched by those whose expertise is in the disciplines—for all the reasons that resulted in the creation of SoTL" (p. 9). As Shulman (2005) notes, disciplines and professions often develop signature pedagogies which

> implicitly define what counts as knowledge in a field and how things become known. They define how knowledge is analyzed, criticized, accepted, or discarded. They define the functions of expertise in a field, the locus of authority, and the privileges of rank and standing
>
> *(p. 54)*

Disciplinary experts exploring these pedagogies through DBER can provide insight into not only content knowledge but also the assumptions about a discipline or profession. As McKinney (2013) notes, "SOTL began, primarily, as a discipline-based movement that included a few multi-disciplinary conversations" (p. 2).

However, these multidisciplinary conversations are a key strength of SoTL that may not be possible in pure DBER. As Mary Taylor Huber and Sherwyn Morreale (2002) note, SoTL "draws strength from being situated in a discipline and its particular style. But growth in knowledge also comes at the borders of disciplinary imagination" (p. 2). Huber and Morreale (2002) introduce another important metaphor for SoTL, the idea of a "trading zone" between disciplinary territories where we could learn from each other (p. 19). Reichard and Takayama (2013) argue that "cross-disciplinary conversations are a defining feature of SOTL, a signature pedagogy and methodology" (p. 170). These conversations illuminate disciplinary assumptions and practices because "it is easier to see the shapes of disciplines in comparison to each other" (Middendorf & Shopkow, 2018, p.7). Weimer (2008) cautions that focusing only on DBER limits the potential impact of insights into teaching and learning practices that transcend specific disciplines, practices like group work or study strategies. Similarly, Poole (2013) argues that SoTL "requires the crossing of disciplinary boundaries" if we are "to clearly understand phenomena related to teaching and learning" (p. 147). He argues not just for toleration of differences (in discipline, methodology, purpose, and assumptions), but for respect (p. 149).

Judging SoTL

But how do we judge the quality of SoTL work given its diversity? After all, as we've seen, some consider it on a continuum with scholarly teaching, others see it as related to more traditional educational research—each conceptualization has very different evaluative measures. Add to this what Peter Felten (2013) describes as an "amateur culture" (p. 1) where faculty from different disciplines investigate research questions in their own contexts, often with very little formal training. And these disciplines may have radically different assumptions about what knowledge is, how teaching and learning occurs, and what acceptable scholarship looks like.

Nonetheless, scholars have tried to articulate evaluative criteria responsive to the diversity of SoTL. Glassick, Huber, and Maeroff (1997) argue that all scholarship, regardless of type or discipline, should have clear goals, adequate preparation, appropriate methods, significant results, effective presentation, and reflective critique. These criteria provide a starting point for judging SoTL, and can be observed in various conference and journal vetting processes, but they are very general and can be applied to many activities beyond scholarship.

Felten (2013) offers some helpful (and widely cited) guidelines: SoTL should be "(1) inquiry into student learning, (2) grounded in context, (3) methodologically sound, (4) conducted in partnership with students, and (5) appropriately public" (p. 121). Felten's first principle distinguishes between SoTL and the many other types of inquiry possible in higher education, for example, higher education policy or demographic trends. Some have argued that SoTL should be understood to include educational development or educational leadership, a position we take in this book. Felten's second principle recognizes that teaching and learning is a profoundly contextual construct, difficult to generalize, but it also recognizes that scholarship needs to be grounded in the scholarly literature of what has been learned before.

This book focuses primarily on Felten's third principle: creating SoTL that is methodologically sound. As Felten argues, "Regardless of the methods employed, good practice in SoTL requires the intentional and rigorous application of research tools that connect the question at the heart of a particular inquiry to student learning" (2013, p. 123). Whether qualitative or quantitative methods are used, whether positivist, realist, interpretive, or critical worldviews shape the analyses and findings, SoTL researchers must address questions of reliability and rigor in terms and through processes consistent with the methodology chosen. We explore how to do this in the chapters that follow. Felten's fourth principle, that SoTL should be undertaken in partnership with students, means that, as a minimum, SoTL needs to follow good practices of human research ethics, including the idea of informed consent. We explore some of these ethical concerns in the next section. More than that, however, Felten promotes students as partners in the research rather than merely participants in the inquiry process. The Students-as-Partners movement has gathered momentum over the past decade (Cook-Sather et al., 2014). Felten's final principle argues for "appropriately public" dissemination, leaving the form of the dissemination open. Whether through peer-reviewed article, presentation, teaching portfolio, or conversation, SoTL seeks to enhance our knowledge of teaching and learning.

What Are Some Common Ethical Concerns in SoTL?

In the previous section, we mentioned that SoTL needs to follow good practices of human research ethics; of course, the particular processes will depend on your national context. In many jurisdictions, SoTL projects will need to go through some form of institutionally mandated review (i.e., Institutional Review Boards in the USA, Human Research Ethics Boards in Canada, and so on). The process of applying for ethics review can be very helpful in developing the research project, as typically we have to describe the proposed research design, including research questions, method, and methodology. We go into more detail about these elements in Chapters 2 and 3.

Here we want to outline some common ethical principles and concerns that SoTL practitioners need to consider. Faculty members new to SoTL, especially if they are from disciplines outside of the Social Sciences, often identify ethics review as one of the key challenges or barriers they face (Hubball et al., 2010), but good ethical practice doesn't end with Institutional Review Board approval. It is an important part of all aspects of the research process from initial research project design through dissemination as, increasingly, publishers want to know that the project was conducted according to acceptable human research principles.

Ethical Principles

Research involving human participants involves ethics. We make choices and have to consider the effects of those choices on others. Ethical principles, then, are generalized statements that help us judge whether our actions are ethical when we are faced with particular situations. Research ethics developed in response to events in the past and continue to develop today (see Resnik (2022) for a broad timeline). For example, the Nuremberg Code (1949) responded to experimentation in Nazi Germany while the Belmont Report (1978) was influenced in part by the Tuskegee Syphilis Study. Institutionally mandated review of research ethics began in biomedical fields, but has now expanded to include all research involving human participants. Incidents like the infamous Stanford Prison experiment, where college students role-played being prisoners and guards, demonstrate that pressing ethical issues are not limited to biomedical research. Research ethics evolve over time; however, three key principles articulated in the Belmont Report—respect for persons, beneficence, justice—continue to provide a moral framework for research ethics. As Canadians, we focus on ethical review in a North American context, but many other jurisdictions are concerned with similar principles.

Respect for persons includes respecting individuals' autonomy and providing them with accurate information about what the research involves, thus allowing for free and informed consent. No one should feel compelled to participate in a research project, or not know what their participation entails. Beneficence, or as Canada's Tri-Council Policy Statement (2018) phrases it "concern for welfare," involves the researcher's responsibility to do no harm. Of course, sometimes there are risks to participants, but it is the researcher's responsibility to try to minimize risk and maximize benefit, and not all risks are physical; risks may include "social penalties" (MacLean & Poole, 2010, p. 5) or loss of privacy. Justice involves a sense of fairness—burdens should not be imposed unfairly on some, and benefits should not be denied to others. The researcher must treat people equally. Many institutionally mandated ethics review processes are built upon these basic principles.

These principles may seem self-evident when considering biomedical research; obviously, an individual should have the right to consent or refuse consent to experimental treatment after being fully informed of the risks and benefits; deception shouldn't be used to gain consent; and it's not fair that one person not be given adequate treatment because researchers want to amplify their study results. But if the case is clear in biomedical research, it is sometimes harder for people learning about SoTL to see how these principles apply to them. After all, as Healey at al. (2013) note,

> a majority of SoTL practitioners lack formal training in ethics because they do not have philosophy backgrounds, come from disciplines where undergraduate or graduate training in human research ethic is the norm, or work with human participants in their disciplinary scholarship.
>
> *(pp. 23–24)*

They may struggle with the distinction between what they would do as scholarly teachers, trying and evaluating new teaching techniques, and the more formal ethical requirements of scholarship (MacLean & Poole, 2010). Some may come from disciplines where research is only considered valid if control groups are employed, which is difficult to design ethically in an educational context. They may not see the point of institutionally mandated ethics review; they may believe that they can get formal review later if necessary; or they may think the review board is just trying to block their research for no good reason (Stockley & Balkwill, 2013). And, indeed, some review boards struggle with how to adjudicate SoTL (Martin, 2013). Still, most review boards are looking for evidence that the SoTL researcher has thought through potential ethical issues.

A Dual Role

Many of the ethical issues SoTL practitioners face are related to the fact that they often have a dual role—they are simultaneously teachers and researchers. SoTL practitioners must keep this dual role in mind when planning all aspects of the research, everything from recruitment and consent, to types of data gathered, to confidentiality and privacy. As MacLean and Poole (2010) note, "The teacher's responsibility to hold students' educational interests paramount provides an important perspective when considering ethical issues for research in teaching and learning" (p. 3). As researchers, we may want our students to complete various research activities during class time; however, they didn't sign up for the course in order to participate in our research. The primary focus must be their learning in the course, even if we firmly believe that our research will improve the teaching and learning environment. In practical terms, this means that activities that seem like a normal part of teaching may have to be approached differently when viewed through the lens of research.

For example, while it may be a normal part of scholarly teaching to reflect upon how students have performed on a particular assessment over multiple terms, students must be given the opportunity to give or refuse consent to participate in research. While all students in a class may be required to complete a particular assessment connected to the learning outcomes of that course, not all students will consent to have that same assessment used in research. Consent has to be informed—that is, students need to know what we are doing with their work; and students need to feel free to participate or refuse without worrying that we or others will think less of them if they do. In practical terms, that means we have to provide participants with information before they consent, someone else might talk about the study and collect consent forms while the instructor isn't present, the instructor might not know until after the course is over who has agreed to participate, and the identities of those who have agreed to participate are carefully guarded throughout the process.

As we work through the chapters of this book, we will address ethical concerns that researchers need to be aware of when employing particular methods and methodologies along with some practical suggestions. Your own institution will probably provide more specific guidance, but you might find some of the following resources interesting. In particular, Pat Hutchings's *Ethics of Inquiry* (2002) offers case studies into ethical issues and how particular researchers chose to deal with them. Fedoruk (2017) provides some practical strategies for ethical practice in SoTL from a Canadian perspective, but many of the strategies are widely applicable. Finally, Healey et al. (2013) offer an ethical framework that moves beyond considerations of how to get projects through institutional review to consider how we can develop personal ethical fitness in an ethical climate through reflection. As they point out, "Being ethically minded is about striving to make the right choices, not simply following institutional regulations" (p. 31).

Key Concepts

- The Scholarship of Teaching and Learning is a remarkably diverse field of inquiry occurring in many countries around the globe.
- Despite this disciplinary and national diversity, SoTL can be evaluated using broadly accepted criteria.
- Methodological soundness is an important criterion (and one we will focus on throughout this book).
- Good ethical practice is another important criterion. As SoTL researchers, we must demonstrate respect for persons, beneficence, and justice.
- SoTL researchers must always be aware of the ethical conflicts inherent in their dual roles.

Further Readings

On SoTL

Bass, R. (1999). The scholarship of teaching: What's the problem. *Inventio: Creative Thinking about Learning and Teaching*, 1(1).

Felten, P. (2013). Principles of good practice in SOTL. *Teaching and Learning Inquiry*, 1(1), 121–125. https://doi.org/10.20343/teachlearninqu.1.1.121.

Hutchings, P. (Ed.) (2000). *Opening lines: Approaches to the scholarship of teaching and learning*. Carnegie Foundation for the Advancement of Teaching.

McKinney, K. (2007). *Enhancing learning through the scholarship of teaching and learning: The challenges and joys of juggling*. Jossey-Bass.

On Ethics

AHRECS. (2014). SoTL Resource Books. Available at https://ahrecs.com/previous-projects/sotl-resource-booklets/ (Australia and New Zealand).

Boling, W., Berlin, K., Rahn, R., Vogelzang, J., & Walter, G. (2018). Institutional review board basics for pedagogy research. *Pedagogy in Health Promotion*, 4(3), 172–177. https://doi.org/10.1177/2373379918793400 (USA).

Fedoruk, L. (2017). *Ethics in the scholarship of teaching and learning: Key principles and strategies for ethical practice.* Taylor Institute for Teaching and Learning at the University of Calgary. https://taylorinstitute.ucalgary.ca/sites/default/files/Ethics%20in%20SoTL-Taylor%20Institute%20Guide.pdf (Canada).

Fedoruk, L. M. (Ed.). (2022). *Ethics and the scholarship of teaching and learning* (Vol. 2). Springer Nature.

Healey, R. L., Bass, T., Caulfield, J., Hoffman, A., McGinn, M. K., Miller-Young, J., & Haigh, M. (2013). Being ethically minded: Practising the scholarship of teaching and learning in an ethical manner. *Teaching and Learning Inquiry*, 1(2), 23–33. https://doi.org/10.20343/teachlearninqu.1.2.23.

2

DEVELOPING SOTL INQUIRIES

This chapter discusses how to develop a SoTL research inquiry project, beginning with where good SoTL questions come from. We will introduce question typologies used in SoTL, including some foundational work SoTL researchers should be familiar with. We will then provide advice for developing a problem statement, refining a research question, and conducting literature review. Finally, we provide an exploration of learning theories (broadly categorized) as one potential source of theoretical frameworks for SoTL inquiries.

The first stage of any research involves identifying a theoretical or practical problem, and beginning to refine this into a topic or research question. In the case of applied research such as SoTL, it is usually the latter. In our work with new SoTL researchers, we are often asked what makes a good SoTL question. Those who teach encounter daily, significant questions about their students, their practice, and about teaching and learning. But which of these questions are suitable for a SoTL study? How should a researcher refine their curiosities into a workable question for a research study? What other sources of questions are there?

In this chapter, we will explore this process, present typologies of SoTL questions developed in the literature, and consider the different levels or contexts within the university that might provide sites of inquiry. We will discuss strategies for conducting literature review in the context of SoTL. A review of the literature should be started at the beginning stages of inquiry, and continues as an iterative process throughout the life of a study. We then introduce the role that a theoretical framework plays generally in a well-designed SoTL research study. We suggest learning theory as an important framing element (Steiner & Hakala, 2021): the assumptions being made by

DOI: 10.4324/9781003447054-3

the SoTL researcher about how learning occurs often have an important relationship with the research question and methods chosen. Finally, we will present broad categories of learning theory, which explicitly or otherwise underlie classroom pedagogy. Perspectives on learning, too, have a strong influence on research design in SoTL and indeed the research question itself.

Asking SoTL Research Questions—Where Do Good Questions Come From?

As Gary Poole (2018) and others have written and talked about, daily work in educational settings inevitably leads to many questions about "what is or isn't going on" (p. 7). These questions are often discussed with one or two close colleagues in what Roxå and Mårtensson (2009) have called small "significant networks" (p. 556). The SoTL movement intended in the first instance to move these questions from the conversational sphere into systematic inquiry. Poole suggests that the act of teaching is "so cerebral, so academic, and so social" that it is "impossible to engage in it" without developing beliefs about what's happening, leading to curiosities that "in turn become the origins of SoTL projects" (p. 7). He asks, "What if inside every teaching was a scholarship of teaching and learning (SoTL) project waiting to be brought to life?" (p. 7).

We need not today, however, restrict SoTL to individual classrooms. SoTL is, at its heart, practitioners' research, whether the practitioner is a classroom instructor, educational developer, or program administrator. The field continues to broaden its definition, the scope of questions researchers ask, and the contexts in which the questions can be asked. SoTL inquiry can be fruitfully applied to experiential elements of higher education, or work experiences. SoTL can be conducted at a program, institutional, or cross-institutional level. In the scholarship of educational development (SoEd), SoTL sensibilities and approaches are applied to the work of educational developers. While having its own tradition of teacher practitioner research, the K–12 system has begun to show interest in SoTL—which has been traditionally defined within a post-secondary context. It makes sense for these contexts to be speaking to one another. As authors we believe that SoTL is, can, and should be extended out from individual classroom studies. However, the heart of the work remains in the classroom, so we will begin there.

So how do we develop good SoTL questions in our teaching and learning contexts? Beginning at a classroom level, in an article often cited from the early days of SoTL, Randy Bass (1999) points out that we tend to think of a problem in teaching as a bad thing, while problems in research are the exciting starting point for inquiry. He suggests that SoTL can help us reframe problems in teaching and bring them into the teaching commons, rather than be a source of private shame. From these early days, however,

SoTL has expanded outward into broader concerns. Bass (2020) revisits his earlier article in an update entitled "What's the Problem Now?" where he writes:

> The framework for appreciating SoTL at the time of my original essay, as a way for teachers to understand their students' learning as a rich field of investigation, has expanded in the last 20 years as a robust, diverse, and potentially transformative portfolio of tools and practices, the richness of which matches the urgency of the times. What are we to make of this convergence of knowledge, tools, and urgency? ... We need to think of the problem of learning—and by implication, the problem of higher education—as a complex, *wicked* problem.
>
> *(pp. 5–6)*

In exploring what he means by wicked problems, Bass quotes the Austin Center for Design (2019) explaining that these are social or cultural problems that are difficult or impossible to solve. Bass argues that understanding teaching and learning as a "complex or high-stakes problem" rather than a "tame or solvable one" helps us to think more ambitiously about our work (p. 6). Further, Gary Poole (2018) points out that "we should not fall into the trap of believing that all SoTL projects should solve a problem. Some will provide elegantly insightful descriptions of a learning process or environment" (p. 8).

Anthony Ciccone (2018) outlines five conditions for good SoTL questions that are "meaningful for ourselves; our students; our colleagues; and ultimately, for advancing the field" (p. 16). The first condition outlined is "that our question should arise from a troubling, surprising, or perplexing teaching and learning experience that seems to defy a simple solution" (p. 16). These experiences in the classroom tend to be rich fodder for SoTL inquiries. They are the things that the teacher puzzles about on the way home or may keep them up at night. The very troublesome nature of the problem speaks to its potential richness. In calling for exploring "wicked problems," Bass (2020) argues, "how complexly we understand the problem of learning and education will shape the next urgent phase of transformation in higher education" (p. 9). The stakes, then, are high. The second condition outlined by Ciccone is related to the first—when something truly perplexes us, it is also likely to be important: the question will "arrive at something truly consequential to us as teachers and to our students as learners" (p. 17). Investigating something truly consequential in our contexts is, by extension, likely to be consequential to other educators within their own contexts.

The third condition put forth by Ciccone has to do with novelty—not necessarily something no one else has investigated before, but rather, "when we find ourselves required to gather new and different information about our students' learning or at least look differently at what we've been getting and thus to teach and assess differently" (p. 17). The fourth condition speaks to the open-ended, provisional nature of SoTL research: "Our question should raise more questions than it answers and thus invite further research" (p. 19). This connects to the broader audience that Felten (2013) points to, discussed in the first chapter, and relates to the final condition. Ciccone suggests,

> the fifth condition for a good SoTL research question is fulfilled when ... our question shows the potential to go beyond the problem from whence it arose to elucidate some key insights into the big issues about student learning and the frameworks that would explain them.
>
> *(p. 20)*

By all of these conditions being met in a worthwhile SoTL study, we learn more about our students and about teaching and learning, and have contributed these insights in a meaningful way to other educators and SoTL practitioners.

From an alternative standpoint to Western knowledge systems, an Indigenous research paradigm, which we will introduce in Chapter 3 and develop further in Chapter 11, is always guided by a set of values. These values not only frame the questions asked and the possibilities envisioned, but also the relational responsibilities that are embodied through an Indigenous research methodology. Indigenous standpoint theories (Moreton-Robinson, 2013) invite us into a values-based analysis of our teaching as the site of research and challenge us to imagine our research relationships based in a shared humanity which helps to minimize power imbalances.

SoTL Questions—Typologies to Draw From

Types of Research Questions

In 2000, Pat Hutchings delineated a heuristic of four kinds of SoTL questions. This heuristic is ubiquitous in the SoTL literature, so it is useful to be familiar with it, and it can be helpful in thinking about possible directions for SoTL work in traditional single classroom studies and beyond. It can also help to suggest direction for research methodologies, as you can think about whether the kind of question you want to ask is answerable by this or that methodology or research design (see Chapter 3). The four questions are:

1. *What Works* questions: these are SoTL questions that attempt to collect evidence demonstrating whether this or that teaching intervention/pedagogy/approach is effective or creating an impact. Hutchings notes, "not surprisingly, this is where many faculty begin" (p. 4). She observes

that this is a type of question that often has a "ready audience" in contexts where we are always trying to improve our students' learning.

2. *What Is* questions: these are questions about "what is going on" in the classroom or for learners. For example, you might wonder about student study habits or approaches to reading texts or problem solving. Answering these sorts of questions helps to provide insight that can lead to different pedagogical approaches in order to improve learning, or simply to understand students better. Hutchings explains, "Here the effort is aimed not so much at proving (or disproving) the effectiveness of a particular approach or intervention but at describing what it looks like, what its constituent features might be" (p. 4).
3. *Visions of the Possible*: this is currently a less common type of SoTL question, but considers new directions to go in the classroom, and is more transformational in orientation. It is interested in "what might be"—moving outside of, for example, disciplinary norms, transforming a limiting view of students, or exploring how "difficulties can be used to uncover what is most essential to understanding" (p. 5).
4. *Theory Building*: this is work that systematically builds on previous work to theorize about teaching and learning—developing "new models and conceptual frameworks" that "generate new questions that can, in turn, enrich the scholarship of teaching and learning and extend its boundaries" (p. 5). Hutchings pointed out in 2000 that "This type of question is, thus far in the scholarship of teaching and learning 'movement,' under-represented" (p. 5). More than twenty years later, this is still the case, but examples might be found in such theories as threshold concepts (Meyer & Land, 2005).

If you are reading SoTL studies, this heuristic will be very familiar, as researchers commonly define their studies as addressing one of these types of questions, citing Hutchings.

Later work by Kreber (2013) suggests that we need to go further, and situate SoTL studies in a broader context of significance. She suggests that SoTL might be "enacted as an extended form of professionality" and thus should be informed not only by learning theory, "but by a wider repertoire of theories that invite us to ask questions of value and what we are doing this work for" (p. 13). In directing our gaze more broadly, Kreber connects with Bass's notion of wicked problems. As we will discuss later in this chapter, this is where important theory from your discipline might come into play. Kreber goes on to argue,

> The Scholarship of Teaching and Learning is enhanced when linked to ethical considerations, specifically questions of what we think we are committed to in higher education teaching, what we consider its

> purpose to be and whether the educational opportunities we presently provide for students are likely to bring about those capabilities and internal qualities that will make a difference to society … In this lies the real transformative potential of the Scholarship of Teaching and Learning.
>
> *(pp. 13–14)*

Taken together with the Hutchings taxonomy, this can be a powerful reminder of the potential inherent in SoTL—meaning as well as understanding, transformation as well as effectiveness. Part of what we can be doing in SoTL is examining our own intuitions and beliefs about teaching and learning which we may have taken to be natural or self-evident, as Poole (2018) reminds us: "In teaching and learning, we must systematically examine what we take to be obvious because it so often turns out to be anything but" (p. 9).

Context and Audience for SoTL questions

Another way to think about types of SoTL research questions is the group or context the question is asking about. You might be interested specifically in individual student learning within the context of your own course. Or, you might be interested in how students interact in socially situated learning contexts, for example, how group dynamics operate in collaborative test taking. Another approach is to ask questions about student learning in a larger context across multiple courses (either similar courses at the same institution, courses across a program at different levels, or courses across multiple institutions). A final type of SoTL, also sometimes termed Scholarship of Educational Development (SoEd), involves faculty learning about teaching or about SoTL. SoEd studies, while in some ways distinct from SoTL, are also often published in SoTL journals and presented at SoTL conferences.

Keith Trigwell (2021) divides up types of SoTL studies in a different way, describing the scope of the investigation. The three levels of investigations he identifies are:

1. An investigation to inform oneself about an aspect of their teaching/learning. This will result in the production of *personal* knowledge.
2. An investigation to inform a group within one or more shared contexts (typically department or faculty, institution) about an aspect or their teaching/learning. This will result in the production of *local* knowledge.
3. An investigation to inform a wider (international) audience about an aspect of their teaching/learning. This will result in the production of *public* knowledge (pp. 293–294).

The idea of producing public knowledge links to a more recent development in SoTL toward public scholarship. Nancy Chick, at her closing keynote address at the 2019 International Society for Scholarship of Teaching and Learning (ISSOTL) conference, challenged the field to become more engaged in public forms of dissemination and efforts to engage with changemaking in society. (We will discuss this further in Chapter 14.) Building on this call to action, in their introduction to *Going Public Reconsidered: Engaging With the World Beyond Academe Through the Scholarship of Teaching and Learning* (2022), editors Friberg and Chick identify two reasons and processes for engaging in this work:

- the first describes how SoTL scholars can "support and extend the scholarship they produce, allowing them to share their work most broadly," and
- the second presents how SoTL scholars can "inform and affect public issues and events that unfold in our society" (p. 5).

So as you begin to refine a research question, it is worth thinking about the context of the question, the scope of the investigation, and the audience you ultimately hope to reach. How can your SoTL work effect change, and where are you most passionate about seeing that change take effect? In the next sections, we'll walk through how to go about refining your question, conducting literature review, and working with a theoretical framework.

Developing a Problem Statement and Defining a Research Question

Merriam and Tisdell (2016) outline a helpful process in arriving at a defined research question. Once you have a topic in mind, they argue that "it would be a fruitless undertaking to embark on a research journey without first identifying a research problem" (p. 76). Earlier in the chapter, we looked at how a "problem" in your teaching can become a place to begin SoTL work. In crafting a problem statement, "move from general interest, curiosity, or doubt about a situation to a specific statement of the research problem" (p. 77). This is a "funnel"-shaped process—broad at the top, narrow at the bottom—which helps you to refine that broad concern into a question that is answerable through research inquiry (see Figure 2.1). Along the way, you will need to become familiar with what the literature has already said about this topic. Has someone else already answered this question in a way that is satisfying to you? Is there a gap in the literature? Sometimes the question has been answered but in a different context. Other times the limitations of previous work leave room for a differently designed study. Occasionally you find such a plethora of established work that you realize your planned study isn't needed, and it sends you back to the drawing board.

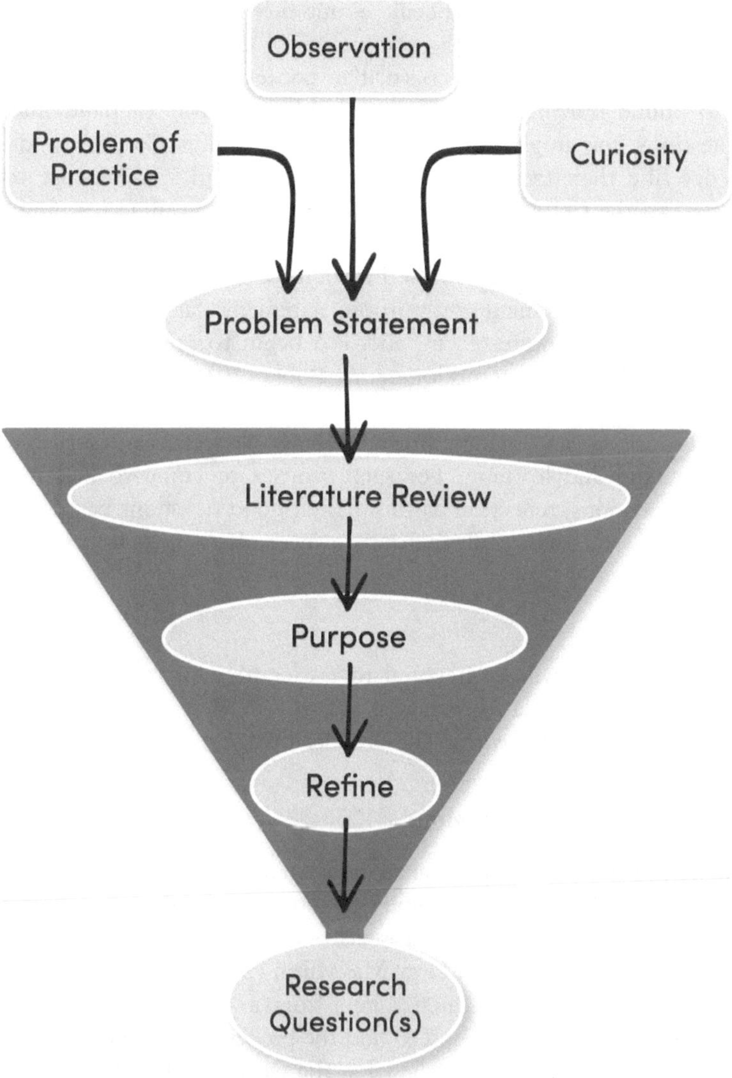

FIGURE 2.1 The process for developing and refining a research question can be represented as a funnel.

Once you've found out what we don't know about a particular topic, and specific problem, you can craft a purpose statement. This identifies what your study sets out to do. For example, it might be something like, "The purpose of this study is to understand the social experience of students doing online learning during the pandemic." At this stage, you are ready to write a research question, or possibly a main research question with several sub-questions. The research question should be specific about the context of the work. Your main research question in this example might be, "What were the social experiences of students in a particular context during the unexpected pivot to online learning in the first part of the Covid-19 pandemic?" As sub-questions you might ask, in this example, things like "How do students describe their experience? What strategies did students use to stay connected to their classmates? How did the pivot to online learning affect their relationship with their instructors?"

Taking this time to refine your broad topic down, with the help of a research problem statement and purpose statement, can help to hone in on what you are really interested in, and also begin to guide you in terms of your research design or methodology. As Poole (2018) describes,

> SoTL projects can originate from the things we feel, hear, and see related to teaching and learning. For such projects to come to life, we must become curious, reflect on all this, design good questions based on those questions, and then craft appropriate methods to help us answer those questions.
>
> *(p. 13)*

Much of this book will be devoted to the crafting of methods. Spending time with the literature at this stage is also key, so that you understand how your developing idea fits within the broader field.

Conducting Literature Review

Beginning to read on the topic you are interested in developing into an inquiry is a critical part of the process as you develop your question. Sometimes new SoTL scholars feel daunted at the prospect of delving into what, for many, is an entirely new literature, and as Margy MacMillan (2018) points out, "Unfortunately, the literature review often suffers from a sort of benign neglect, as researchers (understandably) tend to find the process of conducting their own study … more exciting than synthesizing the work of others" (p. 23). However, the importance of overcoming this tendency cannot be overstated. We often see new SoTL researchers wanting to embark on projects investigating phenomena already well understood, only to find out later they don't have much new to contribute. MacMillan outlines multiple benefits of a robust literature review, as it "not only strengthens the final product of a project but also benefits the entire process. Understanding the relevant theory and prior work can help researchers design studies that align more closely with their questions" (pp. 23–24). It can also save you time: "by providing examples of qualitative or quantitative instruments and protocols, criteria for analyzing results, and models for writing" (p. 24).

Like any field of study, it takes time to become familiar with the conversations happening in the field. This is additionally complicated by the overlap we explore in Chapter 1 between SoTL, DBER (disciplinary-based educational research), and educational research. All of these sources are likely to have literature on just about any topic you can imagine in teaching and learning. You might look both for literature on the topic you want to investigate, but you might also look for how theory has been applied to this topic in other studies, and/or what methodologies were used. As a strategy, we recommend first looking in the SoTL literature to find out the status of the conversation in this arena—you might start with journals that have SoTL in the title (it's worth becoming familiar with several of these), but broaden your search using your topic as a search term. Look to see in your disciplinary educational journals whether the problem has been tackled—chances are, if you are encountering a problem with your students you wish to solve, it's likely that others in your discipline have encountered the same thing. Finally, depending on whether you feel you have a strong grounding from the first two arenas, also look in the educational/higher education literature. Sometimes the K–12 literature can be of enormous help, as there is an analogous practitioner research to SoTL that has been done in schools by practicing teachers. Sometimes the very study you are interested in pursuing appears in the K–12 literature, and is just waiting to be applied in the post-secondary context.

Literature review is something that you will need to do iteratively through the life of your study, and it appears in multiple sections of your research when you write it up. Often, there will be a dedicated section near the beginning, where you situate your topic and research question as described above in the previously existing work. As MacMillan expresses it, "the literature sets the stage for the work" (p. 24), and she points out that just as SoTL researchers come from a wide range of disciplines, so too does its audience, and you can't assume a working knowledge of the literature you are referring to. She suggests that "in fact, it is reasonable to proceed as though a paper were the very first SoTL work a reader has encountered" (p. 24). This is a chance for you to summarize, analyze, and critique previous work, and point out the gap that you are addressing. But literature review appears in other places, too—as early as the introduction, where you are setting up the need for the study. Later, when you discuss your findings, you will bring back the literature to speak to what you have found. As Cappello and Miller-Young (2020) note, "Reviewing the work of others is also critical to the researcher's own thought process as it helps the researcher make meaning of and explain their own results, both expected and unexpected" (p. 4). How this is done will depend to some degree on the research paradigm and methodology you are working within. However, there is really no case that we can think of where you would be conducting research without situating the work in what others have done, said, or thought about.

A question often asked is, how much literature is enough? As we will discuss later in the chapters on collecting data, in qualitative research there is a notion of "saturation"—where the data you are collecting is repeating what you have already seen, for example, that you are not really hearing anything "new" from additional interview participants. The same kind of notion can be helpful in the literature review. As you read, take note of when you start to feel you are encountering the same ideas again and again. Also ask yourself whether you have identified who some of the key thinkers or researchers are in the topic area, and whether you can point to the major theoretical work and know when it was conducted. As you go, do take note of the year of publication of what you're reading. The expectation for the recency of the work you are citing will vary somewhat by the research paradigm and the individual journal. As disciplinary practices and expectations vary in this regard, so too do expectations depending on the audience for your work.

As in disciplinary research, remember to track what you read. Some researchers use software tools to keep track of the literature and share with co-researchers; others keep copies (whether digital or hard copy) and make lists. Find an approach that works for you; however, it is critical that you have systematic strategies for being able to find citations easily, put your hands quickly on something you have read and need to refer to, as well as create accurate reference lists, using a variety of citation styles depending on the journal's guidelines.

Using Theoretical Frameworks in SoTL Research

Once you have decided at least provisionally on the research question, and begun reading the relevant literature in SoTL, DBER, and potentially the broader educational research, you are on the path to choosing the most appropriate research methodology. SoTL practitioners benefit from understanding the range of lenses and methodologies that have been applied to educational and higher education research. They do better SoTL when they are aware of their philosophical approach and theoretical assumptions about learning because it will help them ask new questions, design better studies, and also more strongly articulate their findings, especially to colleagues with different worldviews. Theoretically grounded work is one way for SoTL to achieve broader impact across studies and make new contributions to knowledge about teaching and learning beyond single classrooms.

Along this path, selecting a theoretical framework for your research can be immensely useful in developing the kind of congruence that is a hallmark of high-quality work. However, this can be a difficult idea at first, and can be further confused by the fact that the terms "theoretical framework" and "conceptual framework" are commonly used interchangeably (Merriam & Tisdell, 2016). With Merriam and Tisdell, we prefer the term theoretical framework as it provides a broader lens, and is inclusive of concepts and models.

Understanding the role of theoretical framework can be tricky at first. As Merriam and Tisdell (2016) comment, "although it is relatively easy to spot the lack of a theoretical framework, it is considerably more difficult to explain what it is and how to go about incorporating it into your study" (p. 84). They further explain,

> a theoretical framework underlies all research. Theory is present in all qualitative research because no study could be designed without some question being asked (explicitly or implicitly). How that question is asked and how it is worked into a problem statement reflect a theoretical orientation.

While Merriam and Tisdell are explicitly talking about qualitative research here, quantitative designs also involve a theoretical framework, where theory provides a rationale for the choice of variables to be studied. As Kara notes, however, "theory in qualitative research operates differently from theory in quantitative research" (p. 34). She explains that in quantitative work, "theories exist to be tested and then, based on the test results, either verified, modified, or rejected" (p. 34). Theory is thus used as a tool to draw from and make decisions, whereas in most qualitative work the theoretical framework is more like an orientation through which the entire project is approached. As Kara explains in qualitative research, "theories exist to increase our understanding by offering different ways to look at, think about and organise data and findings" (p. 34).

The theoretical framework can be thought of as the lens through which the study is conducted (Creswell & Plano Clark, 2017). For example, if your study is trying to assess how students were transformed through a field experience, your theoretical framework might be transformational learning. It would be useful, then, to draw from the theoretical literature on transformational learning to help you design the methods of the study, and it probably helped you (or could have helped you) to design the pedagogical experience and assessment of students. Below we will provide a short summary of learning theory categories that can be helpful as a potential source of theoretical frameworks. However, you are not limited to these. Consider, also, important theories from your own discipline that resonate with you or that underlie your teaching. Perhaps reader response theory, or specific aspects of feminism, or a particular process of architectural design might provide a lens to ground your study. Such theory can provide a bridge for your disciplinary colleagues to your SoTL work, and it can also open up to you research methods and analysis strategies from your discipline as well.

Merriam and Tisdell (2016) point out that since researchers have been socialized into their discipline, the theory within that discipline will color how they view the classroom, and what questions they will be drawn to:

> The frameworks of your study will draw upon the concepts, terms, definitions, models, and theories of a particular literature base and disciplinary orientation. This framework in turn will generate the "problem" of the study, specific research questions, data collection and analysis techniques, and how you will interpret your findings ... All aspects of the study are affected by the theoretical framework.
>
> *(p. 86)*

Using disciplinary theory is one way SoTL can be hospitable across disciplines as the "big tent" where disciplinary lenses and methods can be brought to bear on the classroom. For example, see Halasz and Kaufman's (2008) paper on "Sociology as pedagogy: How ideas from the disciplines can inform teaching and learning" as a demonstration of how principles from the field can be utilized to structure pedagogical decision making.

Alternatively, SoTL researchers may not see an applicable theoretical lens they wish to explore from their own discipline, or may wish to take a different perspective. Since SoTL is about teaching and learning, learning theory provides a potential framework that is cross-disciplinary in its application. A SoTL practitioner's perspective on learning can often become a potential source for the theoretical framework of their study. Whether conscious or not, beliefs about how learning works undergird pedagogical choices in the classroom, and thus, the question the practitioner wants to investigate. We will briefly outline the major categories of learning theories and methodologies and the importance of congruence between them; we then provide examples of SoTL studies in this framework—this is intended as a primer rather than an exhaustive guide.

Learning Theories

A learning theory can provide a potential framework upon which researchers base their assumptions about the nature of learning. Faculty members may teach for decades without formal study about learning theory; however, realizing it or not, they operate from a set of basic assumptions about how people learn. Often, these follow what are sometimes termed the "signature pedagogies" (Shulman, 2005) of their discipline. For example, many disciplines follow experiential learning principles: interior design programs with studio courses, chemistry with labs, nursing with clinical practice. Law is commonly taught through cases, and mathematics through problem solving. Indigenous ways of knowing are transmitted through a relational theoretical framework that is based in inclusive teaching practice and the pursuit of balance (Bastien, 2016; Battiste, 2002). Although we tend to think about these as pedagogical strategies, underlying them are assumptions about how learning works.

Consciously or unconsciously, these assumptions will naturally influence a practitioner–researcher's SoTL work. The type of question pursued, the kind of data collected, the form of analysis—all of this will be influenced by the discipline (i.e., what the discipline considers to be evidence of learning) and the researchers' assumptions about learning. This phenomenon can also be seen at play in the "signature" or typical assessment practices of various disciplines (Yeo & Boman, 2017). These patterns or habits are not necessarily fixed, however, especially when a SoTL researcher has the opportunity to examine their assumptions about learning. This examination can open new avenues for inquiry and potentially exciting new pedagogical approaches. This is one of the strengths of SoTL—it is by nature cross-disciplinary, breaking down traditional silos in the academy.

One helpful way to broadly categorize learning theories is into behaviorist, cognitivist, constructivist, humanist, and perhaps even Indigenous perspectives, although the latter resists categorization into Western theoretical schemas. While exact agreement does not exist on "how many learning theories there are or how they should be grouped for discussion" (Merriam et al., 2006, p. 277), these broad categories are relatively well accepted and present contrasting assumptions. It is useful, when reading a SoTL study, to understand the basic assumptions of the researcher in terms of how learning works and how this framework can be employed to think about these assumptions and their implications for classroom practice. In conducting SoTL research, being explicit about the learning theory behind the study can guide the methods and methodologies chosen, and help to create study alignment.

Behaviorism

This perspective on learning developed in the early 20th century and suggested that all behavior is based upon external stimuli—or the idea that environmental changes lead to behavioral change as evidence of learning (Gurung & Schwartz, 2013). Behavior was seen as being shaped by positive and negative reinforcement. "Pavlov's dog" is a well-known example demonstrating classical conditioning leading to a physiological response (Gurung & Schwartz, 2013). Subsequently, Edward Thorndike "proposed the law of effect, which helped to explain the trial-and-error mechanism underlying behaviors that are more likely to occur again" (Gurung & Schwartz, 2013, p. 35). Watson, who was at one time a student of Dewey, "influenced a school psychology he referred to as 'behaviourist', due to this view of learning as based on observable and measurable changes in behaviour" (Stewart, 2021, p. 5). Mid-century, the influential B. F. Skinner further developed the theory of operant conditioning, which is more applicable in classroom settings as it focuses on the shaping of behavior (rather than physiological responses) through reinforcement, "if the reinforcer is contingent upon the learners' behaviour" (Naested et al., 2004, p. 74). All of these processes are assumed to be in response to external stimuli, and the perspective is that since internal processes are very difficult to view and measure, that behavior is the most objective indicator of learning (Badyl & Singh, 2017).

We see many powerful vestiges of the approach in our schooling systems, such as the reward of grades for student work, which can lead to students emphasizing the specific grade over the pursuit of knowledge. Most classrooms will include at least some behavioral elements, thinking about "repetition, feedback, and reinforcement of corrections needed in behavior so corrections are done and sustained" (Badyl & Singh, 2017, p. S1). A profound influence of behaviorism is the writing of learning outcomes that can be assessed through observed behaviors (Stewart, 2021). Disciplines that require psycho-motor skills, such as lab work in chemistry (O'Connor, 2015) or clinical skill development in nursing, are taught through careful repetition, "skill and drill" techniques (Badyl & Singh, 2017). In cases where there is a "right way and a wrong way for students to work" (O'Connor, 2015, p. 10), for example when there are safety considerations for practice, behaviorism is particularly useful. Often studies that take approaches borrowed from the field of psychology will take a more behavioral approach. In these studies, learning is defined in behavioral terms, for example, collecting data on how students might be motivated to attend class regularly through the use of pop quizzes or gamified elements.

One exemplar SoTL study that is grounded in behaviorist assumptions is April McGrath's (2014) study, "Just checking in: The effect of an office hour meeting and learning reflection in an introductory statistics course." We consider this study primarily in the behavioral category since the intervention was largely targeted to improving students' study habits. The researcher hypothesized that, based on previous research, the opportunity to build professor–student rapport would improve learning outcomes—in this way rapport becomes a motivator for changes in behavior. What was being measured was results on subsequent exams, rather than, say, interview data regarding student perceptions.

Cognitivism

Cognitivism considers learning as a mental process involving the creation of schema, structures and models, replacing behaviorism as the dominant paradigm in the 1960s. However, as suggested above, the replacement in educational theory is never complete—theories rise and fall in significance and prevalence, but never really disappear. In cognitivism, the mind is seen as a "black box" or information processor with "a focus on a person's own mental activities rather than on the environment" (Gurung & Schwartz,

2013, p. 36). The orientation is towards understanding changes in internal states of knowledge through thinking processes, rather than trying to predict responses to stimuli.

Cognitivist theories prioritize memory, thinking, and problem solving, and "directed psychologists to examine the determinants of learning and memory, with an emphasis on understanding the acquisition of knowledge in humans" (Gurung & Schwartz, 2013, p. 36). Learning is defined as a change in a learner's schemata, and "the learner uses cognitive tools, such as insight, information processing, perceptions, and memory to facilitate learning" (Badyl & Singh, 2017, p. S1). There is an interest in how learners code and structure knowledge, and "the learner is viewed as a very active participant in the learning process" (Ertmer & Newby, 2013, p. 51). Benjamin Bloom's (1956) well-known and still-utilized taxonomy of educational goals (knowledge, comprehension, application, analysis, synthesis, and evaluation), and the initial work in Decoding the Disciplines (Middendorf & Pace, 2004) are examples of cognitivist perspectives in practice.

Janice's first SoTL study was founded in a cognitivist perspective on learning (Miller-Young, 2013). She was interested in the difficulties first-year engineering students experienced when learning to visualize the three-dimensional structures in their textbooks. The study asked students to participate in a think-aloud interview, a protocol from cognitive psychology in which participants are asked to talk out loud about what they are thinking while working on a task (Streveler et al., 2008). The intent of the study was not to test a teaching intervention, but rather to identify typical challenges students encounter when learning the skill so that instructors can be more responsive to these difficulties. With this cognitivist approach, she was primarily interested in gaining better access to and understanding of learning processes as they occur—how students "think through" a complicated problem.

Constructivism

Constructivism builds on cognitivism, viewing learning as an active, "constructive" process, with even more emphasis on the role of the learner and their meaning-making process. In the latter part of the 20th century, it became the dominant educational theory (Ertmer & Newby, 2013), particularly in K–12 education. Under this learning theory, new information links and builds upon prior knowledge through meaning, and subjective representations of reality are created for the learner. While having elements in common with cognitivism in terms of an interest in mental schemas, "constructivists contend that what we know of the world stems from our own interpretations of our experiences. Humans *create* meaning as opposed to *acquiring* it" (emphasis in the original, Ertmer & Newby, 2013, p. 55).

In constructivism, an interest is taken on how past experience and cultural factors influence learning—within this perspective, the learner is understood in a context rather than as merely an individual. Ertmer and Newby (2013) explain that "both learner and environmental factors are critical to the constructivist, as it is the specific *interaction* between these two variables that creates knowledge" (emphasis in the original, p. 55). Jean Piaget was a key theorist in constructivism (also often associated with cognitivism), active from the 1920s through the 1970s and beyond. In his work on understanding how learning works, assimilation and accommodation are key processes to creating new understandings (Badyl & Singh, 2017; see also see Marchand, 2012 for a more thorough discussion of Piagetian constructivism). These are slightly different but related processes the learner uses to connect new learning to previous learning. Assimilation is when the learner adds new learning to previous learning structures. Accommodation, on the other hand, is when prior learning structures must be altered based on new information.

The learning theory was also influenced heavily by theorists such as Lev Vygotsky (1896–1934), known in education for the Zone of Proximal Development, where the optimal "zone" for learning occurs just beyond a student's level of competence, and John Dewey (1859–1952), often considered the father of experiential learning (Naested et al., 2004), who called for a more democratic and learner-centered approach to education (Stewart, 2021). Social constructivism is a further development, which recognizes the impact of interaction with others on learning. An example of social constructivism in action would be to think about how a child learns their first language from their family: through context and meaning making, motivated by a desire to communicate and have needs met, through modeling and practice in interaction with others.

Pedagogical approaches such as group work, now almost ubiquitous in the classroom, are based in constructivist learning theory. Experiential learning, a familiar concept to most educators, was written about by Dewey in *Experience and Education* (1938). Kolb (1984) influentially developed a model he called the experiential learning cycle—this is an inherently constructivist model, which emphasizes the learner's active interaction with the environment in a cycle of concrete experience, reflective observation, abstract conceptualization, and active experimentation (leading to more concrete experience).

Theories such as situated learning (Lave & Wenger, 1991), connectivism, and networked learning (Jung, 2019) are rooted in constructivist and socially constructivist principles, further refining and extending them. As it has gained predominance in acceptance, constructivism has led to a proliferation of teaching methods. Problem-based learning, active learning, and communities of practice are all examples of constructivist and socially constructivist pedagogies. These pedagogies provide rich ground for SoTL investigations, as researchers explore the sense-making of their students.

Karen conducted a study of students' choices in reading strategies through examining students' reflective reading logs in a course on critical writing and reading where she provided direction, prompts, and feedback (Manarin, 2012). She had students write ten reflective log entries where they described how they read different essays and reflected on the choices they made. Using her own disciplinary method of close reading, she identified five categories of actions students took in reading, and used patterns based on the purpose of the reading and whether the content was something students could personally connect with. This study then has constructivist/socially constructivist underpinnings, although they are not explicitly stated, because of the recognition that learning is done contextually and in conversation with others, in this case mainly through feedback from the instructor on the reading logs. The importance of students' prior learning experiences is acknowledged, as is the importance of personal meaning-making. A dialogical process in the reading logs is described.

Humanism

Humanism, a paradigm that also emerged in the 1960s, is based upon ideas of freedom, dignity, and the potential of human beings. Maslow's hierarchy is the well-known model (Maslow, 1970, please see next section regarding Blackfoot origins). This model is typically presented as a pyramid, with physiological needs at the bottom, moving through safety, love and belonging, esteem, need to know and understand, aesthetic needs, and finally self-actualization (Naested et al., 2004). The perspective here is that people act with intentionality according to their core values, but one set of needs has to be fulfilled before the learner can move on to the next. This has important implications for learning, because it suggests that learners must have their basic needs for food and shelter, as well as feeling safe and like they belong before they can effectively learn. Focusing on the whole learner and their relationships, rather than only the "thinking" aspect of the person, is key. Humanist pedagogies are common in professions such as nursing and social work. Examples of specific theories that fall under this umbrella are Mezirow's (1991) transformational learning, self-determination theory (Deci & Ryan 2012; Ryan & Deci, 2000), and narrative identity theory (Brockmeier & Carbaugh, 2001).

In SoTL, the current Students-as-Partners movement frequently demonstrates a humanist orientation, focusing on breaking down the power relationships between teachers and students to create empowering learning environments. Example work is Haney et al.'s (2021) podcast and associated essay on "Power, voice, and positionality," or Marquis et al.'s (2021) "'It's a little complicated for me': Faculty social location and experiences of pedagogical partnership."

Indigenous Perspectives—With Gabrielle Weasel Head

Indigenous pedagogies have much in common with both social constructivism and humanism, in the sense they are relationally and experientially oriented, and take into account the entire being of the learner. Indeed, it has come to light that Maslow developed his ideas on the hierarchy of needs when studying the Blackfoot (Blackstock, 2011)—one colonial example of knowledge being taken without credit. However, the Blackfoot concepts have many important differences from Maslow's formulation, highlighting fundamental differences between Western and Indigenous understanding of the world. Blackstock explains that Maslow did not fully situate the human being in the context of community the way it is understood in Blackfoot worldview, and that if he had, "the model would be centered on multi-generational community actualization versus on individual actualization and transcendence" (p. 4).

As settler–scholars, the authors of this book do not have the authority to fully explicate Indigenous pedagogies; however, now more than ever there is a critical need for all in education to acknowledge and appreciate the rigorous and complex nature of Indigenous perspectives on learning in higher education, and to educate ourselves. For this reason, we are grateful for the contributions to this section of our Indigenous colleague, Gabrielle Weasel Head, as introduced more fully in the Preface. Gabrielle also contributes to the Indigenous research methodologies sections in Chapters 3 and 11. Some of the elements present in the literature and in our learning from Indigenous colleagues include: on-the-land learning (Calderon, 2014; Simpson, 2014; Tuck et al., 2014), relationality, positionality, spirituality (Bastien, 2004, 2016), centering Indigenous knowledges, being attentive to story, and learning from Elders (Pete et al., 2013). Ermine (2007) suggests an ethical space between Western and Indigenous thought, "in a manner where they are poised to encounter each other" (p. 194). Further reading suggestions are provided at the end of this chapter, but it is also important to acknowledge that Indigenous perspectives are highly local and contextual; therefore, it is the responsibility of the practitioner to learn about local Indigenous groups and perspectives on pedagogy. An exemplar of this kind of effort can be found in Pete et al.'s (2013) "Decolonizing our practice: Indigenizing our teaching."

To put it together, a good SoTL study begins with a good question, often rooted in the curiosities and problems that arise in teaching. There are various taxonomies and levels that can help think through the types of questions that might be asked, and it's worthwhile to keep in mind Kreber's reminder that SoTL should be situated in a broader context of significance. A stepwise process of identifying a topic, problem statement, and purpose statement can help to refine a research question (or series of questions). All of this should be situated in the literature. A theoretical framework is chosen to anchor the work—this theory can come from a variety of sources, but one common source to consider in SoTL is learning theory.

Key Concepts

- SoTL inquiries often originate from questions arising from teaching and learning practice.
- Typologies of SoTL questions can help narrow down the focus and context of the inquiry.
- A well-developed SoTL inquiry includes a defined problem, research question, and exploration of previous literature.
- A theoretical framework provides a lens to choose a research methodology or design, and select appropriate methods for the SoTL study.
- One source of a theoretical framework is learning theory.
- Indigenous pedagogy and research methodologies provide an alternative framework to Western knowledge systems.

Further Reading

Research Questions and Literature Review

Cappello, A., & Miller-Young, J. (2020). Who are we citing and how? A SoTL citation analysis. *Teaching and Learning Inquiry*, 8(2), 3–16. https://doi.org/10.20343/teachlearninqu.8.2.2.

Ciccone, A. (2018). Learning matters: Asking meaningful questions. In N. L. Chick (Ed.), *SoTL in action: Illuminating critical moments of practice* (pp. 15–22). Stylus.

Galvan, J. L. (2012). *Writing literature reviews: A guide for students of the social and behavioral sciences* (5th ed.). Pyrczak.

MacMillan, M. (2018). The SoTL literature review: Exploring new territory. In N. L. Chick (Ed.), *SoTL in action: Illuminating critical moments of practice* (pp. 23–31). Stylus.

Merriam, S. B., & Tisdell, E. J. (2016). *Qualitative research: A guide to design and implementation.* Jossey-Bass.

Poole, G. (2018). Using intuition, anecdote, and observation. In N. L. Chick (Ed.), *SoTL in action: Illuminating critical moments of practice* (pp. 7–14). Stylus.

Learning Theory

Bastien, B. (2004). *Blackfoot ways of knowing: The worldview of the Siksikaitsitapi.* University of Calgary Press.

Miller-Young, J., & Yeo, M. (2015). Conceptualizing and communicating SoTL: A framework for the field. *Teaching & Learning Inquiry*, 3(2), 37–53.

Steiner, H. H., & Hakala, C. M. (2021). What do SoTL practitioners need to know about learning? *Teaching and Learning Inquiry*, 9(1), 79–85. https://doi.org/10.20343/teachlearninqu.9.1.7.

Stewart, M. (2021). Understanding learning: Theories and critique. In L. Hunt & D. Chalmers (Eds.), *University teaching in focus: A learning-centred approach* (2nd ed.) (pp. 3–28). Taylor & Francis Group.

Wilson, S., & Shellhammer, B. (2022). *Indigegogy: An invitation to learning in a relational way*. WBG Academic. https://files.wbg-wissenverbindet.de/Files/Article/ARTK_ZOA_1028844_0001.pdf.

3

THINKING ABOUT SOTL RESEARCH FRAMEWORKS

This chapter introduces a research framework representing a continuum of research paradigms, from a positivist and post-positivist approach on one end of the spectrum to a transformative approach on the other, with critical realist and interpretive approaches in between. All of these paradigms are rooted in the worldview of the researcher and their orientation towards knowledge. We first explain the framework, and then briefly describe each category with specific research designs and methodologies introduced, each of which will be discussed more fully in subsequent chapters. This chapter is intended to give the SoTL researcher a sense of the full range of research designs and methodologies available—which should be chosen in alignment with the research question as well as the worldview of the researcher.

In this chapter, we delve into a full range of potential methodological approaches to SoTL research, mapping a continuum of research paradigms rooted in the worldview of the researcher, their academic discipline, and previous training. "Paradigms" reflect perspectives on the nature of knowledge—what knowledge is considered of most worth—and how it can be known (see Kuhn, 1962), relating to "the beliefs, assumptions, values and practices shared by a research community" (Braun & Clarke, 2013, p. 4). Paradigms are also sometimes called worldviews (Creswell & Plano Clark, 2017, p. 35), and can include ontology (nature of reality, our being-in-the-world), epistemology (nature of knowledge) (Merriam & Tisdell, 2016, p.8), and axiology (values, especially ethical implications and assumptions) (Lincoln et al., 2018; Wilson, 2008).

As discussed in Chapter 1, SoTL is often referred to as a "big tent"—a metaphor meant to suggest that SoTL is hospitable to the full range of research

DOI: 10.4324/9781003447054-4

paradigms. This hospitality is one of the appealing elements of working in SoTL, but it can also create complications because with such a broad range of methodological possibilities, it can be difficult as a beginner to choose. Further, SoTL researchers at the same conferences or even within the same research team can find themselves engaged in cross-talk rooted in different views about how research should be conducted. Indeed, despite having worked together for many years, given our own diverse disciplinary backgrounds, we found we had profoundly different understandings of foundational elements in the process of writing this book. In particular, our conceptions of how theory should be understood and used in research and what is an empirical observation (see Miller-Young et al., forthcoming) required a great deal of discussion. Similarly, it can be difficult for reviewers, editors, and authors alike when worldviews clash during the review process, sometimes without the players being aware of the difficulty; for example, a reviewer might ask the researcher to demonstrate the generalizability of findings, which may not be appropriate in their qualitative study. Therefore, having a basic understanding and mental map of the range of research paradigms, and the priorities and assumptions of each, can be helpful in navigating the big tent of SoTL, both for newcomers and also for those communicating their work to a multidisciplinary audience.

Objectivity Versus Subjectivity

One important distinction to make is that some research paradigms prioritize objectivity on the part of the researcher, while others embrace subjectivity, arguing that all experience is interpreted. The valuing of objectivity, for example in the scientific method, is such a dominant paradigm in Western culture that assumptions made about the predominance of the scientific method as the approach by which the world can be known, has become tacit within the paradigm as an obvious "given." When doing science, researchers typically do not talk about their underlying philosophical assumptions or describe the scientific method—that part is all assumed. While few scientists today would claim that science is purely objective, they still attempt to describe the world as objectively as possible. In contrast, research paradigms that value subjectivity think about the world as something co-created through our perception, seeing reality as constructed or interpreted (Kara, 2022). These research paradigms are more common in disciplines that study the social, rather than natural, world.

However, there is a recognition in most paradigms that a complete separation between the world and the subjective knower is not possible; indeed in many streams, science, too, has evolved towards this understanding. While distinguishing the objectivist and subjectivist position is important, we also see it as a somewhat false binary. The world is always known and interpreted by *someone*, and who that person is and their context matter. But the question is whether objectivity is *sought* on the part of the researcher, and the answer to this question is in part what creates dividing lines between research paradigms. How the idea of objectivity versus subjectivity is taken up, and how fully the subjective or objective perspective is embraced and with what level of priority, will vary depending on the goals of the research paradigm, the theoretical framing, and the underlying worldview.

We considered attempting to place these values on two axes, plotting objectivity versus subjectivity against an interest in the individual versus populations, which also can be a distinguishing feature of different paradigms. In practice, all of these attempts to represent research paradigms in opposing terms break down quickly, illustrating the dangers of false binaries. Also, we realized there are more than two axes, or as Janice would put it, they can't be mapped to a two-dimensional space. Therefore, the rest of this chapter, and indeed the remainder of this book, is aimed at describing the continuum of research paradigms, methodologies, designs, and methods in a way that is at once simple, yet cognizant of nuance. We encourage readers to consider all of our descriptions as a continuum rather than firm categories, understanding that all of these paradigms have evolved historically and continue to do so as the social context changes. For every rule we might try to articulate, there are enough exceptions to make the rule unhelpful. However, we believe that these kinds of frameworks are needed as a heuristic to help interpret and place the work you might encounter in SoTL, to consider your own position in your disciplinary thinking, and also to give you potential directions to travel as you plan your own SoTL inquiry.

In what follows, we present a framework for understanding the range of research methodologies, which is inclusive of many disciplines and research traditions. We have found this framework helpful in our practice of working with both developing and experienced SoTL practitioners. We will introduce the range of methodologies and research designs here at a high level, while later chapters will address design, methodology, and method in more detail.

Research Paradigms

Research paradigms, like learning theories, can be placed broadly into categories representing a continuum: positivist/post-positivist, critical realist, interpretive, and what we are calling transformative, which includes such diverse approaches as critical, postmodern, and Students-as-Partners. While the Indigenous research paradigm holds elements with all of the above, excluding positivist/post-positivist, it should be understood as comprising its own paradigm due to its diversion from the Western paradigms. Each of these paradigms is associated with different worldviews on the nature of reality (or ontology), different understandings about the nature of knowledge and how it can be known (or epistemology), and the values and ethical stance of the researcher (or axiology). Each paradigm tends to be associated with particular research designs, although there can also be a great deal of variation. For example, critical work, while always interested in dynamics of power in society, can encompass research methodologies across the spectrum, including quantitative and qualitative designs.

Below is a table summarizing these research paradigms, their associated worldviews, and goals. Yet as Merriam and Tisdell (2016) point out, “there is overlap in actual research design and orientations” (p. 9). While the categories and distinctions we discuss in this chapter are useful to map the landscape of research methodologies, there are no absolutes, and much crossover and crosstalk—in part as a response to larger socio-political dynamics in the larger society over time.

Therefore, we cannot emphasize enough that it is better to understand these as a continuum, with ideas clustered like family trees surrounding each paradigm, rather than rigid categories with firm delineations.

Perhaps because SoTL draws from disciplines across the spectrum in higher education, one can find examples of studies from across the continuum. In the “big tent” of SoTL, all are possible and accepted, although we argue that certain approaches are more suitable for some questions and contexts than others. Researchers tend to be heavily influenced by their own disciplinary background and training, and indeed if they wish their SoTL work to reach an audience of their disciplinary peers, it makes sense to work in ways that will be accepted within that discipline. We now turn to discussion of each research paradigm presented in the table, the associated views of reality, and the goals of each.

Positivism/Post-Positivism

Positivist perspectives assume that there is a single truth or knowable world which is independent of context, observer, or the observed, a view traditionally associated with the natural sciences (Hempel, 1965), seeing reality as “observable, stable, and measurable” (Merriam & Tisdell, 2016, p. 9), and having “the capacity to be fully understood” (Kara, 2022, p. 19). Kara (2022) points out that the scientific method developed in step with positivist philosophy and “for much of the 20th century they seemed to go hand in hand” (p. 19). However, she also notes that “positivism and the scientific method were not as secure and homogenous as they appeared, and philosophers of science provided debating points which helped to widen the field of thought” (p. 19). For example, even disciplines like physics do not have universal laws: what applies at the atomic scale does not apply at human (e.g., Newtonian) or cosmic scales.

Through influential philosophers of science such as Paul Feyerabend, Thomas Kuhn, and Karl Popper, in Euro-Western thought a more flexible approach has replaced earlier classical positivism (Kara, 2022). Kuhn (1962,

TABLE 3.1 Research Paradigms

Research Paradigm	*View on Nature of Reality*	*Goals*
Positivist/ Post-positivist	Single reality exists in an external world and can be objectively known (positivism), or sought but imperfectly known (post-positivism) ↓	*Predict, determine cause–effect*
	Measurable/observable reality, researcher tries to be impartial and objective	*Generalize, test and refine theory; describe, understand, explain phenomena and populations*
Critical Realist	Single reality exists but knowledge is dependent on socio-historical contexts ↓	*Test and refine theory, describe, understand, explain phenomena*
	Researcher seeks the truth, is explicit about use of theory, theory is constructed, and context matters	*Gain an understanding of complex situations in contexts*
Interpretive	Multiple realities as perceived by individuals, common understanding built through intersubjectivity (shared understanding), reality is seen as constructed/interpreted ↓	*Describe, understand, interpret experience*
	Researcher values closeness and subjectivity; researcher often considered an additional participant	*Unpack individual and shared experience of complex phenomena, in contexts as perceived*
Transformative ***Critical***	Differential experiences of reality depending on social location, determined through power relationships (one position is privileged): through social, political, cultural, economic, and gender values	*Change, emancipate, empower*
Postmodern	Reality can never truly be known (questions the very assumption of a knowable reality), multiple realities	*Deconstruct, disrupt, problematize*
Indigenous	Reality is deeply relational and interconnected with the natural world, others (human and non-human)	*Restore (re-storying), heal, reconcile, reconnect, reciprocate*

1979) is widely credited for identifying major paradigms of thought within science and for pointing out that theory is socially constructed within the scientific community, meaning "truth" is that which is accepted by the community at a given point in time. Instead, the researcher addresses the extent of the generalizability of a theory, the limitations of measurement techniques, and the influence of their own assumptions: this is often referred to as the post-positivist turn (Philips, 1990). There is still a belief in a single reality that should be sought as objectively as possible by the researcher, but also an understanding that reality can only ever be partially understood (Kara, 2022).

In a SoTL context, both quantitative research and qualitative empirical studies can be conducted within a post-positivist paradigm: both attempt to describe, understand, or explain a phenomenon or the impact, for example, of a teaching intervention. Quantitative designs will attempt to test and refine theory by finding patterns within larger sets of data, and to control for bias through research design and statistical methods, knowing it can't be fully eliminated; qualitative empirical studies use a more focused lens, leaving it to the reader to determine the transferability of their findings. More on these later in the chapter.

Critical Realism

Critical realism developed in the third quarter of the 20th century, initially through the influence of Roy Bhaskar's ontological work (1975). This paradigm rejects both the subjectivist, but especially the objectivist, view dominating social science at the time. It is not just a combination of the two perspectives, but rather an independent position that is theory-driven: interested in contextual, stratified explanations of phenomena. By stratified we mean that critical realists think about the different levels a phenomenon might operate, for example, individual, group, institutional, and the broader society. For this reason, it can be very useful in higher education for efforts such as institutional or program evaluation, and aligns well with studies taking a systems thinking, complexity theory, or social network–informed approach.

Kara notes that this paradigm "views facts as always questionable and laden with theory. Knowledge is seen socially and historically produced" (p. 21), with the importance of context emphasized. Kozhevnikov and Vincent (2019), citing Fleetwood (2014), suggest that it "offers an opportunity to reject objectivist ideas about universal laws without accepting a subjectivist belief in multiple realities" (p. 3). Unlike interpretivists, critical realists do expect that findings of their research could be replicated, if the context were replicated (Kara, 2022). There is an interest in something called generative causation, meaning that we can find out how phenomena operate in society by uncovering "hidden mechanisms" and "identifying the influence of contextual factors" (Kara, 2022, p. 22).

In critical realism, there is a complex understanding of the world as having different layers of reality—the *empirical*, which can be observed; the *actual*, which are the processes and events happening; and the *real*, which are an aggregation of casualties (Archer et al., 1998). This is a complex paradigm that is theoretically driven, and does not necessarily have a set of research methodologies directly associated with it. Rather, it takes a pragmatic approach, and uses various study designs depending on the question being studied. However, critical realism is often very compatible with a mixed methods study design, described with more detail in Chapter 9.

Interpretive (Detailed in Chapter 10)

Interpretive approaches derive knowledge claims from the interpretation of contextual experiences, assume that social reality is locally, specifically, and co-constructed (Lincoln et al., 2018), and that the knowledge produced is idiographic in nature, meaning that it relates to those things that are contingent, unique, concrete, and specific. The interpretive paradigm follows from a different philosophical tradition, usually traced back to philosophers such as Kant, Husserl, and Heidegger. In interpretive research, the world is seen as made up of people experiencing multiple subjective realities, and our collective understanding of those realities is what constitutes knowledge: sometimes termed "inter-subjective"—meaning shared understanding "derived from community consensus regarding what is 'real': what is useful and what has meaning" (Lincoln et al., 2018, p. 113). In interpretive methodologies, methods and approaches emerge and are adjusted during the study. Rather than judging interpretive research on criteria such as validity and generalizability, quality in interpretive research must be judged through trustworthiness.

Using Hutchings's (2000) taxonomy, most interpretive studies would tend toward a "what is" type of question. Ethnography, hermeneutic, narrative inquiry, and phenomenological approaches are examples of interpretive methodologies, and will be explored further in Chapter 10.

Transformative Approaches (Detailed in Chapter 11)

Critical

The critical perspective examines power relationships present in society and, therefore, recognizes truth in multiple subjective realities, since truth defined by those in power is different than by those who are marginalized. These "virtual" realities are shaped by "social, political, cultural, economic, ethic, and gender values, crystallized over time" (Lincoln et al., 2018, p. 110). Kreber (2013) suggests that discourse in SoTL has been so oriented to "what works" that it tacitly ignores questions of social justice and ethics. She argues that such questions are inseparable from "what we think we are committed to in the scholarship of teaching and what we consider its purpose to be" (p. 858). This perspective then leads us towards a critical approach which is designed to illuminate inequities and could ask questions about race, class, and gender and how they play out in a pedagogical space, i.e., mainly humanist and potentially socially constructivist kinds of questions. Researchers engaged in critical approaches are interested in "critique, transformation, restitution, and emancipation" (Lincoln et al., 2018, p. 110).

Students-as-Partners (Detailed in Chapter 11)

The Students-as-Partners movement (SaP) has gained important momentum within SoTL over the last decade. It makes an authentic effort to unravel the power dynamic between academic faculty and students, bringing students into the research process as full partners, rather than merely as participants or even research assistants—the distinction may be expressed as researching "with" instead of researching "on" students. SaP is based on the idea that students are legitimate knowers in post-secondary contexts, and sees them as key stakeholders in the educational experience. Engaging students as partners in SoTL means inviting them to shape, deliver, and disseminate the work alongside faculty partners.

Postmodern

Postmodern analyses include diverse and contradictory critiques that "resist, subvert, and refuse any structural formation" (Denzin & Lincoln, 2013, p. 455). The related term post-structural tends to be most associated with literary theory, but is rooted in the same, postmodern perspective. Postmodern discourses are deconstructive in that they seek to make us skeptical about beliefs concerning truth, knowledge, power, the self, and language that are often taken for granted. The purpose is to deconstruct existing "grand narratives" or theoretical frameworks that describe social behavior, and the outcome is a reconceptualized description of a phenomenon. This research methodology might indeed reject the notion of a unifying learning theory and challenges the researcher to consider a multiplicity of perspectives, including an individual's potential resistance to learning (Ellsworth, 1997). Merriam and Tisdell (2016) describe:

> Postmodernists celebrate diversity among people, ideas, and institutions. By accepting the diversity and plurality of the world, no one element is privileged or more powerful than another. Congruent with this perspective, postmodern research is highly experimental, playful, and creative, and no two postmodern studies look alike.
>
> *(p. 11)*

Currently, postmodern research in SoTL is rare. However, as Merriam and Tisdell point out, citing Grbich (2013), most qualitative research has a postmodern version (and here is where we can see overlap in the categories and paradigms—ethnography, feminist research, and phenomenology, for example, all have postmodern versions). SoTL researchers, particularly those from disciplines that play with postmodern and poststructural approaches, may want to consider what a postmodern SoTL study could entail.

Indigenous Research Methodologies (Detailed in Chapter 11)—With Gabrielle Weasel Head

In Canada, the final report of the Truth and Reconciliation Commission in 2015 set in motion a focus within post-secondary institutions on decolonization and Indigenization. Similar movements are underway, in various stages (some much further ahead than Canada) in places such as New Zealand, Australia, and South Africa. The move towards recognizing Indigenous research methodologies may be more of an urgent public discourse depending on your local context; however, we encourage all engaging with SoTL to learn about these perspectives.

Margaret Kovach (2018), in her chapter "Doing Indigenous Methodologies: A Letter to a Research Class," describes both the epistemological and methodological requirements for "doing" Indigenous methodologies. She first makes a distinction between Indigenous research, which "concerns itself with Indigenous matters," (p. 215) and Indigenous methodologies, which she argues "asks more" (p. 217). She writes, "Indigenous methodologies require exploration of identity, an ability to be vulnerable, a desire for restitution, and an opening to awakenings" (p. 217). The researcher must first be willing to confront the ubiquity of the Western gaze, and begin to destabilize it. This requires a deconstruction of colonialism and the ideologies that shape it in order to illuminate its influence in academia, which also aligns with a postmodernism/post-structuralism. Indigenous methodologies include, in Kovach's description, Indigenous epistemologies (beliefs about knowledge such as holism and interconnectivity), Indigenous theory principles (beliefs about values and actions), relational actions (beliefs about conduct and actions), and re-storying/interpretations and representations (responsibility in witnessing and relating events and meaning). Relationship is at the heart of Indigenous methodologies—and Johnston et al. (2018) note, "relationships in Indigenous research extend beyond human agents to include all beings, what Western science would call 'living' and 'non-living.' Relational accountability includes literally all relations" (p. 13).

Positionality

We encourage all SoTL researchers to consider your own positionality, meaning your identity/role, context, and relationship to your research question. Including this kind of statement when you write up your work is expected in some paradigms, like the interpretive paradigm, while it has been historically uncommon in post-positivist and especially positivist dissemination. This can be seen as a reflection of the subjective/objective lens. For studies using a highly objective lens, the research might be described in a distant way from the researcher, and may be written in third person. In more subjective paradigms, first person is the expected stance, as is a detailed positioning statement. In critical realism, the researcher would likely write their positionality statement in the first person, acknowledging how the context and their relationship to the research informed their research question and choice of theoretical lens, while the methods, analysis, and discussion might be in the third person. For Indigenous research methodologies, it is common to see a very detailed and nuanced discussion of the author's relationality, as described in Chapter 11. Expectations can also vary by the journal, so this is something worth looking for and becoming familiar with before you start writing (more on how to choose an appropriate journal for your SoTL study in Chapter 12).

As we have shown, the research paradigm represents important differences in worldview, which leads into epistemology (how the world can be known) and axiology (values and ethics). Each of these paradigms is associated with various research methodologies and designs, although this correspondence is loose rather than absolute, since the methodologies can and are used across the continuum. We next introduce some major types of research methodologies that can be utilized in SoTL studies. These will all be explored in more depth in later chapters.

Research Methodologies

In Chapter 2, we introduced how a theoretical framework is used to underpin a research inquiry. It is important that SoTL researchers have an awareness of the research paradigm they are operating under, but depending on the paradigm, this may or may not be explicitly stated. However, a second element that needs articulation is the methodology of the study. This should be seen as distinct from methods, which is simply a description of how the participants were selected, and the data collected and analyzed. A well-designed and persuasive SoTL study is inherently rigorous. As discussed in Chapter 1, Felten (2013) provided a list of widely cited guidelines for good practice in SoTL: principle three is "methodologically sound." But what does this mean? In part, it suggests that the study is coherent—in other words, there is alignment between the pedagogical orientation of the teacher, the research question, the research design or methodology, and the research methods used. We distinguish between methods and methodologies in this way: methods are the tactical choices made by the researcher in terms of what and how data is gathered and analyzed, whereas methodology is the underlying design or approach (for example, mixed methods or phenomenology). These methodologies carry with them basic assumptions about the nature of the world and how it can be known. For example, do we learn about the world primarily through observation? Through learning about the perceptions and perspectives of others? Through our own engagement with multiple sources of knowledge both seen and unseen? Are we concerned about power and how it affects the learning endeavor? Answers to these more philosophical questions will have implications for the most suitable research methodology and design, but so will the research question itself.

Other terms researchers will commonly use include "research design," which Creswell and Poth (2018) explain "means the plan for conducting the study" (p. 49), while the "research process" includes all phases of the work, "including the introduction to a study through its purpose and research questions, data collection, data analysis, report writing, and standards of validation and evaluation" (p. 2). The methodology explains why it was done this way, and articulates the assumptions and world view of the researchers (Burton, 2002, p. 4), which falls into this or that research paradigm (more on that below). As Berenson (2018) comments,

> awareness of our research paradigm helps us see and defend to others the rigor of our work, including what counts as evidence, how we generate and analyze that evidence, and the claims we make about the broader relevance of that work.
>
> *(p. 42)*

Put another way, Creswell and Poth (2018) describe methodology as the conceptualization and assumptions of the research process for which the study purpose, questions, and methods must be cohesive and congruent (p. 50). While many SoTL studies may collect work samples or interview students, what is done with this data and what is looked for depend largely upon the methodology. For example, if a quantitative approach is taken, relationships between variables will be sought, whereas in a critical study, the researcher is attuned to questions of privilege and power. In most qualitative approaches, generalizability is not an aim of the research but rather a rich, contextual ("thick") description to ensure trustworthiness or credibility (Tracy, 2010). The onus is then on the reader to determine whether the findings are transferable to other contexts. Please see Figure 3.1 for an illustration of how we conceptualize the relationship between methodology and method.

FIGURE 3.1 Visualizing the relationship between methodologies and methods, where the big picture worldview of methodology drives tactical decisions about methods.

Qualitative Versus Quantitative Research

A simple distinction is often made between qualitative and quantitative research—university courses about research, and methodology texts, are often titled with these terms. However, in trying to define differences between these research designs based on worldviews, we encountered all kinds of difficulties, demonstrating that the distinction between qualitative and quantitative research is not as simple as it appears. On the surface, it seems obvious that quantitative research is interested in "quantities"—in measuring and observing the world, while qualitative research tends to use words and images (created by people) as data. For example, Braun and Clarke (2013) as well as Divan et al. (2017) claim that the quantitative researcher uses numbers as data while the qualitative researcher uses words as data, but on the other hand it's certainly possible to turn words into quantitative data, for example, when a researcher counts and reports how many times a particular word or concept is used. It's also possible to use non-verbal artifacts, like photographs or drawings, as qualitative data, or turn them into quantitative data through content analysis. So the number/word distinction is insufficient. Whether a study collects quantitative or qualitative data alone is not enough to identify the associated research paradigm—as Janice continuously reminded us, "It's not about the data!" What we can say is that a quantitative researcher is interested in reducing complexity in order to find patterns amongst variables and populations, while a qualitative researcher is interested in qualities and complexity. Mixed methods seek to combine these approaches in a dynamic way.

We need to look at other qualities, then, to define these terms and to distinguish research paradigms. Additionally, Braun and Clarke (2013) make a helpful distinction between "Big Q" qualitative research—research conducted within a qualitative paradigm—and "small q" qualitative research, that is, research that uses qualitative techniques without sharing all the values of an interpretive paradigm; the data may be used to inform questionnaire design, as part of mixed methods research designs, or to quantify qualitative data in content analysis (pp. 4–5). In this book, we explore both "Big Q" and "small q" qualitative research in different chapters.

Inductive Versus Deductive Processes

While quantitative studies are deductive by definition, meaning that data is collected to test an already existing theory or hypothesis, qualitative research can be either deductive or inductive (see Chapters 7 and 8 for more detail). Inductive means working from the bottom up: "researchers gather data to build concepts, hypotheses, or theories" (Merriam & Tisdell, 2016, p. 17), rather than top down, as in deductive research. Figure 3.2 illustrates the relationship between theory and data through either inductive or deductive process. Importantly, however, with the exception of grounded theory

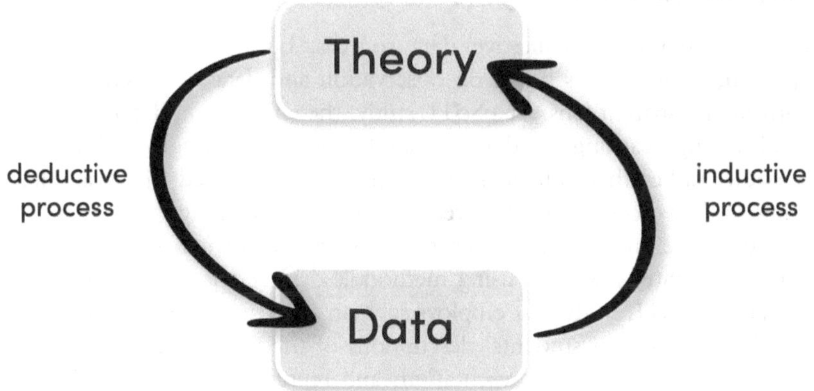

FIGURE 3.2 Deductive vs. inductive processes: where data can be used to test or generate theory.

research, most individual studies following an inductive process contribute to, rather than fully develop, theory.

Quantitative Designs (Detailed in Chapter 7)

As stated above, quantitative research is interested in measuring quantities (how much, how many), and typically uses statistical analysis to support findings. While research paradigms across the spectrum make use of quantitative data, it is most often associated with positivist/post-positivist and critical realist paradigms. This type of research is hypothesis-driven, and its purpose is to find relationships among variables and/or to define cause and effect. It can be described as "variable-centered"—the process involves objective measurement and observation of deductively predetermined variables, and determining whether there are, for example, statistically significant differences between groups, or average effects of a variable on an outcome. The methods and variables are defined in advance, informed by previous research and/or theory. The choice of measurement tools, sample, and data analysis must address validity, reliability, and generalizability (see Chapters 4 and 7 for further detail). In this book, we describe three common quantitative designs.

In SoTL, because we are working in the environment of the classroom in which for both practical and ethical reasons variables cannot be fully controlled, the quantitative work may be post-positivist in its orientation, meaning that the researcher is attempting to approach understanding an observable reality, knowing that it can never be perfectly known, or more commonly may be conducted with a critical realist lens, where theory is explicit and phenomena are understood in context.

Qualitative Empirical Design (Detailed in Chapter 8)

Some research uses qualitative data sources, but is still empirical in its approach, meaning it is based on observation and data is viewed through a relatively transparent lens. In a SoTL study, the emphasis in data collection is on observing learning as demonstrated (such as through a think-aloud interview) rather than inferring that learning has occurred (for example, by asking students to self-report or reflect upon their learning).

A qualitative empirical approach may also be taken to analyzing "small q" data such as interview data, using methodologies such as phenomenography. An example SoTL study that employs such an approach is Brett McCollum et al.'s (2016) study on students' descriptions of their experiences when introduced to new symbolic representations and representational technologies in chemistry. While the researchers are interested in experience, it is experience as described by participants at face value, which the researcher then "observes." Phenomenography is interested in delineating clear categories, where the researcher takes an objective stance while using inductive processes. McCollum et al. (2016) explain that while they acknowledge that "the experiences of the researcher will influence the research process, from design of the research question through analysis of the data and formulation of conclusions," that "the researcher must address these unavoidable biases, and where possible implement controls or checks on his/her interpretations" (p. 108). They note that "the outcome of any phenomenographic analysis is a set of well-defined and logically related categories" (p. 108) in an inductive process that "emerges from the data once analysis starts rather than being predicted prior to data collection" (p. 108). This is a good example of a qualitative empirical approach.

Whether using deductive or inductive processes, "small q" qualitative empirical studies tend to collect non-quantified data such as interviews, think-alouds, or artifacts, applying a range of empirical approaches—some of which apply strict and objective rules; others are still focused on trying to observe an external reality but are heading towards more interpretivist practices without fully embracing "Big Q" qualitative research. This is one of many places where we should think in terms of a continuum rather than strict categories.

Mixed Methods (Detailed in Chapter 9)

Mixed methods research (sometimes abbreviated as MMR) means that both qualitative and quantitative data are collected within the same study, but in a process that integrates the findings of both in a dynamic way, where the results of one inform the other. Mixed methods is likely to have one foot in either a post-positivist or critical realist perspective, and, on the qualitative side, it sometimes shifts into an interpretive frame, particularly when the qualitative data component is emphasized. Depending on the specific type of mixed methods study, and the disciplinary orientation of the researchers, exactly where mixed methods should be placed may vary paradigmatically. This makes sense when we consider:

> for these researchers, MMR is characterized by eclecticism, paradigm pluralism, a celebration of diversity, a rejection of dichotomies, an iterative approach to inquiry, an emphasis on the research questions, and a focus on signature MMR design and analysis strategies.
>
> *(Denzin & Lincoln, 2018, p. 314)*

Mixed methods can be a valuable option in SoTL research. Some advantages of the approach are that questions can be tackled that can't be answered by either quantitative or qualitative data alone, and it capitalizes on the common scenario where SoTL research teams are made up of researchers from a diversity of disciplines, research paradigms, and methodological skill sets.

Qualitative ("Big Q") Methodologies (Detailed in Chapters 10 and 11)

Most research texts written about qualitative research (for example, Merriam & Tisdell, 2016; Creswell & Poth, 2018) are exploring work within the interpretive category—this is what we can think of as "Big Q" qualitative research (Braun & Clarke, 2013). Saldana (2011) describes qualitative research as:

> an umbrella term for a wide variety of approaches to and methods for the study of natural social life. The information or data collected and analyzed is primarily (but not exclusively) nonquantitative in character, consisting of textual materials such as interview transcripts, fieldnotes, and documents, and/or visual materials such as artifacts, photographs, video recordings, and Internet sites, that document human experiences about others and/or one's self in social action and reflexive states.
>
> *(pp. 3–4)*

In this definition, Saldana lists many qualitative data sources, but he also brings in some other qualities of qualitative research—that it involves a wide variety of methodologies, which we will explore briefly below and in later chapters, and that it explores human experiences in complex social contexts. Many other definitions of qualitative research expand on these qualities. For example, Merriam and Tisdell (2016) identify four key characteristics of qualitative research: "The focus is on process, understanding, and meaning; the researcher is the primary instrument of data collection and analysis; the process is inductive; and the product is richly descriptive" (p. 15). Creswell (2007) adds the idea that "Qualitative research is a form of inquiry in which researchers make an interpretation of what they see, hear, and understand" (p. 39) and that "Researchers are bound not by tight cause-and-effect relationships among factors, but rather by identifying the complex interactions of factors in any situation" (p. 39). These definitions demonstrate how well suited qualitative research can be for scholarship of teaching and learning. In the following table, we note the qualities identified by different qualitative research texts as being important aspects of the work.

Most scholarship of teaching and learning takes place, not in a lab where the researcher can control for different variables, but in the fluid and relational terrain of the classroom or specific course where it's much more difficult to list, let alone control, all of the different factors at play. Quite often researchers are not only key instruments but also factors within the teaching and learning environment. Qualitative research, like teaching, is emergent, complex, contextually bound, and hopefully theoretically informed.

Most qualitative data tend to focus less on the final result or product of a process, for example, whether a particular learning outcome was achieved,

TABLE 3.2 Qualities of Qualitative Research

Qualities	*Creswell (2007)*	*Merriam & Tisdell (2016)*	*Braun & Clarke (2013)*	*Saldana (2011)*
Natural setting	X			X
Researcher as key instrument	X	X	X	X
Inductive process	X	X	X	
Emergent design	X	X	X	X
Interpretative and descriptive	X	X	X	X
Complex	X	X	X	X
Many types of data	X	X	X	X
Context important	X	X	X	X
Theoretically informed	X	X	X	X

and more on the process and meaning of achieving that outcome. It involves how individuals make sense of their world, how they interpret their experience, and as such, it cannot be objective. For interpretive researchers, as discussed above, this lack of objectivity in the data is not a problem; indeed, they recognize that they bring their own biases and subjectivity to the inquiry and explore how their own subjectivity affects their interpretation of the data. This interpretation moves from observations to understanding or theory in an inductive process. This doesn't mean that the interpretive researcher begins without any ideas about the area or theoretical framework; indeed, as we've seen in Chapter 2, so much of the research design depends upon our theoretical lens and literature review, but qualitative researchers spend a lot of time working with the specific details of their data. They move back and forth between bits of data and more abstract ideas as qualitative research involves both description and interpretation. Creswell (2007) describes the qualitative data analysis process as a spiral where the loops include data management; reading and memoing; describing, classifying, and interpreting; and representing and visualizing: "one enters with data of text or images (e.g., photographs, videotapes) and exits with an account or a narrative" (p. 150).

Understanding the landscape of research paradigms and methodologies is an important first step in conceptualizing your inquiry, aligning these components of your research with your refined research question and theoretical framework. This all might sound complicated, but remember that the relationships are not random: each component has something to say to the others, and they work together as we have suggested, like a series of family resemblances. The next section will be more practically oriented, as we present different methods to generate and collect data for SoTL research.

Key Concepts

- Approaches to research design and methodology reflect paradigms or worldviews about the nature of the world and how it can be known.
- There is a continuum of research that values objectivity and attempts to know about a "real" world through observation, and research that values subjective knowledge related to individuals experiencing that world. The importance of context to the research varies along this continuum, and theory is utilized in different ways depending on the research paradigm.
- Data can be either quantitative or qualitative, and data analysis can follow deductive or inductive processes. While more commonly associated with particular paradigms, these descriptions do not necessarily determine the paradigm, category, or research design/methodology.
- Research design, methodology, and methods are all distinct terms and should not be used interchangeably.
- Broad categories of research paradigms include positivist/postpositivist, critical realist, interpretive, and transformative approaches, which includes critical, postmodern, and Indigenous paradigms.
- The choice of research design or methodology should reflect the research question and align with the researcher's worldview, taking into account the discipline or context in which the research takes place.

Further Reading

Braun, V., & Clarke, V. (2013). *Successful qualitative research: A practical guide for beginners.* Sage.

Creswell, J. W., & Plano Clark, V. L. (2017). *Designing and conducting mixed methods research.* Sage.

Creswell, J. W., & Poth, C. N. (2018). *Qualitative inquiry and research design: Choosing among five approaches* (4th ed.). Sage.

Chick, N. L. (Ed.). (2018). *SoTL in action: Illuminating critical moments of practice.* Stylus Publishing.

Ermine, W. (2007). Ethical space of engagement. *Indigenous Law Journal*, 6(1), 193–203.

Kara, H. (2022). *Qualitative research for quantitative researchers.* Sage.

Kovach, M. (2018). Doing Indigenous methodologies: A letter to a research class. In N. K. Denzin & Y. S. Lincoln (Eds.), *The Sage handbook of qualitative research* (5th ed.) (pp. 214–234). Sage.

McKinney, K. (Ed.). (2013). *The scholarship of teaching and learning in and across the disciplines.* Indiana University Press.

Merriam, S. B., & Tisdell, E. J. (2016). *Qualitative research: A guide to design and implementation.* Jossey-Bass.

Miller-Young, J., Yeo, M., & Manarin, K. (forthcoming). Navigating boundary experiences in SoTL: Pinch points, paradigms, and perspectives. In J. Miller-Young & N. L. Chick (Eds.), *Becoming a SoTL scholar.* Elon University, USA.

PART II

Generating Data for SoTL

4

GENERATING QUANTITATIVE DATA AND CONSTRUCTING QUESTIONNAIRES

This chapter discusses generating quantitative data and the most common tool for doing so, the questionnaire. We begin by emphasizing the need to carefully consider how to generate data that is valid and meaningful. We also discuss choice of scale, which has implications for both the quality of data and type of analysis. We then apply these principles to the development, implementation, and evaluation of a quantitative questionnaire, and make recommendations for writing and incorporating open-ended questions.

Instructors evaluate learning quantitatively all the time by assigning marks and grades. So it is not surprising that a common place for new SoTL practitioners to start is to consider making a change to their teaching, and looking for a corresponding change to their students' performance on an assignment or exam. Let's talk about some of these processes in quantitative research terms. First, how to measure learning depends on the type of learning the instructor is interested in, in other words, how they define or conceptualize progress. Learning can be defined as a process that takes place in the mind, involving an increase in understanding of a concept, an ability to apply knowledge to a new situation, or a change in knowledge, beliefs, behaviors, values, or attitudes, as just a few examples (Ambrose et al., 2010). Many of these things cannot be observed directly, so the instructor has to infer them by identifying behaviors that would indicate the type of learning they are interested in, designing an activity that provides evidence of that behavior, and developing an assessment. To develop quantitative assessments, they choose indicators that are thought to be closely related to learning, and that are observable, and then decide how to translate those observations into a number. As a simple example, a student being able to solve a certain problem on an exam is an indicator that they

DOI: 10.4324/9781003447054-6

understand a particular concept. The instructor might develop a rubric that will help them reliably calculate a number based on the extent to which the students' solution meets certain criteria. (The research term for the tool that is used to facilitate the quantification process is "instrument.") Finally, because they know that a single measure will not adequately capture the students' learning, they probably also have multiple assessments over the semester and/or multiple questions on an exam that help the instructor quantify the learning and assign a grade (or even a "pass" score in the case of competency-based grading or ungrading). There are multiple levels of assumptions here: that the teaching, or better put, the learning activity, is responsible for the learning, that learning (or an aspect of learning) is acceptably quantifiable, that the observable indicator is representative of that learning, and that the procedures used to translate the observation into a number on a scale are valid and objective (Figure 4.1). In other words, while the indicators are observable, that is, the data is empirical, the researcher is not directly measuring the phenomenon they are interested in: learning. Scientists and quantitative researchers tend to be very clear about this distinction, and use theory and previous research to frame the relationship between the indicator and the phenomenon. When generating quantitative data, the researcher therefore needs to be able to articulate, and address to the best of their ability, all of these assumptions and processes. Although the example we use above is grading, the basic process is the same any time we want to generate a number that can be used as data for quantitative analysis.

Quantitative data is most typically used in quantitative and mixed method research designs, when there are large enough participation numbers to generate statistically significant results; alternatively, it may also be used in qualitative, empirical studies when triangulated with other sources of data. In any of these cases, by making the assumption that learning (or a variable assumed to be related to learning, such as motivation) is associated with one or more indicators that can be observed and quantified, the researcher is

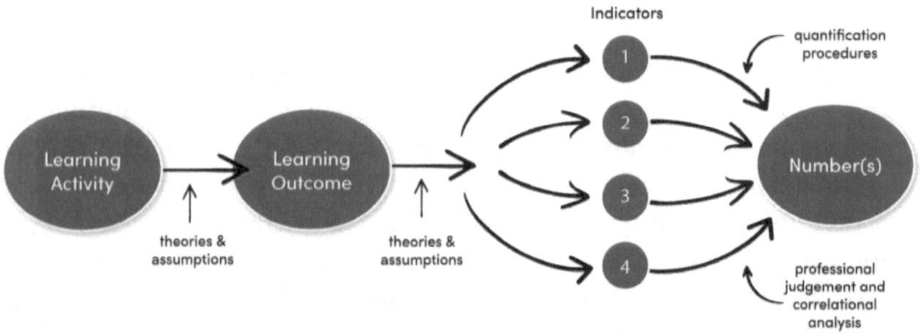

FIGURE 4.1 Generating quantitative data involves multiple layers of assumptions and judgment, which are informed by theory and statistical analysis.

likely using theory to inform their decisions, whether explicitly or implicitly. We encourage SoTL researchers to be explicit about theory because it will help them consider and communicate their assumptions about learning, decide what variables they want to measure, and test the validity and reliability of their measurements. As discussed in Chapter 3, this would put most quantitative SoTL research within a post-positivist or critical realist paradigm, where the researcher is trying to be as objective as possible in their generation, collection, and analysis of data, but needs to explain their choice of theoretical framing.

Because of this need for theoretical framing and careful choice of quantification processes, the hard work of conducting quantitative research happens before the data is collected. It is relatively easy (and therefore tempting!) to analyze quantitative data once you have it, but first you need to know that the numbers are actually meaningful. There are many pedagogical resources for developing rubrics and assessments (e.g., Suskie 2018); therefore, this chapter will focus on the most common means of generating data for SoTL studies: the questionnaire (Divan et al., 2017; Manarin et al., 2021). In the first section of this chapter, we discuss general principles and definitions for generating quantitative data, which are applicable to any instrument including questionnaires; in the second section we apply these principles to questionnaire development and implementation. Questionnaires can also yield qualitative data, which is also addressed in this chapter; however, because of the additional work required to generate meaningful quantitative data, we first focus on quantitative data.

Principles for Generating Quantitative Data in Research

Any time we quantify something we are essentially measuring it according to some underlying theoretical definitions and assumptions. Let's say an instructor is interested in redesigning an aspect of their course to improve student motivation. How do they define motivation? Who has written about motivation and what factors might affect it? What would qualify as evidence that students are motivated or not? Again, theory and literature review is a useful place to start when thinking about what data to generate and collect. Further, established learning theories often have more than one variable associated with them. For example, according to self-determination theory, intrinsic motivation is affected by innate needs for self-efficacy, autonomy, and relatedness (Ryan & Deci, 2000). So, if an instructor's underlying assumptions are that their particular teaching strategy might help support students' intrinsic motivation in their course, and therefore student performance on a final exam, they could find and use scales that measure these three constructs in addition to (or instead of) using exam marks as data. In other words, finding an appropriate theory or a theoretical framework from the literature can help SoTL researchers think more carefully about the complexity of what they want to study and, as a result, choose to generate additional data that might be related to their research question, thus strengthening their study and deepening their understanding of the phenomenon they are interested in. Further, multiple sources of data can also help reduce what is called common method bias, which is common in survey research and occurs when all data are collected using the same method or from a single perspective, such as when using surveys and self-reported data (Podsakoff et al., 2003).

Generating Quantitative Data: Who Does the Generating?

Some data already exist in quantitative form or are easily quantifiable. Examples include almost anything with a digital footprint: student records data such as student demographic characteristics (e.g., ethnicity, gender, age, year in school), student performance (e.g., GPA, grades in prerequisite or follow-on courses), LMS data such as video watching behaviors, number/length of posts composed/read in a discussion forum (Bronniman et al., 2018). However, it can't be used as research data unless we have ethics approval to use it. The SoTL researcher still needs to think carefully about whether this data is necessary for answering their research question, and articulate their assumptions: for example, students accessing various aspects of the LMS (the observable behavior) might be an indicator of engagement (the variable of interest). How and why can the researcher assume that? Again, literature and theory can help make this case.

Some data is instructor/researcher-generated. The students produce some kind of indicator of learning through course assignments, projects, and exams, but the instructor turns it into a score by evaluating it with some kind of rubric. Most instructors do not question the potential for bias in their marking process, but this could be checked for by having colleagues or research assistants also do some of the marking, and then assessing correlations through statistics.

Finally, some data is student-generated, such as responses to a questionnaire. This is called self-reported data. This approach is most suitable for asking students to describe their perceptions, experiences, opinions, attitudes, and/or intentions, as well as their recollections of current or recent behavior (Harel & Wentland, 2017). For example, the further in the past a particular event you are asking about is, the less likely students will recall it accurately. Further, students are often not good at evaluating their own learning, either recently or in retrospect; for example, students tend to rate active learning as less helpful to their learning because it feels more difficult, even though objectively it can be shown that they learned more (e.g., Deslauriers et al., 2019). Finally, self-reported data is subject to all kinds of potential for bias. Generally known effects include social desirability (the tendency of survey respondents to answer questions in a manner that will be viewed favorably, such as by over-reporting "good behavior"), sequence effects (order of questions can affect responses), contrast effects (respondents tend to answer a second question more or less favorably because they are influenced by the topic of a previous question), and the halo effect (when the overall positive impression of something positively influences our feelings in another related area). The literature on student evaluations of teaching has further demonstrated potential sources of bias specific to teaching and learning, including grading leniency and difficulty of course material (Ellis et al., 2004; Marsh & Roche, 2000), and the possibility to manipulate responses (Hessler et al., 2018), not to mention an instructor's attractiveness, race, age, and gender (Ambady & Rosenthal, 1993; Hamermesh & Parker, 2005; MacNell et al., 2015; Adams et al., 2022).

We don't intend to scare SoTL researchers away from using self-reported data because, of course, students' feelings and perceptions are very important. However, researchers need to carefully consider the limitations of this type of data. In summary, if a SoTL researcher wants to assess something using a survey, they need to be aware that student responses portray their perceptions, and will likely be influenced by their emotions at the time they respond. If a SoTL researcher is interested in understanding student learning rather than their perceptions of teaching and learning activities, we strongly recommend correlating or triangulating self-reported data with other types of data.

Generating Quantitative Data: What Type of Scale to Use?

Scales of measurement comprise the different ways indicators can be scored, or assigned a value, using an instrument. The type of scale has implications for the quality of a question as well as which statistical test(s) will be used for data analysis. In this section, we discuss the different types of scales and give examples of when it is most appropriate to use them.

Categorical scales are used for one or more categories of description. A nominal scale has no order to the categories, for example, gender (male = 1, female = 2, other = 3), yes/no questions, students' program, etc. Since there is no order to the categories, averages, partial scores, and relative magnitudes are not calculated because they are meaningless. The other kind of categorical scale is the ordinal scale, where scores can be ranked but do not correspond to a consistent magnitude of difference. Some examples would include asking students to rank a list of options from most important to least important, or to report their year in a program (students in 2nd year do not know twice as much as students in first year); Likert scales (strongly agree to strongly disagree) are usually ordinal data as they are typically not so well-defined as to describe numerically uniform increments (unless previous research has shown that the distance between each value on the scale is equal). For example, when assessing student learning using concept maps, Watson et al. (2016) used a rubric with a 3-point scale to assess students' maps for comprehensiveness, organization, and correctness. They also described how two researchers did the scoring independently and discussed until consensus was reached, and showed examples of high- and low-scoring maps. The key consideration with categorical scales is that it doesn't make sense to calculate averages and other descriptive statistics; frequencies of different scores should be reported instead.

Continuous scales are assumed to have equal distance between the options, for example, the difference between 70–75% is the same as 80–85%. For interval scales, there is no meaningful zero (a mark of zero on an exam does not mean the student didn't learn anything), whereas for ratio scales, there is a true zero. For example, in LMS data, when scoring the number of times a student accessed a particular video, zero means never.

Different types of scales are appropriate for different purposes. When asking students to self-report their satisfaction, attitudes, or values about something, continuous scales provide the most variation of responses and therefore lend themselves to stronger statistical analysis (Creswell & Guetterman, 2019). Ordinal scales with a wider distribution of responses are also more desirable for statistical reasons; Likert scales typically use 1–5 or 1–7 scales, but sometimes 1–3 is useful as well. A shorter scale may reduce the burden on students and increase data reliability. If desired, even-numbered scales can be used to force a respondent to "choose a side" (e.g., agree or disagree, with no middle). Both the choice of scale and the distribution of data will influence the choice of statistical analysis; this is discussed in Chapter 7.

Evaluating Quantitative Data: Validity and Reliability

Any time we want to "measure" something by turning an observation into a number, there will always be a certain amount of error. When discussing quantitative data, the terms validity and reliability refer to how well a measurement reflects "reality." Validity refers to accuracy, in other words, whether or not an instrument really measures what it is supposed to measure. Validity is also closely bound up with reliability, which refers to the precision of the instrument, in other words, whether it consistently produces the same result if used multiple times.

There are several common strategies to minimize and check for the potential error in measurements. One is to correlate a new measurement with a previously established measurement of a similar or related variable—if there is a strong correlation, this increases the researcher's confidence in the new measurement. Second, if the potential sources of bias are minimized, then the average error over many measurements should be close to zero. This means that researchers can also improve the validity of their measurements by using multiple indicators of the variable they are interested in, such as giving a quiz on a particular concept more than once and comparing the results (test, retest), or having multiple questions related to a concept on an exam or questionnaire, and checking their correlations.

In the next section we will explore how the principles described above can be applied to the design of questionnaires, especially those that heavily rely on quantitative questions.

Constructing Questionnaires

A questionnaire is a useful means of collecting information from students by asking them to respond to quantitative (closed-ended) and/or qualitative (open-ended) questions. First, it is important to define some terms. Although the terms "survey" and "questionnaire" are often used interchangeably, they are not the same; we use the terms differently here to distinguish between research approach and method. The purpose of a survey design is to collect enough data from a sample that you can make inferences about a population (see Chapter 7). Because of the large number of participants needed, less time-consuming methods of collecting data are most often used for survey studies, such as the questionnaire. In research terms, the questionnaire is the instrument; each question on a questionnaire is called an item. To be even more specific, a questionnaire could be administered in multiple ways (such as by interview), but most commonly they are self-administered, meaning that participants fill them out themselves on paper or online. For the purposes of this book, survey refers to the overall research approach, and questionnaire refers to a self-administered instrument of data collection.

Questionnaires are an efficient tool for gathering data, which is likely the reason that they are the most common data collection technique in SoTL studies, with 43% of these studies asking both quantitative and qualitative questions (mixed mode), 40% using quantitative questions, and 17% using qualitative questions (Divan et al., 2017). Despite their common use, questionnaires are subject to all the sources of error and bias discussed above. A purely quantitative questionnaire requires substantial expertise and resources to develop if the researcher wants to be confident in the validity and reliability of the data; standard psychometric procedures such as factor analysis can be found in textbooks and online resources (e.g., Harel & Wentland, 2017; Jhangiani et al., 2015). A purely qualitative questionnaire is rare and usually very specific to the context in which it is being deployed; the main disadvantage of such an instrument compared to other strategies for qualitative data collection is that there is no possibility to probe deeper into responses. This section will focus on important aspects of creating a mixed mode questionnaire for a SoTL study, including defining the scope, writing (or using/modifying) good questions, organizing them well, administering the questionnaire, and evaluating. SoTL researchers interested in developing purely quantitative questionnaires should also refer to the section on exploratory sequential mixed methods research designs in Chapter 9; those interested in a purely qualitative questionnaire might consider conducting an interview instead.

Orientation and Scope

The selection, modification, or development of a questionnaire starts with the researcher: what is the researcher's orientation and what information needs to be obtained in order to answer their research question(s)? Because questionnaires are an efficient way of collecting data in large quantities, much of the literature on questionnaire design assumes quantitative items and a post-positivist or critical realist approach (e.g., Benson & Clark, 1982; Jhangiani et al., 2015). Because of the work necessary to produce valid and reliable data, quantitative researchers usually recommend finding and using an existing, validated questionnaire from the literature (e.g., Maurer, 2018). In a contrasting view, Creswell (2007) suggests that qualitative researchers do not rely on survey instruments developed by other researchers (p. 38) because of the highly contextual nature of qualitative research. Again, the SoTL researcher will have to decide what approach and balance to take based on their orientation and research question, as well as what other sources of data they are using. Based on these decisions, they next need to decide on the scope of the questionnaire.

While it is tempting to ask survey participants about as much as possible, limiting a questionnaire to concepts related to the research question will help keep it a reasonable length, thus increasing the chances that participants will complete it. On the other hand, it is also good practice to have more than one question about each concept or construct, especially on a quantitative questionnaire. There is no hard and fast rule about how many questions per concept of interest, but generally more complex ones require more questions. There is also a cost/benefit trade-off such that more questions may make your measurement more precise, but also increase the length of the questionnaire, which could reduce completion rates. We recommend using similar, previously developed questionnaires, your own experience, and student feedback from a pre-test as guides.

As Maurer (2018) recommends, if you are considering using a quantitative questionnaire for your study, it is best to start by searching the literature to find an existing questionnaire that suits your purposes or could be easily adapted. Compendiums of scales that measure key psychological variables already exist and have been validated; one such compendium includes scales for academic self-efficacy, self-regulation, critical thinking, metacognition, motivated strategies for learning, depth of processing, lifelong learning, procrastination, study behaviors, and textbook assessment, just to list a few (Jhangiani et al., 2015). However, note that validity is not a characteristic of the questionnaire by itself but is related to the context in which it is used. Therefore, if using a previously validated questionnaire, SoTL researchers will want to check that it was validated in a similar context to which it is to be used and/or with questionnaire takers defined by similar demographics, linguistic or other relevant attributes (Padilla & Benítez, 2014); if not, then they may want to modify by, for example, using more context-appropriate terminology. And finally, they will still need to evaluate their data after collecting it.

Validated questionnaires typically measure related variables and often deal with only a few related variables at a time. If, however, a SoTL researcher is interested in additional variables or in students' perceptions of a specific activity or assignment in their class, then they will likely need to develop some of their own questions. For SoTL studies it sometimes makes sense to put together a new questionnaire by using items from a number of validated questionnaires, plus adding some context-specific questions (e.g., Miller-Young et al., 2021a). If doing so, consider both quantitative and qualitative questions. For example, after a series of quantitative questions related to the quality of collaboration within a team, include an open-ended question such as "Please explain your response(s) to the above question(s)," "Describe a time when you felt your team was working well together. What made it memorable?", and/or "Is there anything else you'd like to say about your team experience?"

Writing and Organizing Questions

Each question must be specific enough to ask for one piece of information only. Avoid vagueness, ambiguity, complexity, and jargon. Although instructors may believe they know how students will interpret certain words and questions, this is quite possibly not the case (e.g., Lauer, 2012). Conducting a pilot study or some focus groups will help you determine that students are understanding the questions in the way you intend them to.

Second, be sure to only ask questions about students' own perceptions and experiences, not others'. For example, if an instructor wanted to know whether they created an inclusive environment in their classroom, they wouldn't ask, "Was the classroom an inclusive environment?" (This question is also worded for a yes/no answer, which doesn't leave any room for nuance.) A better question would be to ask students how strongly they agreed or disagreed with the statement "I felt welcome in the class."

Because of the potential for error with quantitative questions, include multiple questions related to the same concept or issue. It is also good practice to include some positively worded and negatively worded questions about a concept. This has two benefits: it can reduce acquiescence, the tendency to agree with questions if you don't have a strong belief about the topic (Tourangeau et al., 2000), and it will also help you determine if students are reading the questions carefully. As discussed above, different formats and scales are most appropriate depending on the information you are seeking; most quantitative questionnaires use a mix of categorical and continuous scales. It is also important to ensure you are giving respondents all possible options to answer a question. Therefore, consider whether providing a "not applicable," "not sure," or "other" response might be useful.

Finally, questions asking about similar topics should be grouped together to aid recall and reduce cognitive burden on the respondent. Consider adding headings for the subsections of your questionnaire, to help students see the connections between the questions and the overall purpose of the survey, and to aid with completion and thoughtfulness of responses. Questions should also be organized in a logical order, from most general to most specific. Exceptions to this rule include demographic information. Put these questions at the beginning of the survey if these responses are important for answering your research question; otherwise, you risk not being able to use responses from students who do not complete the entire questionnaire. Knowing demographic information will also help you determine how representative your sample is of your target population, although for ethical reasons you should only ask questions about variables which are important to the study. Finally, it is usually most useful to add any open-ended questions to the end of a section, to give students the opportunity to expand upon or explain some of their previous responses.

Open-Ended Questions

Qualitative questions are also called open-ended questions, that is, questions "without a pre-determined set of answer choices" (Albudaiwi, 2017, p. 1716). Open-ended or qualitative questions on a questionnaire have both advantages and disadvantages. Rather than clicking on a Likert scale or choosing words selected by the researchers, participants are able to respond to the prompt in their own words. This can lead to much greater variation in the responses, and if the purpose of the questionnaire is to understand a phenomenon from the perspectives of the participants, this variation could be important. Participants may also bring forward issues or ideas that the researchers haven't thought of. Finally, if a researcher is interested in student perspectives on a sensitive topic, they may choose a qualitative questionnaire because students can remain anonymous and therefore may be more comfortable revealing issues that they would hesitate to raise in an interview or focus group.

However, open-ended questions can also be more challenging to analyze because of the richness possible. Certainly, they will take more time to analyze whatever methodology is chosen as the SoTL researcher will have to read and reread the participants' responses to try to understand their perspectives. It's also possible that the participants may only give one- or two-word answers to a prompt that would elicit a lot of discussion if given in an interview or focus group. That's why we sometimes recommend using a questionnaire initially and then asking follow-up questions in an interview or focus group. Alternatively, terms discovered through the interview process can help inform survey questions. After all, multiple forms of data provide a sort of triangulation that helps us feel more confident in our findings.

Some published instruments can be useful for SoTL practitioners interested in qualitative questionnaires depending on their research questions. Stephen Brookfield's Critical Incident Questionnaire (1995), for example, was originally developed as a way to receive formative student feedback at the end of a lesson, but can also be used to gather qualitative data for a research project, recognizing that, as always, the researcher has to think through issues of confidentiality and consent. Various classroom assessment techniques (Angelo & Cross, 1993) can also be adapted to generate qualitative data for SoTL projects.

To increase the chances that our participants will provide rich and interesting responses to survey questions, we need to pay attention to how we construct the prompts. In general, we want to:

- Avoid questions that could be answered in one or two words. After all, the point of qualitative data is to understand how participants make meaning of their experiences. We want them to slow down and reflect. Instead of asking, "Did the group work help you reach your goals in this course?" you might ask, "Give a specific example of how group work helped or hindered you in this course."
- Use words like "Why" or "How" to invite participants to go deeper into their personal experiences and opinions.
- Make the prompt unambiguous. Sometimes researchers don't want to be too directive, so they leave their prompts wide open. But if your research project is about a particular aspect of teaching and learning, that's what you want to get opinions and perspectives about. Asking "What is the best or worst thing about this class?" may be a useful classroom assessment technique, but it's unlikely to produce usable qualitative data for a research study.

Administration and Ethical Considerations

When and how you administer your questionnaire will affect both the response rate and quality of data obtained. Major decisions to make include whether to do it in class or outside of class time, at what point during the semester, whether it will be online or on paper, and whether it will be anonymous or not. Consider, also, what else is going on in your program or at your institution during this time—survey fatigue can affect students' responses. Giving time during class will likely increase the response rate as well as the time students spend on it, although there are ethical issues with using class time for research activities. However, if the SoTL researcher can make the case that they're interested in students' perspectives for the purposes of teaching as well as research, then it is perfectly reasonable to use class time. In this case a research assistant would need to collect the questionnaires so that participants are kept anonymous to the instructor until the course is over (and there is little likelihood of teaching the same students again). Other considerations for ensuring students can offer free and informed consent to participate in the research would still need to be followed. Alternatively, depending on the size of the class and the sensitivity of the research question, it may be important for students to have a stronger assurance of anonymity so that they feel they can honestly respond to questions. If so, then administering the question online and at the end of the semester may be a better option.

If a questionnaire is administered during class, it could be on paper or online, depending which is most appropriate for the context. If it is done outside of class, then online is likely more convenient. Also, if there are a lot of respondents and/or the questionnaire consists of many quantitative questions, then an online version might be preferable because the data would already be recorded in a spreadsheet format and therefore more readily available for analysis. Although survey software exists, freely available platforms such as Google forms also work well for online questionnaires.

Finally, consider whether the questionnaire needs to be anonymous or not. Again, being truly anonymous might help improve students' comfort responding to sensitive questions. However, if the researcher wants to triangulate their questionnaire responses with other sources of data, then the respondents' identity must be recorded somehow. If the questionnaire is administered during the semester, a research assistant should keep participants' identity confidential until at least the end of the semester.

Evaluating the Questionnaire

Traditional (quantitative) questionnaire design requires three types of validity testing: expert reviews, response process validation, and pilot testing (Artino et al., 2014; Harel & Wentland, 2017; Maurer, 2018). These types involve, respectively, having experts in the content or method provide feedback on a draft questionnaire, determining (usually through interviews or focus groups) whether students interpret the questions the way you intend them to, and using psychometric procedures to assess validity of pilot data

(Artino et al., 2014; Deng et al., 2021; Padilla & Benítez, 2014). This is a long process; depending on your time and resources, it may or may not be realistic. However, getting expert and student perspectives on a questionnaire before implementing it is always a good idea.

After you collect the data, the questionnaire should be evaluated again based on the quality of data received. The test reliability of a quantitative questionnaire (or quantitative sections of a questionnaire) can be assessed using two simple tests commonly found in statistical textbooks: item-total-correlation indicates the correlation between a single score and the total score for a particular construct or variable (a low correlation would tell you that the question, or item, does not relate to the overall construct you are interested in); Cronbach's alpha is used to estimate how consistent a test is across multiple items, in other words, how closely all items relate to the construct. Both are commonly used measures in quantitative research. More comprehensive validity testing is definitely necessary when developing a purely quantitative questionnaire, and especially if you intend to use it for quasi-experimental or correlational research designs (see Chapter 7). If this is the case, we refer you to the further readings section at the end of this chapter. Otherwise, consider a mixed mode or qualitative questionnaire, and taking a qualitative empirical approach to analysis by triangulating multiple sources of data, integrating quantitative responses with the open-ended responses to your questionnaire, and following up a questionnaire with some interviews.

Finally, a decision about the extent of validation required may also depend on where you intend to disseminate your results; for example, a SoTL journal from a quantitative discipline is more likely to ask for extensive evidence of validation than a SoTL journal from a qualitative discipline where reviewers may be more accustomed to triangulation of data. Check previous articles in your target journal for a sense of what to expect.

Key Concepts

- Evaluating and reporting the validity and reliability of quantitative data is an important aspect of quantitative research.
- The use of different types of scales has important implications for quantitative data analysis.
- Questionnaires may use quantitative, qualitative, or a mix of both types of questions.
- Good questionnaire items relate to predefined indicators and are as specific as possible about one aspect at a time.
- The organization of questions and the length of a questionnaire are critical considerations.
- The timing and administration of the questionnaire can affect response rate and quality of data.

Further Readings

Allen, S., & Knight, J. (2009). A method for collaboratively developing and validating a rubric. *International Journal for the Scholarship of Teaching and Learning*, 3(2), n2. https://doi.org/10.20429/ijsotl.2009.030210.

Blair, J., Czaja, R. F., & Blair, E. A. (2013). *Designing surveys: A guide to decisions and procedures.* Sage.

Dawson, P. (2017). Assessment rubrics: Towards clearer and more replicable design, research and practice. *Assessment & Evaluation in Higher Education*, 42(3), 347–360. https://doi.org/10.1080/02602938.2015.1111294.

Jhangiani, R. S., Troisi, J. D., Fleck, B., Legg, A. M., & Hussey, H. D. (Eds.) (2015). *A compendium of scales for the scholarship of teaching and learning.* https://teachpsych.org/ebooks/compscalessotp.

Julien, H. (2008). Survey research. In L. M. Given (Ed.), *The Sage encyclopedia of qualitative research methods* (pp. 847–848). Sage.

Harel, D., & Wentland, E. (2017). Survey use in academic contexts: Considerations and guidelines. In *Handbook on measurement, assessment, and evaluation in higher education* (pp. 517–528). Routledge.

Maurer, T. W. (2018). Methods and measures matter: Meaningful questionnaires. In *SoTL in action: Illuminating critical moments of practice* (pp. 71–81). Stylus.

Meade, A. W., & Craig, S. B. (2012). Identifying careless responses in survey data. *Psychological Methods*, 17(3), 437. https://doi.org/10.1037/a0028085.

Suskie, L. (2018). *Assessing student learning: A common sense guide.* John Wiley & Sons.

5

INTERVIEWS AND FOCUS GROUPS

This chapter explores generating qualitative data for SoTL projects through interviews and focus groups. Both methods can provide rich, self-reported data. We provide some advice on when and how to set up interviews and focus groups before suggesting some basic data management practices.

While surveying participants through questionnaires has historically been the most common way of generating data in SoTL studies, interviewing participants, whether individually or in focus groups, is another common way of generating data (Divan et al., 2017; Manarin et al., 2021). Interviews and focus groups allow researchers to interact directly with participants and can generate rich qualitative data. They are compatible with many different methodologies—from post-positivist and critical realism through interpretive and more transformative frameworks. Of course, the particular form of the interview will vary based on methodological approach, as the researcher's stance towards the area of inquiry differs. In this chapter we will describe some of the basics of setting up and conducting a semi-structured interview, recognizing that later chapters will provide more detail about methodological variation.

Before selecting interviews or focus groups as a method for gathering data, however, it's important to recognize some of their limitations. Like questionnaires, interviews and focus groups generate self-reported data. Sometimes, that's exactly what is needed to answer a research question, for example, what people think about a particular issue or how they experience something. On the other hand, sometimes self-reported data is not enough to answer a research question. In those cases, interview and focus groups data might be supplemented with other data sources, like observations or artifacts. Unlike questionnaires, where a lot of time is spent up front

DOI: 10.4324/9781003447054-7

developing and validating the instrument, interviews and focus groups are very time-consuming to conduct, transcribe, and analyze. However, interviews and focus groups can generate rich and provocative data for SoTL projects.

As with other data gathering strategies, the research question will dictate who should be approached. If the research question is about student study strategies, it makes sense to ask students; it might also make sense to ask instructors or learning skills specialists about their perceptions of student study strategies. Quite often SoTL researchers will be interested in what is happening in their own classes, and so they need to be aware of their dual roles and the power relationships they have with potential participants. In most cases, an instructor will not interview current students because students could feel pressured to participate. Sometimes it is possible to wait until after the course is over to interview participants, or to have another person (whether a colleague or a research assistant) conduct the interview. Braun and Clarke (2013) discuss the importance of thinking about the power dynamics of interviewing in advance. Indeed, most institutional review boards will require the researcher to explain how and when participants will be recruited and informed about the study, so that participants can provide informed consent; they will also want to know who will conduct the interview or focus groups, when and where they will be held, what sorts of questions will be asked, and how data will be recorded and safeguarded. There are a lot of decisions to make before conducting an interview or focus group.

Which Is Better, Individual Interviews or Focus Groups?

SoTL researchers need to consider what type of interview works best for their research question. One of the first decisions is whether to have interviews with individuals or whether to conduct a focus group, where there are multiple participants. Focus groups often have between six and ten participants; the facilitator should be aware of and comfortable dealing with different group processes and dynamics (Merriam & Tisdell, 2016, p. 114). When setting up focus groups, it's important to remind participants that their responses should be kept confidential.

One advantage of individual interviews is that it is possible to focus more on the particular details of an individual's experience. Another advantage is that an individual may feel more comfortable speaking with one person once trust has been established. A disadvantage is that individual interviews are more time-consuming. Focus groups can be more efficient in terms of time; they also give participants the opportunity to build off of each other's comments, perhaps surfacing issues or themes that might otherwise go unnoticed. However, focus groups can also be challenging to facilitate depending on the group composition, as the facilitator tries to make sure one or two individuals don't dominate the group. Sometimes focus groups wind up reinforcing a sort of "group think" where individual interviews might lead to more variation in answers.

So how do you decide whether to conduct individual interviews or focus groups? In part it depends on the topic being explored. Merriam and Tisdell (2016) argue that focus groups are "a poor choice for topics that are sensitive, highly personal, and culturally inappropriate to talk about in the presence of strangers" (p. 114), but you might also want to consider whether the research question involves something that people typically experience alone (for example, reading) or together (for example, a particular classroom technique) when deciding whether to plan for individual interviews or focus groups. As Morgan (1997) notes, "an interest in individual behavior might not be well served by data from group interviews. Similarly, a research interest in group behavior might not be well served by data from individual interviews" (pp. 12–13). In part, it also depends on your confidence about being able to facilitate a group of people or conduct an interview. With focus groups, the researcher has less control over how the conversation will evolve, which can be either a strength or a weakness (Morgan, 1997).

Traditionally, interviews and focus groups are held in person. Ideally, the interview location should be convenient, confidential, safe, and quiet. Sometimes, interviewers select somewhere public like a coffee shop as sort of neutral ground, but it might not provide enough privacy for participants to feel comfortable, and it will be difficult to record a conversation. Herzog (2012) notes that selecting interview locations is not merely a matter of logistics, but also involves socially negotiated power. Consider, for example, the difference between conducting an interview with former students in a faculty member's office versus a bookable study room. In-person interviews and focus groups have several advantages, including being able to observe participants' body language and perhaps making them feel more at ease by sharing food or (non-alcoholic) drink. The disadvantages include difficulties in scheduling and concerns about well-being; for example, during the COVID-19 pandemic, much data gathering moved online due to public health measures.

Given these concerns, more researchers are conducting online video interviews and focus groups through a variety of platforms. The advantages include safety, geographical freedom, and ease of scheduling; however, there are disadvantages to consider. Some participants may not have stable or private internet access. They may feel uncomfortable sharing their video with others. Phone interviews (or online videos with the cameras off) offer another option; however, without visual cues, it is very difficult to facilitate a focus group. Merriam and Tisdell (2016) note that it is also possible to consider asynchronous interviews or focus groups, perhaps by using email or discussion board structures. The advantages include saving the researcher time and money in transcription while still allowing for some back-and-forth discussion unlike a questionnaire; however, it is even harder to interpret responses given the lack of non-verbal cues, including tone and pauses. It can also be harder to build rapport with participants. Braun and Clarke (2013) note the importance of maintaining momentum in asynchronous interviews while also respecting other demands on participants' time. They emphasize the importance of explicit acknowledgment that you are interested in what participants are saying and polite check-ins if they would like to continue (pp. 102–103).

How Do I Structure an Interview or Focus Group?

Another important decision is how structured the interview or focus group should be. Atkins and Wallace (2012) talk about the differences between respondent and informant interviews. The respondent interview is highly structured, as "The only questions to be explored are questions the interviewer has thought to ask," while the informant interview allows "the participant to *inform* the research in ways the researcher may not have anticipated" (emphasis in the original, p. 88). In most SoTL interviews, we are hoping that the participants will inform the research by talking about their perspectives and experiences. Other scholars talk about three basic forms of interviews: structured, semi-structured, and unstructured (Merriam & Tisdell, 2016; Braun & Clarke, 2013; Qu & Dumay, 2011; Norton, 2009). In the structured interview or focus group, the interviewer/facilitator goes through a predetermined set of questions in a particular order. Essentially, it's an oral questionnaire, and, as Qu & Dumay (2011) note, it positions the interviewee as "a truth teller" and the interview as a tool allowing knowledge transfer (p. 241). Because the questions and order are determined ahead of time, this type of interview is easier to conduct, and the results are standardized and thus easier to compare; however, a lot of potentially rich data is lost because the interviewer does not follow up on interesting responses. In a semi-structured interview, the interviewer has a series of key questions that they want to ask, but they also have the freedom to use additional prompts and deviate from the script to ask follow-up questions where appropriate. In the unstructured interview, the interviewer comes with the desire to learn more about the participant's experience but without specific questions. Typically, unstructured interviews require greater levels of trust on the part of the participants and greater levels of expertise on the part of the interviewer as relationships are carefully built over time. Unstructured interviews are particularly appropriate for certain methodologies and epistemologies, for example, Indigenous ways of knowing (Kovach, 2009). However, unstructured interviews are challenging for the novice interviewer. Qu & Dumay (2011) suggest that semi-structured interviews are consistent with a wide range of epistemologies (p. 243). Thus, we will focus on preparing for the semi-structured interview here.

Preparing for a Semi-Structured Interview

Whether you've decided to use individual interviews or focus groups, a successful interview involves preparation. Before the interview, decide who you would like to interview, whether you will conduct individual interviews or focus groups, whether it will be in person or another modality, how structured it will be, how you will recruit and inform participants, and whether you might follow up with them if you have additional questions. These decisions will be documented in your institutional ethics review.

For a semi-structured interview, you will also come up with an interview guide or protocol that identifies the main questions you will ask. There is no set format for an interview protocol; however, most will include basic information about the study and interviewer, information about how the interview will be conducted, and the main questions to be asked. These questions should connect to the main research questions. Eric Chan, working with Janice to explore how students from underrepresented groups experience engineering education, developed a matrix to map the main interview questions to the research questions. The matrix helped him ensure that particular areas of interest were covered during the interviews.

As you can see from Table 5.1, the types of questions you ask are connected to your research question(s). In this example, the first question after each research question serves to get the participant thinking about the topic before moving into the more specific questions about their experiences. Similarly, the question asking participants to think about belonging generally serves as a transition to their experiences of belonging in the program. You'll also notice that the interviewer explicitly gives the participant the opportunity to identify other areas they want to talk about.

So how many main questions are appropriate? Really, it varies, depending on the research questions and experience of the interviewer. Often, fewer broad questions can elicit more interesting answers than a lot of more specific questions, but the interviewer has to be willing to probe further. Creswell (2007) recommends coming up with around five open-ended questions by focusing on the research question and sub-questions; these form the core of interview protocol. Merriam and Tisdell (2016) note that

> Having fewer, broader questions unhooks you from the interview guide and enables you to really listen to what your participant has to share, which in turn enables you to better follow avenues of inquiry that will yield potentially rich contributions.
>
> *(p. 126)*

TABLE 5.1 Sample Interview Questions

Research Q #1: How do students who self-identify as being from multiple underrepresented groups describe …	*… their engineering experience?*	*… their design team experience?*	*… their feelings of belongingness?*
Tell me some more about your engineering experiences?	X		
What is your experience with team-based design projects?		X	
How do you manage conflict or disagreements in your design team projects?		X	
When you think of the word "belonging," what comes to mind?			X
Based on your thoughts about belonging, do you feel that you belonged in your design team? Why or why not?			X
Research Q #2: How do their perceived experiences influence their …	*… engineering identity?*	*… self-efficacy?*	*… institutional integration??*
In your opinion, what does it mean to be a successful engineer?	X		
How closely do you personally align with your vision of what a successful engineer is?	X	X	
Do you feel like you fit in with the engineering culture in your department/faculty? Why or why not?			X
To what extent do faculty members, professors, or academic staff influence your idea of what it means to be an engineer?	X		X
What pushes you to keep going and to believe in yourself when things get difficult?		X	
Before we wrap up the interview, is there anything else that you feel we should elaborate on with respect to your engineering experiences, identity, design team, or feelings of belongingness?			

Adapted from Chan and Miller-Young (2022).

The quality of the data largely depends on the quality of the questions and the quality of the interviewer/interviewee interactions.

As when creating open-ended survey questions, researchers should avoid using jargon, double-barrelled or ambiguous questions, leading questions, and questions that can be answered in one or two words. Instead, qualitative researchers typically try to encourage the participants to talk more through a combination of core questions and follow-up probes. Merriam and Tisdell (2016) offer some helpful frameworks for generating productive questions, including Patton's (2002) typology of questions about experience/behavior; opinions/value; feelings; knowledge; senses; and demographics. They also describe how participants might be asked to imagine a hypothetical situation, to play devil's advocate, to imagine an ideal situation, or to check on preliminary interpretations. For example, students in a SoTL study about student perceptions of academic integrity might be asked what they would do if they saw someone else cheat; they might then be asked to play devil's advocate and imagine a different response before reflecting on the pros and cons of each response. They might then be asked to talk about the ideal situation. Each question will likely uncover different elements of their perceptions, experiences, and values.

Good interview questions allow us to explore many different types of knowledge. Miller-Young (2018) notes that

> Students' knowledge can be classified as semantic (knowing facts, meanings, concepts), procedural (knowing how to do something), integrative (being able to connect and synthesize multiple knowledge models), or metacognitive (being able to think about and control one's cognitive and learning processes). Whichever aspect is of interest, it is important to develop interview questions that require students to demonstrate that kind of knowledge.
>
> *(p. 93)*

Depending on the research design, you might also show the participant something, and ask them to talk about it. For example, you might follow up on questions previously answered in a survey, or you might ask participants to talk about a particular assignment they have already completed. These types of prompts can encourage the participant to explain what they meant and reflect more deeply.

Along with planning the core questions, it can be helpful for novice interviewers to think through, and indeed to practice, what they might say to elicit more detail from participants. For example, an interviewer might have a few phrases jotted down on the interview protocol in case needed; something like, "That's really interesting, could you give me an example?", "What do you mean?", "Can you tell me more about that?", or even non-verbal prompts like nodding and smiling can elicit more detailed responses. No matter what types of questions are chosen, it's a good idea to practice with friends and colleagues before the real interviews.

In almost all cases, participants will have some idea of what the interview will be about; after all, that's an important part of the informed consent process and primes participants to be thinking about particular topics. Sometimes, however, researchers give the interviewees the actual questions in advance. Doing so allows the participants to prepare answers ahead of time. Giving participants the questions in advance makes the oral interview closer to a questionnaire; that is, the process becomes more structured, which may be appropriate for some post-positivist or critical realist research. At the same time, however, giving the questions in advance may close off other possible responses. Responses may also come across as somehow less "authentic" because they have been rehearsed, which may challenge a post-postivist approach. Interpretive or transformative methodologies are less likely to give the questions in advance as the researchers' participation in the conversation is seen as important, and researchers are more likely interested in a spontaneous rather than planned response. Stanlick (2011) offers further pros and cons to the question. If you decide to give the questions to your participants ahead of time, this decision should be discussed in any dissemination.

During the Interview

The interview itself involves several stages. As Norton (2009) notes, before asking questions, you need to put the participant at ease, explain the research and how the data will be used, and gain consent. In most cases, that will involve having participants read through a consent form and ask any questions they might have. You should also get explicit permission to record the interview or take notes (p. 101). We recommend recording the interview where possible as it is extremely difficult to take detailed notes while also interviewing. Recording also allows for direct quotations in analysis and dissemination.

Merriam and Tisdell (2016) recommend beginning the interview with some neutral or descriptive prompts to put the participant at ease before moving to the participant's opinions or emotions; they also note the importance of pace: "the interviewer should avoid pressing too hard and too fast. After all, the participant is being interviewed, not interrogated" (p. 123). Sometimes participants might get emotional or flustered during an interview. Although you might feel uncomfortable, "Do not ignore or discount the distress; provide encouragement and supportive comments that the feelings expressed are valid, that you appreciate the honesty, and that you are there to listen and not to judge" (Saldana, 2011, p. 44) After all, interview data depends upon the interactions of interviewer and participant. Positioning the participant as someone who has something important to say, regardless of whether or not you agree with the content of what they say, helps build rapport. Saldana (2011) emphasizes the importance of respect: "The researcher is always a sympathetic and empathetic listener, someone who does not pass judgment on what the participant says, but one who provides a forum for a voice to be heard" (p. 40). Of course, the interactions between the interviewer and interviewee are mediated by multiple factors, including biases, social roles, and physical characteristics like gender, race, and age.

As the interview draws to a close, it can be useful to ask participants some version of "is there anything more you'd like to say", or "if you could sum up your experience with X, what would you say", or "what do you really want people to understand about X?" You're also going to want to thank participants for their time, and describe what happens next as far as the interview recording/notes. You might confirm contact information if you are offering individuals the opportunity to check over their transcripts. During all of this, we recommend you keep the recording going because sometimes participants will think of other things they want to share.

After the Interview—Dealing With Transcripts

After the interview, you may want to jot down a few notes. If the interview was recorded, it will probably need to be transcribed. There are several different techniques possible, depending upon how much time, money, and skill researchers have. Of course, transcribing interviews verbatim is very time-consuming if you are not practiced at transcribing; an advantage, on the other hand, is that you come to know your data very well. For some types of projects, you might decide you don't need a verbatim transcript; that it is enough to identify key themes or concerns. If you are interested in a verbatim transcript, you might find it worthwhile to hire someone to do it. Given improvements in technology, you might also investigate different voice recognition software packages for transcription. Some packages require that the software be calibrated to a particular voice. Merriam and Tisdell (2016) offer a workaround where the researcher listens to the recording and then parrots back the participant's responses, so the software can transcribe responses into text more accurately (pp. 132–133). Some virtual interview platforms, like Zoom, have the ability to provide automatic transcription, though, of course, the researcher will need to correct errors.

Once you have the transcription, you will also want to add some identifying information on the first page of the transcript, what Saldana (2016) calls attribute coding. That is, you will want to include some basic descriptive information about the participant and the interview. For example, if, as is often the case, the transcript is de-identified (i.e., personal identifiers like the participant's name are removed), you would want to include a participant code or pseudonym. You might also include when or where the interview took place, and any other important demographic information. This information helps researchers keep track of who said what when.

Some researchers will send the transcript back to the participant for them to look over; this decision depends in part on your research question and will be documented in your ethics application, but it is one way to enhance the data credibility. When sending transcripts to participants, it is important to phrase the invitation to comment on the transcript in such a way that they don't have to give you permission a second time to use the transcript because many times a participant won't respond. Instead, share the transcript and ask them to contact you by a specific date if they have any comments or wish to make changes. Occasionally a participant will contact you to withdraw consent entirely, and it is ethically important to respect their wishes. More often a participant will clarify responses or simply thank you for the opportunity to participate. Reading and reflecting on interview transcripts can be a meaningful learning experience for participants.

Interviews and focus groups allow researchers to ask participants about their perceptions, opinions, and experiences. Novice researchers are often surprised at how rich this data can be; even a few interviews can provide a lot of material. Recordings, notes, and transcripts allow researchers to remember and reflect on what participants have shared. How the researcher treats these records during analysis will depend upon the methodological underpinnings of the study; we will say more about this in Part III: Analyzing SoTL Data. Here we just want to emphasize the importance of good data management practices.

Data Management Practices

When working with interviews and focus group data, actually when working with all types of data, the researcher needs to keep track of decisions made during the research process with some basic data management practices.

1) Create a system to keep track of your data

Regardless of the type of data you are working with, we recommend that you keep track of what data came from where (and when). As you collect the data, use a standardized format. If, as is often the case with qualitative data, you need to anonymize it, for example, by using pseudonyms or assigning codes to participants, you will still need to have a key that links particular participants with their consent forms. In most cases, you will want to store the consent forms and key separately from the data. And, of course, data must be kept secure—either through password-protected computers/accounts or under lock and key.

2) Record your thoughts and decisions

We recommend that you keep track of your thoughts and impressions as you gather and begin to work with the data. Saldana (2016) describes the importance of such analytic memos as "a place to 'dump your brain' about the participants, phenomenon, or process under investigation by thinking and thus writing and thus thinking even more about them" (p. 44). Such memos can even become part of the data you are analyzing. Because they allow you to keep track of your ideas and choices as you make them (like an audit trail), it's helpful to date each memo. You want to remember what you did and what you thought at different times during the data collection and analysis, recognizing that you may change your mind about the significance of particular themes or ideas during the research process. As you continue the project, you might want to categorize the different memos you generate; for example, we put ideas for related research projects into a "parking lot."

Consider Methodological Rigor Throughout the Research Process

Both quantitative and qualitative SoTL researchers want to conduct methodologically sound inquiries. For quantitative research, that includes a focus on reliability, that is, the possibility of replication. Qualitative researchers, on the other hand, strive for consistency, that is, the findings are consistent with the data collected. In both cases, decisions made and documented throughout the process, from planning, data gathering, and analysis, through dissemination, impact the methodological rigor of the inquiry. We provide more specific details, including epistemological assumptions underlying particular approaches, in relevant chapters.

Key Concepts

- Like questionnaires, interviews and focus groups elicit self-report data.
- Interviews and focus groups generate rich qualitative data.
- Conducting interviews or focus groups requires ethics review in most jurisdictions.
- Focus groups allow participants to build off each other's comments.
- Interviews allow participants to go into more depth about their individual experiences.
- Successful focus groups and interviews require planning and practice.
- Interviews or focus groups can be categorized as structured, semi-structured, or unstructured, depending upon the amount of freedom the interviewer has in posing and following up on prompts.
- Semi-structured interviews or focus groups are appropriate for a wide range of methodologies.
- Good data management practices are important.

Further Readings

Chick, N. (Ed.). (2018). *SoTL in action: Illuminating critical moments of practice.* Stylus.

Gubrium, J. F., & Holstein, J. A. (Eds.). (2001). *Handbook of interview research.* Sage.

Krueger, R. A., & Casey, M. A. (2015). *Focus groups: A practical guide for applied research.* Sage.

Webb, A. (2015). Research interviews in the scholarship of teaching and learning. *Transformative Dialogues: Teaching and Learning Journal*, 8(1).

6

ARTIFACTS, OBSERVATIONS, AND REFLECTIONS

This chapter focuses on data that goes beyond participants' self-reported responses to specific questions by exploring artifacts, observations, and reflections as data sources. These types of data sources can provide important insights about teaching and learning. Artifacts include things that already exist in the teaching and learning context, like assignments or outlines, but can also be generated specifically for the research project. Observations may involve a whole class or an individual doing a think-aloud protocol. Reflections, whether by participants and/or researchers, can be a powerful source of insight.

While the last two chapters explored how to generate data by asking questions, whether through questionnaires, interviews or focus groups, this chapter focuses on artifacts and various forms of observation before considering reflection as a data source. In each case, the data involves more than the participants' self-reported responses to specific questions. These types of data sources are much less common in SoTL studies (Manarin et al., 2021), but can provide important insights into the teaching and learning environment from various methodological perspectives. On the one hand, they allow researchers to triangulate findings with multiple sources of data, which can be an important strategy for demonstrating credibility for post-positivist or critical realist approaches. On the other hand, this type of observation and exploration can lend itself well to interpretive and transformative approaches, including arts-based research. Since SoTL has as its first principle "inquiry into student learning" (Felten, 2013), it makes sense to explore learning beyond self-reported gains or preferences. Reflection can also be an important data source for some types of SoTL inquiry, including autoethnography and Students-as-Partners projects. This chapter

DOI: 10.4324/9781003447054-8

explores gathering artifacts originally generated for other purposes, also known as secondary use of data; observing participants, in both naturalistic and artificial settings; and setting up reflections as data sources.

Artifacts

Existing Data and Artifacts

If data or artifacts are publicly available, they can be used for SoTL inquiries. Public policy documents, conference programs, and journal issues can provide glimpses into the teaching and learning environment. For example, a research project exploring attitudes towards Universal Design in Learning might have surveys or interviews as data sources, but it might also include analysis of various universities' policy documents or even publicly accessible syllabi. Using these sorts of public documents does not require institutional ethical review in most jurisdictions.

SoTL researchers also have access to rich data sources in their roles as teachers: students interact with course material and each other; students demonstrate their understanding through various assignments; instructors evaluate these assignments, generating feedback and grades; and so on. Written documents, pictures, assignments, exams, and recorded performances completed for particular classes can be wonderfully rich sources of data for a SoTL project, but these artifacts are not public. Using these artifacts in SoTL projects requires ethical review. It's also important to remember that examining these artifacts as data is different from marking them. In a course the assignment is evaluated against a set of outcomes; as artifacts in a SoTL research project, those same assignments can offer glimpses into the participant's learning. One disadvantage to using artifacts as data is that they are highly mediated by contextual factors: "the artifact is not an unmediated representation of the writer's reality, nor does it represent the writer forever. It's a set of choices that occurs in a particular time and context" (Manarin, 2018, p. 102). However, there can be advantages to using artifacts as data. As Merriam and Tisdell (2016) note, artifacts are stable: "Unlike in interviewing and observation, the presence of the investigator does not alter what is being studied" (p. 182). In our experience, participation rates are often higher than they would be for interviews or think-alouds because there is no additional time commitment or effort on the part of participants. Artifacts don't require transcription like interviews or think-alouds. And, perhaps most importantly for SoTL researchers, the artifacts already exist as a natural part of the teaching and learning setting. If we are primarily interested in teaching and learning, it makes sense to explore those forms of data we most commonly use to assess teaching and learning.

Ethical Considerations

While artifacts can be a rich data source for SoTL projects, the classroom is not usually considered a public space where individuals give up their rights to privacy, as demonstrated by various legal frameworks protecting students. Assignments, email exchanges, and discussion board entries created for a class are private, and our role as instructor is separate from our role as researcher. Thus, while students may complete all sorts of assignments for us as part of their regular coursework and while we may have interesting conversations with them about their coursework, this material cannot usually be used as data for research purposes without ethics review. Material students generate for the class must be primarily for the purposes of the class. It is unethical to have students complete assignments intended primarily for our research during class time. However, many times the assignments they complete to increase or demonstrate their learning could also be interesting for our research. If we want to use some of this material as data for research purposes, in many jurisdictions we need to apply to an ethics review board for secondary use of data.

Secondary use of data means that the data was originally gathered for a different purpose (like a course, program evaluation, or even a different research project). The ethics board will require different safeguards depending on the type of data and how difficult it is to connect data with a particular person's identity. In some jurisdictions, if SoTL researchers want to compare grades from a particular class with previous years' performance in that class, the ethics board might ask the researcher to explain how they will gain access to the grades, what safeguards they intend to put in place to avoid breaching privacy, whether the grades will be reported in aggregate, and so on. If it is possible for the researcher to link a participant's data and identity, as is the case in many SoTL studies, SoTL researchers will most likely need to get explicit and informed consent from participants or permission for secondary use of data. Remembering ethical issues around dual role conflicts that we discussed in Chapter 1, this could mean having someone else do the recruiting and waiting until the class is over and the grades submitted before knowing who has agreed to participate. Depending on the type of artifact, it may be impossible to anonymize them. As teachers/researchers, we may recognize particular essays or performances; however, it is still important that we keep the identities of participants confidential, using pseudonyms in dissemination, for example.

Before turning to some practical suggestions about how to use material generated in classrooms as data, we want to say a few words about online artifacts. Salmons (2016) provides a typology of online methods: elicited (i.e., interviews or surveys); enacted (i.e., data created in partnership with participants); and extant (i.e., existing artifacts or unobtrusive observation). As more teaching and learning activities take place online, we need to consider how to deal with online artifacts including email exchanges, discussion forums, social media posts, and so on. Again, the distinction between public and private is crucial, as is a recognition that online data is rarely as anonymous as we may wish to believe. In most SoTL studies, using qualitative data gathered through a Learning Management System (LMS) will require informed consent. Material posted on social media platforms that require a login process is also considered private and requires informed consent, even if participants use pseudonyms. Material posted online without a login process to post or read may be considered public, but quotations of specific posts can easily be traced back to their source using online search tools, and it may be possible to identify the poster through details revealed in other posts. Discussing the ethical issues involved with online artifacts, Merriam and Tisdell (2016) emphasize the term "participants"

> with connotations of inclusion and willing cooperation … as a litmus test concerning ethics. If this term cannot be accurately used—if subjects more appropriately describes the inclusion of unwilling or uninformed individuals under the researcher's scrutiny—then the researcher should honestly reevaluate the methods and procedures of the study.
>
> *(p. 189)*

Remember the criteria of good practice in SoTL include a focus on student learning conducted in partnership with students (Felten, 2013).

Practical Considerations

While SoTL researchers will usually need to get explicit informed consent to use course-generated artifacts, there are different approaches to the timing. Some researchers will outline the research project and seek consent early in the term, recognizing that the instructor cannot know who has agreed to participate until long after the course has ended. Others may seek consent at the end of the term once students have completed most if not all of their assignments so they know what they are consenting to. In either case, someone other than the instructor will have to do the recruiting and hold the completed consent forms securely until the instructor/researcher is no longer in a conflict of interest because of their dual role. For example, if you are likely to have the same students from one term to the next, you might not be allowed to see who has agreed to participate and to have access to their work as data until they are no longer your students. It is also possible to ask for consent from students after the course has finished, and you are no longer in this dual role conflict. However, the main advantage to asking for consent from current students is that you are likely to have higher response rates. Please consult your particular institution for guidance.

Regardless of which approach is taken, the artifacts need to be collected, copied, and stored securely during the course. Again, it is possible to ask participants to send in their work after the fact, but the easier it is for people to participate, the more participants you will have. For our SoTL work, we often collect everyone's work and then destroy the assignments of those who have not consented once we know who has consented to participate. With more electronic submissions, copying and storing work is less of a challenge, but if students complete a lot of assignments by hand or write exams by hand, the instructor/researcher will need to think through a strategy for saving and storing work securely. Again, the ethics board may want to know these details.

Sometimes, novice researchers are worried that they won't have enough data, so they save everything connected to a course. However, the amount of potential data generated by participants in a course can be overwhelming. Rather than the "kitchen sink" approach to data collection, researchers need to return to their research questions and their methodological stances when considering what secondary data might be useful. It is important that question, methodology, and method align. For example, if a researcher believes that knowledge is socially constructed in the give and take of a particular classroom, a comparison of grades achieved across different years is unlikely to be helpful. Researchers might also decide to focus on one particular slice of data at a time, recognizing that there is more that could be said about the same data set later.

Generating Artifacts for the Research Project

Sometimes researchers might ask participants to generate artifacts for the research project specifically. These artifacts could be anything from participants completing a problem set or pre- and post-test outside of the class environment, to creating narratives or keeping diaries, to taking or making pictures. Sometimes it can be useful to pair the creation of an artifact with an interview, which allows the participant to explain what they were thinking about as they created the artifact. What is sometimes called arts-based approaches to research can also involve creating and interpreting visual or performative pieces, often in partnership with participants. The type of artifact being generated will depend upon not only the research question but also the methodological stance of the researcher. In what follows, we briefly identify a few approaches to generating artifacts in order to spark ideas among novice SoTL researchers, but this is certainly not an exhaustive list. More information about these approaches is available in the Further Reading section at the end of the chapter.

Pre- and Post-Tests/Problem Sets

Some SoTL researchers might want to set up pre- and post-tests to see whether a particular intervention had any effect on participants. The chapters on questionnaires and quantitative analysis will be useful here. Sometimes researchers might be less interested in change over time and more interested in how participants approach a particular problem. Examining the rough work generated by participants during problem solving could potentially provide some insight into thought processes. Follow-up interviews using these problem sets as prompts can provide additional insight.

Classroom Assessment Techniques

Many instructors are familiar with Classroom Assessment Techniques, like the minute paper or the muddiest point (Angelo & Cross, 1993). These techniques can also be used to generate data for SoTL research projects from various methodological perspectives, although the researcher will need to think through how to inform participants and how to provide anonymity.

Story Completion Tasks

Participants are provided with a story stem, perhaps a few sentences or paragraphs, and are then asked to write about what happens next. Researchers need to decide how much information to provide in the story stem and how much direction to provide participants in completing the story. While post-positivist or critical realist researchers might see the results as revealing something about participants' assumptions or biases, researchers from more interpretive perspectives will need to address the constructed nature of the narratives themselves.

Diaries

Participants might be asked to complete diaries for the research project. These diaries can vary dramatically in format, everything from handwritten to email, audio or video recorded, to scrapbooks where participants collect meaningful images or texts. In each case, however, participants create regular entries over a period of time. How long and what the entries should look like depend upon the researcher, but it's important to remember that diaries require a significant and sustained time commitment from participants. So while diaries can be a rich source of data for a variety of methodological approaches, they can be difficult to maintain participant engagement.

Photovoice

In Photovoice, participants are asked to photograph scenes illustrating aspects of their experience, and then come together with researchers to interpret the meanings of their images. A technique more prominent in fields like social work, it can be a powerful participatory action strategy (Jarldorn, 2019).

Arts-Based Approaches

The term arts-based approaches to research serves as a sort of umbrella category, recognizing that our attempts to understand human experience need not be limited to discursive or numeric data. As Given (2006) notes, it "is defined by the presence of aesthetic qualities (or design elements) within both the inquiry process and the research text" (p. 30). It is more than using the artistic artifact as a way to elicit participants' responses in interviews or focus groups. Rather the creative process and products are important parts of the inquiry, and researchers engaged in arts-based approaches to research will often present their findings in creative ways. Because such inquiries are always mediated by aesthetic principles, this approach is not often used by researchers who want to focus on an observable reality; rather, it is more common for interpretive or transformative approaches.

Observations

While both interviews and surveys are valuable ways to gather data because they allow participants to share their experiences and perceptions, they rely on participants' self-reports. Depending on the research question, we might want to gather information through direct observation. Saldana (2011) describes the distinction this way: "Participant observation is primarily the researcher's take on social action, whereas the interview is the participant's take" (p. 46). Observations have a long tradition in some types of qualitative research like ethnography. SoTL studies can also involve observation of classroom activities or particular tasks, although researchers must think through the ethical issues involving their dual roles and the need for informed consent. There are also practical issues to consider, including how to decide what to observe, how to ensure information is collected systematically, and how to position the observer and participants. For example, if the researcher is interested in how students interact in groups when solving problems, they need to think through ways to observe and document these interactions, recognizing that multiple groups may be active at any given time, that communication patterns are difficult to document in real time with written field notes, that the group's behavior is likely to change if the instructor is there, and that it is unethical to record and use all students' discussion without their knowledge. Observation is possible, but it requires careful planning and, in many cases if the data is to be used in presentations or publications, institutionally mandated ethical review (Cerbin, 2011).

Norton (2009) identifies three main types of observational research: direct observation where participants know they are being observed, which may influence the behavior; naturalistic observation where participants don't know they are being observed, which creates ethical issues around consent and deception; and participant observation, whether direct or naturalistic, where the observer is a member of the group. Each type of observation has its own ethical and practical challenges. And much depends upon the stance taken by the observer. Merriam and Tisdell (2016) note a range of options from complete participant through complete observer. They also draw attention to the possibility of participants being collaborative partners in the research, what in SoTL has been called the Students-as-Partners movement, where "the investigator and participants are equal partners in the research process" (p. 145). The Students-as-Partners stance offers new possibilities for observation into teaching and learning processes (see, for example, Cook-Sather et al., 2014). Observational research in SoTL can occur in the natural environment of the teaching and learning context (for example, classroom observations) or when a participant demonstrates an activity, perhaps while talking about their thought processes (a think-aloud).

Classroom Observation

Classroom observations are usually framed as a way to improve teaching (Cerbin, 2011; Montgomery, 2012), but they can also be a valuable source of data for SoTL. They do involve particular ethical and practical challenges. In most contexts, the classroom is not considered a public place where ethical requirements for consent might be waived. Remember students have signed up to a particular class to learn something, not to be participants in a research project. They need to be able to make an informed decision whether or not to participate without the undue pressure of wanting to please their instructor. An ethics board will want to know how the instructor/researchers will handle this issue. One possible strategy is having a research assistant or colleague recruit participants without the instructor knowing who has agreed to participate.

A key practical issue involves who will be doing the observation. An instructor trying to facilitate learning or a student trying to learn in a class does not have the ability to also conduct a systematic and thoughtful observation of the entire teaching and learning environment in the moment. As Cerbin (2018) notes,

> We simply cannot attend to multiple students and events at the same time. During on-the-fly observations, we may not see the antecedents of students' responses or understand their comments, and we don't have time to ponder their meanings and implications.
>
> *(p. 83)*

When planning a classroom observation, then, it is important to think about who will be doing the observing, how they will gain consent from those observed, what the purpose and parameters of the observation are, and how the details will be documented. For example, Cook-Sather et al. (2014) describe a Students-as-Partners approach to classroom observation. For some types of observation, it might be possible to use audio or video recording that can eventually be turned into transcripts. Lemieux and Roettger (2019) were able to use recorded student conversations during collaborative exams as data, but only because they worked together. Lemieux gained student consent ahead of time and formed the groups so that consenting students could be placed together without Roettger, the instructor, knowing who had consented to participate. All groups were recorded at their tables; only consenting groups were transcribed. Because recording can be difficult ethically and practically in the classroom environment, classroom observations are often documented in writing. Such notes are both descriptive and reflective. Like an interview transcript, the notes will be analyzed later, so it is important to try to capture as many pertinent details as possible. Observers are more likely to capture those details systematically if they have a plan or protocol going into the observation. This protocol will include details about when and where the observation took place and who was there. A consistent format helps the researcher distinguish between the different types of information documented. For example, the observer might write reflective notes in brackets or in the margin and use quotation marks for participants' own words. In their work on active learning classrooms, Santos and Cheeseman (2019) explored several observational protocols before settling on the Teaching Dimensions Observation Protocol (2015). Cerbin (2018) emphasizes the importance of orienting the observers to the task with an explicit protocol and instructions. Just like it takes practice to be a good interviewer, it takes practice and preparation to be a good observer.

Another practical issue is what precisely should be observed. If we are primarily interested in the instructor's actions, we should observe the instructor (as is the case with much peer observation done for performance evaluation), but if we are primarily interested in the students' learning, we should observe the students, recognizing that we cannot observe thinking or learning directly. We have to make do with indirect proxies—what people say or do. Norton (2009) identifies three approaches to observation: continuous monitoring—the observer records what is happening during the entire class session; time sampling—the observer records what is happening at predetermined intervals; and event sampling—the observer focuses on what is happening when specific behavior occurs (p. 108). Cerbin (2018) recommends that observers focus on a task "that is challenging and generates a range of student performance that allows observers to examine strong as well as weak student performance" (p. 85). As Cerbin (2018) notes,

> by observing students as they engage in a learning task, we can identify their paths to solving a problem or formulating an idea, how they use background knowledge, interpret new information, make decisions, where and how they have difficulty, and so forth.
>
> *(p. 90)*

The goal is to capture as much information as possible about student thinking and performance.

Think-Alouds

The issue of how to make student thinking visible is tackled head-on with think-alouds. Unlike classroom observation, which typically occurs in the natural teaching and learning environment, a think-aloud involves training a participant to verbalize their thoughts as they go through a particular task. For example, a think-aloud might involve a participant talking through the steps they undertake to try to solve a problem. Think-alouds were first developed by cognitive psychologists seeking to understand different cognitive processes. Ericsson and Simon (1993) claim that think-alouds provide an opportunity to access participants' short-term memory. The idea behind think-alouds is that

> Asking participants to state everything they are thinking provides access to unfiltered thoughts as they arise. When thoughts are not verbalized in a moment-by moment manner, they become subject to participants' applying unspoken strategies, which is problematic if you want to study the strategies they are using before speaking.
>
> *(Bohn-Gettler, 2018, p. 5)*

Think-alouds are usually conducted orally rather than having participants write down what they were thinking in the moment or retrospectively as writing involves planning and filtering (Bohn-Gettler, 2018). Investigating the concern that even asking participants to verbalize their thoughts will change those thoughts, Fox et al. (2011) conducted a meta-analysis of published research; they found that "instructing participants to merely verbalize their thoughts during a task did not alter performance, whereas directing them to provide explanations about their thought processes actually improved performance" (p. 333). In both cases, thinking aloud increased the time it took to complete the task. These findings have implications for SoTL researchers who wish to implement think-alouds in their studies. If the research question is exploring how participants typically approach a particular task, researchers should avoid giving detailed prompts or probing for explanations. If the research question is exploring questions of metacognition or self-regulation, such probes may be appropriate.

Setting up a think-aloud, like setting up an interview, requires that the researcher plan carefully with their research questions in mind. Researchers should develop a protocol involving when and how to prompt participants as few participants are used to verbalizing their thoughts spontaneously. For example, if researchers are interested in how participants find online information, they might ask participants to verbalize each time they click a mouse or input information into a search bar; if researchers are interested in how participants solve a mathematics problem, they might ask participants to think aloud each time they write something down, making it clear that participants could also verbalize at other times if they wanted to. The research protocol is guided by the research questions and the practical constraints of the research situation, for example, the complexity of the task.

During the think-aloud itself, again much like the interview, researchers will go through a variety of stages, including welcoming participants, explaining the study, and gaining consent including for recording. Think-alouds are typically audio-recorded as it is too difficult to capture stream-of-consciousness thoughts in notes; depending on the particular task, for example, if the task requires physical manipulation, it may make sense to video record participants. If relying on audio recording, you may still want to make additional notes about actions taken by the participants, for example, if they flip to the end of a reading or return to a graph part way through. Recordings will eventually need to be turned into transcripts for analysis. Transcripts of video recordings will often have participants' actions described; it is important to let the transcriber know what level of detail you require.

Some researchers will also train the participants by modelling how to verbalize during a think-aloud; others believe that such training biases responses. If you decide to model responses, make sure that the modelling includes different types of responses (Bohn-Gettler, 2018). You might also use a practice task with participants just to get them used to speaking their thoughts out loud. Calder (2018) recommends an anagram exercise to get participants comfortable with verbalizing thoughts without predisposing them to a particular type of response in the think-aloud task. If participants ask what they "should" be saying or doing during a think-aloud, reassure them that there is no right answer and encourage them to say what they are thinking. Bohn-Gettler (2018) recommends trying to maintain neutral expressions as a way to reduce demand characteristics where "a participant strives to behave according to their perceptions of the researcher's goals." (p. 7)

Remember that, with the think-aloud, we are trying to get some insight into, perhaps not unmediated, but at least less mediated thought processes.

Reflections

While observations try to capture behavior and less mediated thought processes in the moment, reflections, as the name suggests, are highly mediated as individuals think back and try to make sense of particular experiences, shaping and reshaping their narratives. Nonetheless, reflections can provide a useful data source for some types of SoTL research questions, especially since reflection is often conceptualized as part of the learning cycle (Kolb, 1984; Gibbs, 1988). Reflection allows individuals to consider past experience, gain insight, and move forward to new experiences, as the cycle begins again. As researchers reflect upon the experience of framing the research inquiry, gathering data, and analyzing data, it's worthwhile considering different types of reflection. Donald Schön (1984) distinguished between reflection-in-action and reflection-on-action. Both types of reflection are relevant to the SoTL researcher. Reflection-in-action, a sort of thinking on your feet as you observe situations and problem-solve, is a necessary part of teaching, but it is also part of being an effective researcher. Reflection-on-action, as the name suggests, involves careful reflection after the fact. Such reflection has the potential not only to provide insights into the research data, but also to transform the researcher as Mezirow (1991) argues it is possible to reflect not only on content but also on process and on premises. Using this framework, then, the research reflects not only on the content of the data, but also on the processes of gathering and analysis and, crucially, on the assumptions underlying the research project. As Kreber (2004) notes, "Mezirow's notion of critical or premise reflection involves calling into question underlying presuppositions we have come to take for granted;" such reflection can, but does not have to, involve ideological or political critique (p. 33).

Reflection as a Data Source

Reflections may be a form of secondary data; that is, students are asked to reflect on something as part of their coursework, and then that reflection is used as data in a SoTL inquiry. In that case, many of the comments around artifacts earlier in this chapter would apply.

Reflections can also be used as a form of primary data where the participants or the researchers directly reflect as part of the research project. For example, participants might be asked to reflect on a questionnaire or in an interview or focus group. They might be asked to write reflections on a particular topic. As Jasper (2005) notes, such "narrative and self-reflective written accounts, that are then analysed and interpreted by the researcher, are a well established data source in qualitative work" (p. 253). Finally, reflections of the researchers themselves can be used as data sources depending on the methodology.

Some methodologies, particularly those that value an objective account of the area of inquiry, are less likely to use reflections of the researchers as a primary data source. Some approaches might use researcher reflections as a sort of "audit trail" to enhance credibility or to explicitly account for bias. Some types of phenomenological approaches, for example, try to temporarily "bracket off" or suspend judgment about particular experiences through reflection (LeVasseur, 2003; Ahern, 1999). Still other approaches, among them some interpretive and transformative methodologies, celebrate the subjectivity involved in researcher reflection. From a constructivist and interpretive stance, Jasper (2005) argues that "researchers' reflective writing is central to the research process and therefore needs to be incorporated into any study as a data source and to be considered as central to establishing the trustworthiness of a qualitative study" (p. 257). While research from many different methodological perspectives will benefit from the researcher recording key decisions in analytic memos, only some methodological perspectives will explicitly include reflection as a data source. For those methodologies, reflective writing "offers a method for not only contributing to the trustworthiness of a research study, but that in itself offers techniques to facilitate creativity, critical thinking and strategies for analysis and innovative discovery" (Jasper, 2005, p. 248). Reflection surfaces the researchers' assumptions and construction of reality as they engage with the research project. However, such reflections must be recognized as constructed, rather than naive "true" representations of reality. Braun and Clarke (2013) also note that the conventions of much academic publishing work against discussions of reflexivity, although this pattern is, we believe, changing (see, for example, Cook-Sather et al., 2019).

Reflective Frames

In addition to making sure that reflections are aligned with methodology, researchers may want to consider various models of reflective practice to see what resonates with their experience and meets the needs of their particular research project. Reflection is an important component of multiple domains of knowledge, including but certainly not limited to philosophy and psychology, while some professions like nursing and education explicitly strive to create reflective practitioners. Thus, some SoTL researchers may be familiar with reflective models through their disciplinary identities even if they haven't used these models for reflection in SoTL projects. For SoTL researchers, whose home disciplines put less emphasis on reflective practice, we offer a brief outline of some commonly discussed reflective frames from an education perspective. It is certainly beyond the scope of this book to go into depth about these models or the rich philosophical debates about the nature of reflection. Here, we briefly identify each frame and offer an example of how it could be used to generate researcher reflections for SoTL inquiries.

Four Lenses of Reflection

In *Becoming a Critically Reflective Teacher*, Brookfield (1995) offered four lenses for reflection: self, students, colleagues, and literature. The first involves reflecting upon our own experiences as students, as teachers, and as researchers. Far more than simply anecdotes of the past, these reflections help us understand the basis of some of our choices, both in the classroom and as we are exploring data from the classroom. Reflecting through the lens of students, or participants in a research project, means trying to understand what is happening through their perspectives. In the classroom setting, Brookfield (1998) suggests using data like student evaluations of instruction or classroom assessment tools, like critical incident questionnaires; applying this model of reflection in a research study includes explicitly considering the data from participants' points of view. Participatory action research and Students-as-Partners inquiries require this type of reflection. The third and fourth lenses, those of colleagues and of the literature, involves comparing our interpretations with those of others, as we oscillate between the specifics of our own interpretations and reflections and the broader contexts of professional practice and theory. Ossa Parra et al. (2015) write, reflect on, and share critical incident reports to explore the connections between pedagogy and theory as they move towards a critically reflective teaching method.

Structured Reflection

Christopher Johns' (1995) model of structured reflection builds upon Carpers' ways of knowing in nursing. Like many other frames, it begins with a description of the situation, including identification of specific issues to be addressed, followed by careful reflection. In the reflection section, prompts include what the individual was trying to achieve, why they acted the way they did, and what the consequences are of those actions. The individual is then encouraged to consider both internal and external factors before considering other possibilities and their consequences. Finally, the individual is asked to reflect on how this experience has changed their ways of knowing: scientific, moral, personal, and aesthetic. McConnell et al. (2017) describe using Johns' framework during a collaborative autoethnographic SoTL project; they not only outline their prompts and process but also explore the cognitive and affective impacts of this reflective process.

What? So What? Now What?

The last reflective framework we'll briefly discuss in this section originated in curricular development. Borton (1970) developed a school curriculum involving three simple questions: What? So What? and Now What? This protocol has since been transformed into a reflective framework by multiple scholars, including Driscoll (1994) and Rolfe et al. (2001). Although originally interested in Borton's questions as a way to structure curriculum, Rolfe (2014) saw its potential as a reflective framework: "In particular, it steers the practitioner through the process of analysing, evaluating and synthesising information and facts (What?) into meaningful and organised knowledge (So What?) and subsequently from knowledge to knowledgeable doing or wise action (Now What?)" (p. 489). Rolfe et al. (2001) offer suggestions specifically for nursing and healthcare professionals, but the framework can also be useful for SoTL researchers. For example, Manarin et al. (2015) gathered data about undergraduate reading using the What? So What? Now What? prompts, but also reflected on this data using the same framework; these reflections are an important part of their findings.

This chapter has explored diverse types of data, including artifacts, observations, and reflections. While these types of data are not as common as focus groups, interviews, and questionnaires in SoTL studies, they have a lot to offer SoTL researchers. Researchers need to consider which data sources are compatible with their methodologies and productive for their research questions.

Key Concepts

- Artifacts, observations, and researcher reflections can provide rich sources of data for SoTL inquiries.
- The research question and methodological approach need to align with data sources.
- It's important to distinguish between public and private data sources.
- Artifacts can be divided into primary (that is, created for the research project) and secondary use of data (that is, created for other purposes like coursework).
- Observations can be made in naturalistic or artificial environments.
- Reflections can be primary or secondary data sources for some methodological approaches.

Further Reading

On Artifacts

Braun, V., & Clarke, V. (2013). *Successful qualitative research: A practical guide for beginners*. Sage.

Jarldorn, M. (2019). *Photovoice handbook for social workers: Method, practicalities and possibilities for social change*. Springer International Publishing. https://doi.org/10.1007/978-3-319-94511-8.

Leavy, P. (Ed.). (2018). *Handbook of arts-based research*. The Guilford Press.

On Observations

Calder, L. (2018). Student think-alouds: Making thinking and learning visible. In N. L. Chick (Ed.), *SoTL in action: Illuminating critical moments of practice* (pp. 109–116). Stylus.

Cerbin, B. (2011). *Lesson study using classroom inquiry to improve teaching and learning in higher education* (1st ed.). Stylus.

Cerbin, B. (2018). Classroom observations: Exploring how learning works. In N. L. Chick (Ed.), *SoTL in action: Illuminating critical moments of practice*. Stylus.

On Reflections

Brookfield, S. (1998). Critically reflective practice. *The Journal of Continuing Education in the Health Professions*, 18(4), 197–205. https://doi.org/10.1002/chp.1340180402.

Rolfe, G., Freshwater, D., & Jasper, M. (2001) *Critical reflection for nurses and the caring professions: A user's guide*. Palgrave.

PART III

Analyzing SoTL Data

7

QUANTITATIVE RESEARCH DESIGNS AND STATISTICAL ANALYSIS

This chapter is an introduction to conducting quantitative studies in SoTL. We begin by describing some key terms and goals of quantitative research, as well as important strategies such as sampling. We then describe three common quantitative research designs, which answer different kinds of questions. Finally, we discuss key concepts and implications for descriptive and inferential statistics.

If your research question focuses on describing or comparing relationships between predetermined, measurable variables, then it is best suited to a quantitative research design. As discussed in Chapter 3, researchers who rely on quantitative data typically value objectivity in their research approach and seek to reduce complexity in larger data sets in order to find patterns amongst variables. Using post-positivist assumptions, a phenomenon such as learning can only be imperfectly known because our measures of learning are not direct and because you cannot measure something without altering it. In the critical realist paradigm, a researcher is interested in the underlying mechanisms which generate or explain a phenomenon; in the case of learning, this could include such abstract concepts as motivation, attitude, and identity, all of which can be influenced by context. In other words, the phenomenon (learning) is real but the mechanisms can be abstract, theoretical, and constructed. In both post-positivism and critical realism, quantitative researchers systematically choose methods to try to minimize the possibility for bias and therefore draw conclusions that are independent of the researcher; however, the critical realist acknowledges that theories, especially those related to social phenomena, are not entirely independent of the researcher nor the participants, and therefore can be tested, refuted, or refined over time. In this chapter we explore how in both paradigms,

DOI: 10.4324/9781003447054-10

grounding quantitative research in a theoretical framework helps inform the choice of variables for a study and the study design, and can contribute to knowledge beyond the context of the study.

The benefits of quantitative research are that with precise definition, measurement, and control of variables, one can test hypotheses, test theory, detect patterns, and make inferences from a sample to a population. In order to use quantitative methods, researchers narrow the focus of each study to selected variables, and are expected to provide evidence that their measurements are valid (match reality) and reliable (the same measurement made at two different points in time or by two different researchers will yield the same result). By identifying variables upfront, the process is inherently deductive. Quantitative SoTL studies are often conducted by researchers from STEM and social science disciplines because (a) they align with their disciplinary/professional worldview, (b) there are often large enough classes to achieve statistical power, and (c) there is often enough similarity between various courses and programs that they can collaborate to achieve larger sample sizes and/or expect their findings to be transferable to other contexts.

Can You Achieve Generalizability?

As discussed in Chapter 4, the time-consuming work in quantitative research happens before collecting the data. Because quantitative approaches involve closed-ended methods where variables and measures are defined in advance, quantitative SoTL researchers need to spend a substantial amount of time conducting a literature review and designing a study, including defining variables of interest and how to measure them, determining the validity and reliability of instruments (see Chapter 4), and estimating statistical power. Statistical power refers to how much data is needed in order to be able to *generalize* a set of data to a particular context or population. Put another way, because narrowing the focus of a quantitative study to predetermined, measurable variables is an essential aspect of quantitative approaches, the possibility of bias (in sampling, measurement, or analysis) and/or variability in the data influencing the study findings must be addressed. Sample size formulas help estimate, in advance, the size of sample needed in order to minimize the risk of such errors. As a rule of thumb, Creswell and Guetterman (2019) suggest following Cohen (1992):

* for a survey study, approximately 350 participants,
* for an experimental study, approximately 65 participants in each group,
* for a correlational study, approximately 70 participants.

The actual required sample size will vary depending on the validity, reliability, and scales of measurement used; sample size formulas are available online and in most statistical texts. However, if a SoTL researcher has small classes and no reasonable expectation of getting participation numbers close to those listed above, they should consider a "small q" qualitative approach for their research where they could triangulate the quantitative data with other data sources (see Chapter 8). Note that this would be different from a "mixed methods" study which, despite the misleading name, consists of both quantitative and qualitative *methodologies*; simply collecting both quantitative and qualitative data (multimethod) is not enough to fulfill this requirement, because having statistical power is part of the approach of a quantitative methodology.

Study Validity

The validity of a study refers to whether the inferences drawn from the data are "correct." Therefore, we note that this is a term used in positivist/post-positivist and critical realist paradigms because it aligns with assumptions of measurable constructs and a single reality. Creswell and Guetterman (2019) refer to four different types of validity:

- Statistical conclusion validity: the appropriate use of statistics;
- Construct validity: the extent to which the measurements of the variables match reality;
- Internal validity: how well the research findings match reality within the context of the study;
- External validity: the extent to which the research findings are generalizable to contexts beyond that of the study.

Construct validity is discussed in Chapter 4. Before we turn to the internal validity of a study, which is supported by statistical validity, we first address external validity, and more specifically, the term "generalizability."

A common criticism of SoTL research from those in primarily quantitative disciplines is that context-specific studies are not "generalizable." This term is used differently for different types of studies and research questions, and in our experience, has resulted in much confusion in conversations between SoTL researchers working across disciplines. In the post-positivist and critical realism paradigms, researchers contribute to knowledge by comparing and/or contrasting their findings to what has been demonstrated in other contexts, essentially testing the generalizability of theory, not of a specific study's findings. We have found Yin's work in case study research to be helpful in this regard. Yin (1994) defines two levels of inference in research, which correspond to different forms of generalization (Figure 7.1). Yin defines internal validity as a Level I inference, which we suggest that all quantitative SoTL studies should be able to demonstrate; in this case the findings from the data are being generalized to the context of the study, with a certain level of confidence provided by statistical analysis (statistical

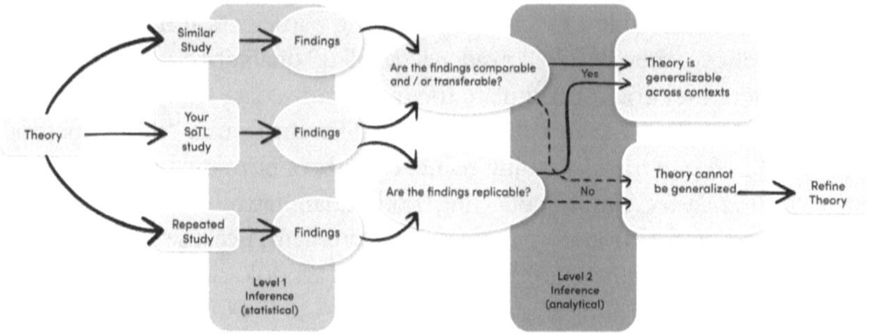

FIGURE 7.1 Well-designed quantitative studies apply theory in a particular context, thereby producing findings that may be transferable to or replicable in other contexts. Each study adds new information which contributes to the generalizability or refinement of a theory (Level 2 inference).

generalization). However, given the contextual nature of SoTL and, indeed, teaching and learning, one wouldn't expect the findings of a single SoTL study to be applicable across all settings and contexts (i.e., high external validity). While Yin's ideas about inferences are typically associated with post-positivist assumptions of causality and stability of relationships between variables, they can be useful in critical realism as well, as we will explore later through example studies.

Similar to Yin, we argue that quantitative SoTL researchers should address internal validity with appropriate design and analysis, and be clear to what population and in what context(s) they expect their findings to be generalizable; they can do so by discussing the expected transferability of their findings to other contexts based on comparability with previous studies (de Leeuw et al., 2022). Yin calls this analytic generalization. Note that these terms all mean something different than replicability, a term frequently used in the hard sciences, where the same study, repeated in a different context and/or with a different data set, is expected to yield the same results (Figure 7.1). Certainly, a SoTL practitioner could choose to try to replicate an existing study in their own context; however, if the particular details of a study are not appropriate or exactly reproducible in their own context, they might reasonably prefer to adapt a study instead, and then discuss the similarities and differences of findings between contexts. A researcher could also conduct a meta-analysis of studies in order to test the generalizability of a theory or findings across multiple contexts or conditions (a Level 2 inference); one well-known example in STEM is a meta-analysis of 225 studies, which concluded that active learning increases student performance compared to lecture-based teaching (Freeman et al., 2014).

In summary, both Level I and Level II types of inferences help contribute to knowledge. However, these ways of comparing, contrasting, and building upon previous studies require that all researchers ground their work in theory, explain their positionality, provide a rich description of the context of their study (terms often used in qualitative research), and discuss any potential mediating variables that could influence their findings. These details will allow their reader to judge the external validity and transferability of their study. In the following sections, we will explore in detail how sampling strategies, study design, and statistical analysis also contribute to the validity of an individual study.

Who Are Your Participants?

In quantitative investigations, researchers ideally randomly select participants in order to minimize the possibility of selection bias. However, in many contexts, including SoTL research, random selection is not possible. Yet there are several choices and considerations beyond simply inviting students from one's own class to participate in a study. This means researchers need to think carefully about who makes up their population, target population, and sample (and they need to be explicit about how they chose these in their dissemination). These terms are most commonly used in survey research, but the principles are applicable to other quantitative designs as well.

Population

A population is a group of individuals who have the same characteristics, and to whom you want to be able to generalize your findings (Figure 7.2). At a minimum, if you are considering a quantitative study, then you would likely want to be able to generalize your findings to the student population in your

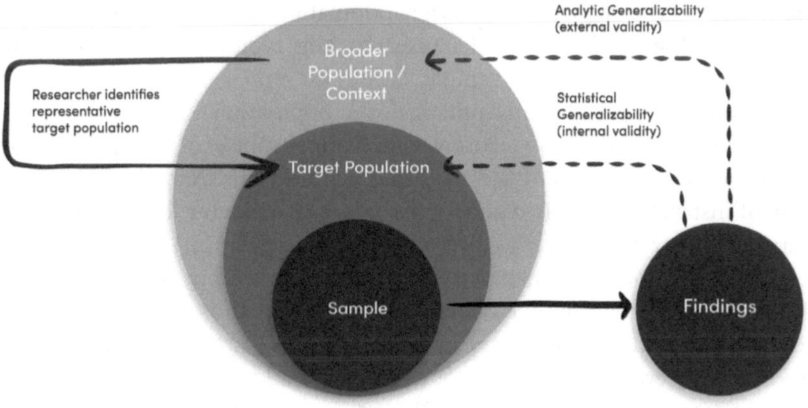

FIGURE 7.2 The population and/or context to which a study's findings can be generalized depends on how much the sample and target population are representative of the population of interest, i.e., have the same relevant characteristics.

class(es); if this were the case, you could expect that your findings would also apply to future cohorts of students in that class (assuming relevant student characteristics don't change much from one semester to the next), and therefore the findings would be useful to you as an instructor but would be very context-specific. If you are considering a larger study, you might hope to be able to generalize your findings to the whole student population in a year of a particular program, or possibly even in a particular discipline. No matter which is the goal, you will then try to choose individuals or groups who are representative of the entire population of interest for your target population.

Target Population

The target population is a group of individuals with the defining characteristics of the population, which you can identify and recruit from (Figure 7.2). It may or may not be a subset of the population. For example, if you want to be able to generalize your findings to the students in your course, the target population would be the same as the population, and therefore you would invite all students in your course to participate in the research. If the goal was to be able to generalize findings to all first-year students in a particular discipline, then the entire population wouldn't be accessible or practical, so you might recruit over multiple semesters or collaborate and recruit students from several institutions.

Sample

The sample is the subset of the target population that the researcher actually studies (Figure 7.2). In SoTL research, this typically means those who volunteer for the study. The sample should be representative of the target population (or, if possible and practical, the population). For this reason, it is common to report how closely the demographics of the participants match the demographics of the target population. For example, in a survey study of instructors who had accessed services of a Center for Teaching and Learning over a three-year period (the target population), the researchers were explicit about how many participants were invited (all of the target population) and the number of respondents minus those who didn't meet the inclusion criteria (the sample); the question of how representative the respondents were of the target population was addressed by reporting the response rates by discipline (Miller-Young et al., 2021b). Even though for SoTL studies convenience and volunteer sampling strategies are most common, it is important to be explicit about how the sample was chosen because it gives the audience a sense of whether there is potential for sampling error.

Sampling Strategies

How research participants are chosen has important implications for the generalizability of the study. Given that this involves communication with potential participants, it is also something the ethics review committee will want to see in detail. The two categories of quantitative sampling approaches are probability and non-probability sampling, where the difference is defined by the purposefulness of the sample.

Probability Sampling

In probability sampling, the researcher purposefully selects individuals who are representative of the target population; this is therefore the more rigorous form of sampling. In simple random sampling, the researcher selects participants randomly such that any individual has an equal chance of being selected (survey), or is randomly assigned into a group (experiment). When a population is imbalanced in terms of an important characteristic (for example, there are far more men than women in engineering), it might make more sense to use stratified sampling. In this case, the researcher divides the target population based on that characteristic(s), and then randomly samples from each subgroup. Neither of these is very common in SoTL studies because of potential ethical concerns. However, we need to be aware that a lack of random sampling is a limitation of our quantitative studies.

Non-probability Sampling

The two most common types of non-probability sampling are convenience and snowball sampling. Non-probability sampling is much more common in SoTL, in both quantitative and qualitative studies. However, it can result in sampling error, in which case the findings cannot be generalized to the target population, let alone the broader population. The larger the sample, the more likely it is that it will represent the target population; however, there is always some potential for error, which should be acknowledged.

With convenience sampling, the researcher selects participants because they are available and agree to participate. This is the most common approach because the SoTL researcher often recruits from within their class (convenient target population), and only uses data from the students who consent (i.e., the sample is those who volunteer for the study). Unless they have a very high participation rate, the researcher cannot say with confidence that the sample is representative of the target population, let alone the broader population.

Snowball sampling is when the researcher asks participants to identify others, or pass along to others the invitation, to participate in the study. In quantitative research, this would be appropriate for studies where the researcher does not have contact information for all members of the target population, and they are trying to recruit large numbers of participants, so it is most common in survey designs. It is less rigorous than a convenience sample because the response rate is unknown, and therefore a researcher is even less likely to know whether the sample population is representative. Researchers also need to be very specific about their inclusion criteria (who, from those who respond, will be included in the sample).

Which Quantitative Design Fits Your Research Question?

The three quantitative designs described in this chapter answer slightly different research questions; they could also each be called a methodology because they imply an observable or measurable reality and comprise certain assumptions about methods of data collection and analysis. However, the term "methodology" is not often used in quantitative research because the objective worldview is assumed to be a given. Instead, the researcher usually names the research design and then describes methods in detail. Whether the study falls into a positivist, post-positivist, or critical realist category will depend on the methodology and the underlying theory and assumptions framing the work. However, for each design, the researcher seeks to quantify relationships amongst variables (or characteristics), and thus poses research questions in terms of these measurable variables:

- survey design: *how is x and/or y distributed within a population?*
- experimental design: *does x cause y?*
- correlational design: *is x related to y?*

The goal of a quantitative study, then, is to answer one (or more) of these types of questions and address internal validity with statistical analysis. Since the analysis is fast once the data is collected, many quantitative studies ask more than one research question at a time. Indeed, all four example studies described in the following sections of this chapter do so, although they each have a design they most closely align with.

Survey Designs: How Is x and/or y Distributed Within a Population?

If your interest is to learn about certain characteristics of your student population, such as students' attitudes or behaviors, a survey design is appropriate. You may also want to correlate variables within that population. Creswell and Guetterman (2019) distinguish survey designs from correlational designs by specifying "their focus is directed more toward learning about a population and less on predicting outcomes, as is the focus in correlational research" (p. 385).

Although the terms are often used interchangeably, a survey is different from a questionnaire. The survey is the design; the questionnaire is the instrument. Because of the large number of participants needed in survey studies, less time-consuming methods of collecting data are most often used, such as the questionnaire, resulting in this confusion. Typically, quantitative data is collected in a questionnaire; however, other data collection methods such as open-ended questionnaire questions, interviews, and structured observations are certainly possible. If qualitative responses or observations are collected, they can be themed and scored for the purposes of quantitative analysis (see "scoring" below, and content analysis, Chapter 8).

Unlike other types of SoTL studies, it doesn't necessarily make sense to recruit participants from your own class or program for a survey design. For surveys it is best to have as large a sample from the population as possible; appropriate sampling methods and high response rates are critical. As an example, if an instructor is considering implementing game-based learning in their class, they might be curious about students' attitudes toward it. Instead of surveying only the students in their class, why not survey all undergraduate students in their program or their institution? For example, Jossan et al. (2021) surveyed undergraduate students from second and third year of a biology program to understand students' views of game-based learning. Because they were also looking for correlations with students' ethnic backgrounds, this could be described as a post-positive approach. In another example, as part of a Center for Teaching and Learning (CTL) self-study, Janice and her team developed a questionnaire to survey instructors who had accessed the CTL in the last three years; we classify this as a critical realist study because it took a complexity-informed approach and a systems-level view of "impact." In other words, it did not assume that the longer-term impacts of the services of the CTL could be reducible to the impacts of its individual programs (Miller-Young & Poth, 2021; Miller-Young et al., 2021b).

When using quantitative data, the validity of the instrument measures is important (see Chapter 4); Jossan et al. developed their own instrument and provided evidence of internal validity using Cronbach's alpha, while Miller-Young et al. performed an exploratory factor analysis. Both of these studies used online, self-administered questionnaires. If an interview is used to conduct a quantitative survey, a structured interview using closed-ended questions is most appropriate, and the protocol should be pilot-tested. The rules of good question construction from Chapter 4 also apply here.

One of the drawbacks of many survey studies is that data is only collected at one point in time (cross-sectional survey design). If you are asking about students' attitudes or perceptions, it is possible they might respond on a day when they happen to feel more positively or negatively than usual for some reason (low reliability). Chapter 4 discusses some administration considerations that will be useful in order to reduce the potential for such bias, and to get higher response rates from students. It is also possible to use a longitudinal survey design where data is collected more than once in order to check the reliability of the measurement(s), or to identify trends in a population over time, or even changes in individuals over time.

Experimental and Quasi-Experimental Designs: Does x Cause y?

If your research question can be worded as "What is the effect/impact of x on y?", then you need an experimental design. This type of quantitative methodology falls more on the positivist or post-positivist end of the spectrum because of assumptions of cause and effect between variables, although it still benefits from being grounded in theory. Experimental designs require careful setup on the part of the researcher (Wilson-Doenges & Gurung, 2013). Ideally, a researcher would (a) randomly assign participants to different groups in order to distribute any bias in the characteristics of the participants equally within each group; (b) control for any extraneous factors that might influence the relationships they are trying to quantify (i.e., check that the groups are equivalent using a pre-test or measure these extraneous variables and control for them statistically); c) give one group the treatment they are trying to measure the effect of (x, or the manipulated variable); and d) measure the difference in outcomes (y, the dependent variable(s)) between groups.

A key feature of a true experimental design is the random assignment of participants, which is difficult to achieve in a teaching context. For example, if there are two different sections of the same class, it is quite possible that students are not equally distributed between them—perhaps students in second year are more likely to be in a certain section than students in first year, because of a scheduling overlap with another second-year class; this could clearly influence the results if trying to make a comparison between the two groups. Even if a researcher is able to randomly distribute participants, they should consider collecting additional information to confirm, post-hoc, the equivalence of the two groups; they would want to check for whatever extraneous factors might influence the findings. For example, in an experimental study of the impact of a voice-over screen-captured learning tool on student learning and engagement compared to a traditional lecture, researchers were able to randomly distribute students into two groups (experiment and control groups) but also collected data about students' awareness and experience with the content, their comfort level with the lecture delivery method, and their perception that technology can enhance their learning. They used the latter measures to double-check that there were no significant differences between the two groups (Schönwetter et al., 2016).

An experimental design that doesn't use random assignment is called "quasi-experimental"; this is more common in SoTL because we often don't have the control to randomly assign students into groups and/or we don't want our students to feel we are favoring one group over another. In this case, it is possible to "control" for possible influential variables using statistical analysis, assuming we have a high enough sample size and statistical power. Some factors to consider controlling for (covariates), depending on the research question, include gender, age, motivation, time spent on task, and incoming GPA (e.g., Barrett et al., 2021).

An experimental or quasi-experimental design is more complex to undertake ethically in SoTL, but it is certainly possible. Since one of the principles of ethical research is to minimize risk of harm to participants, there are several important considerations to reflect upon when designing a study. First, it would be critical to demonstrate, to oneself and to the ethics board, that it is not already known whether the intervention (the manipulated variable) will have a positive, negative, or no effect. As Hersch (2018) argues, "it is only fair to use different teaching methods for different students when there is genuine educational equipoise within the teaching community" (p. 10), or, in other words, there is not already a good basis for choice of intervention in a given context and therefore the study is worth pursuing. Second, a researcher should have a plan for what to do if, partway through or after the intervention, they find that one group does have an advantage over the other. Will the experiment be stopped early and/or will grades of the second group be adjusted (or will the researcher do some other appropriate adjustment) so that students are not disadvantaged?

Another principle of ethical research is that participants should be able to give free and informed consent to participate; by assigning their own students to an intervention or control group, an instructor would essentially be violating this principle. This problem could be mitigated by collaborating with a colleague teaching another section of the course, where it could be argued that different pedagogical approaches can reasonably be expected. In the case of two or more instructors, they would need to work closely with each other to ensure that, as much as possible, all other aspects of the course are kept the same between the two groups. Another option would be to compare a current group of students to a past group(s); this requires some longer-term planning and doesn't allow for random assignment but minimizes the ethical dilemmas, although it still requires ethics review. It also requires that the relevant characteristics of each class would not be expected to change from one semester to another.

In addition to inter (between) group comparisons, it is also possible to do intra (within) group comparisons. Because the researcher is not dividing students into two groups who receive different "treatments," this is also a simpler approach from an ethical perspective. One possible way is to analytically divide a single group into two groups that differ in some characteristic of interest, and compare them by one or more dependent variables (causal-comparative quasi-experimental design). Another common approach is a repeated-measures quasi-experimental design, where a single group acts as its own control group, and multiple interventions and measurements are taken over a period of time. To explore these and other quasi-experimental designs in detail, we recommend Gurung and Schwartz (2009) and Creswell and Guetterman (2019).

Correlational Designs: Is x Related to y?

A correlational design can be used to answer questions about the relationship between variables, where the goal might be either to quantify the strength of that relationship, or to be able to predict one variable if we know the other variable. Because the researcher does not divide the sample into two groups, a cause–effect relationship cannot be determined, and there is no independent or dependent variable. Rather, all participants are analyzed as a single group, and at least two scores are collected from each participant *at one point in time* (one for each variable). Chronologically, this kind of design and analysis developed after experimental designs due to advancements in statistics (Creswell & Guetterman, 2019), but still typically has post-positivist assumptions as it treats relationships between variables as linear and explanatory variables as independent of each other. Today it is possible to test elaborate models containing many variables, but for the purposes of SoTL we still stick to the explanatory correlational design—quantifying relationships between variables.

A correlational design is much easier to conduct in SoTL because it doesn't involve any manipulation of context; data is collected from what is already happening. It can be used to test ideas or theories that are potentially transferable to other situations. For example, finding a lack of research on upper-level blended learning courses, Watson et al. (2020) were interested in how useful the online material was in this type of class in an engineering context, especially since the class in question was made up of second-, third-, and fourth-year students. They analyzed data from five semesters and used total number of online objects accessed and the total number of unique actions taken on these objects as indicators of usefulness, and grades as a measure of course performance. Length of time in the program was positively correlated with course performance but negatively correlated with interactions with the online material; they concluded that a broader range of materials targeted to different levels of students might be more valuable.

Quantitative Analysis

All quantitative studies will involve at least some quantitative analysis (statistics), with the extent and procedures varying depending on the research question(s) and the size and nature of the data set. For questions related to describing a certain population, descriptive statistics may be sufficient; for questions related to comparing interventions, comparing characteristics of different groups, and/or looking for correlations between variables, researchers need to check for normal distribution in the data and then choose an appropriate inferential statistics test. While a quantitative methodology is often portrayed as a linear series of steps, in reality it can be iterative, where a researcher may move back and forth between various stages of data analysis and interpretation as new insights emerge (Figure 7.3). The following sections are intended to give you enough information to help understand and make decisions related to data analysis such as choosing and conducting statistical tests; however, they do not provide detailed mathematical information such as equations. Once a decision is made about which test and software to use, online resources (e.g., American Educational Research Association, 2014) and textbooks will provide any additional information needed. Alternatively, this chapter provides enough information that you should feel confident in hiring a student research assistant with a quantitative background, or consulting or collaborating with a statistician. No matter the research design nor who will do the analysis, an important first step is preparing the data set.

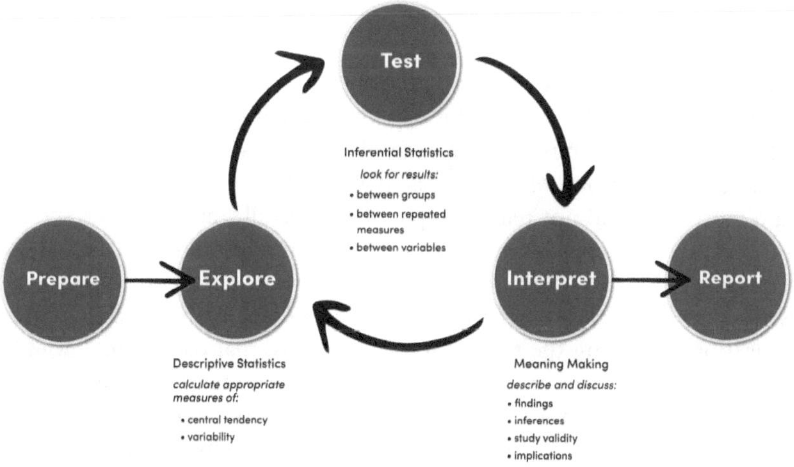

FIGURE 7.3 The five steps of quantitative data analysis, which are ideally, but not always, linear.

Preparing Quantitative Data for Analysis

Before any calculations are performed, you will need to prepare and organize your data. If online software for a questionnaire (e.g., SurveyMonkey, Google Forms) or a gradebook (in the learning management system) was used, the data may already be in a spreadsheet; if not, the first step is to create one. A number should be assigned to each participant and to each variable. Next, score any qualitative data, clean the data, and decide how to handle missing data.

Scoring

The process of converting any observation or qualitative artifact into quantitative data is called scoring. Many qualitative responses, such as to Likert scales (from strongly disagree to strongly agree, discussed in Chapter 4) or answers to categorical questions, such as demographics, can be assigned a quantitative score on the instrument itself. Other steps may include creating new variables such as by calculating averages from a series of questionnaire items related to the same construct, or a series of test questions related to the same concept. Another possibility is conducting a content analysis (see Chapter 8) on short-answer questions from a questionnaire in order to convert the categories of responses into quantitative codes (for example, in order to distinguish the respondents who gave "reason 1" from those who gave "reason 2"). In this case, it is useful to develop a list of codes which names, numbers, gives a definition, and defines the types of scores for each variable.

Data Cleaning

Cleaning the data is the process of screening the data set for any scores outside an acceptable range. One reason for being outside of the range could be an obvious mistake; for example, students reported their age in a questionnaire, and one of the scores says "200." Another reason could be that a participant did not read the questions carefully, and simply responded 4 on a 5-point Likert scale to every single item on a questionnaire. (This is the reason it is good practice to include a few reverse-score questions, as described in Chapter 4—if the participant responded with the same score to all questions including the reverse score questions, that participant should be removed from the data set.) Of course, it is important to be clear and consistent with the criteria for removing data, and these should be reported in any dissemination. It is simple to look for out-of-range scores visually—either use a spreadsheet or a statistics package and sort the data in order for each variable.

Handling Missing Data

In general, missing data occurs when participants don't supply a score for one or more variables. The most common reasons are skipping questions on a questionnaire or leaving the questionnaire before finishing. The best practice is to remove those participants from the data set and report this in dissemination. However, if this greatly reduces the number of participants in the data set, statistical methods can be used to substitute up to 15% of the missing data (George & Mallery, 2019). The best approach to dealing with missing data is to minimize it by carefully designing and pilot testing an instrument.

Once the data is cleaned and missing data handled, response rates and completion rates can be calculated. The response rate is the percentage of participants who responded to the invitation (total responses divided by total invitations), and the completion rate is the percentage of those who contributed a full set of data (number of participants after cleaning and handling divided by total number who responded). Reporting these percentages will help give your reader a sense of the potential for bias in the data. A small response rate does not necessarily mean the responses are biased, as we discuss below, but a low completion rate can be an indicator of an inappropriate instrument which can lead to bias. For example, perhaps only participants who were strongly opinionated about something were motivated enough to complete a very long questionnaire.

Exploring the Data—Descriptive Statistics

No matter which research design you chose, the next step is to explore the data using some descriptive statistics (Figure 7.3). The purpose of descriptive statistics is to describe the information but not to compare or correlate different groups or variables. This is sufficient for descriptive kinds of research questions such as from survey designs, and an important first step for comparison and correlational research questions. Descriptive statistics include reporting both central tendencies in the data (measures that describe a central position within the data for a single variable) as well as variability (how spread out the data is). It is critical to report the variability because it gives a greater description of the data set; for example, if the mean (average) response to a question about student satisfaction was 4 out of 5 on a Likert scale, it would also be useful to know whether all students answered "4" or whether some answered 5 and some answered 1. Put another way, *means mean nothing* on their own. The type of data and spread can also influence which measure of central tendency is most appropriate to use; statistical programs will calculate these, but you will need to decide which to report depending on what most usefully describes the data.

Measures of Central Tendency

Measures of central tendency are single numbers which help describe the location of the "middle" of a set of scores. They are expressed as the mean, median, and mode, and each gives slightly different information depending on the distribution of the data. The mean (average) gives a rough description of the middle of the data set but can be influenced by outliers, especially for small data sets; if this is the case, it is appropriate to also report the median. The median score is the middle score and is especially useful to report for small data sets and/or situations with extreme outliers because it is not influenced by outliers. Finally, the mode is the most common score in the data; it is most useful to report for subjective methods of scoring when grading or scores do not differentiate well between students or for nominal data where the average is meaningless (if students report being in either first, second, or third year of a program, an average of 2.1 is meaningless; a mode of "2" would tell us that most students were in second year). Creswell and Guetterman (2019) recommend reporting all three.

Frequencies

Frequencies count the number of times a specific data point occurs. For categorical data (such as demographic data) and Likert-style perception data (e.g., strongly agree to strongly disagree), reporting means doesn't usually make sense, so it is more accurate and effective to state results in terms of percentages; pie graphs are very useful for this (see Chapter 13).

Measures of Variability

Variability indicates the spread, or distribution, in the scores of a variable. In other words, it offers additional information to measures of central tendency. For example, two data sets could have the same mean, median, and mode, but very different variability; one set could have many of the data points clustered around the mean/median/mode, and another could be very spread out. Typically, the standard deviation is reported, but additional measures could be reported if they provide useful information about the data. Standard deviation (SD) indicates how tightly the data is clustered around the average, with a higher SD meaning the data has a larger spread. It is also used in determining whether a data set has a normal distribution. The variance indicates the dispersion of scores around the mean. It is especially important to check for in some cases; for example, a t-test should only be used when comparing two independent groups with similar variances. Finally, the range is the difference between highest and lowest score; this is particularly useful to report when there are outliers. Knowing the measures of variability will also be important for choosing an inferential statistical test.

Checks for Normal Distribution

The theoretical distribution of mean scores for a variable is called the normal distribution. Many natural phenomena fit this distribution, and many statistical tests are based on an assumption of normal distribution (these are called *parametric* tests). Normal distribution can be checked for by plotting the frequency of scores in a data set (with scores along the x-axis and frequency on the y-axis); the data is normally distributed if it is symmetric around the mean; the mean, median, and mode are equal and at the center of the distribution; and certain percentages of the scores fall within +/– 1, 2, and 3 SDs of the mean (Figure 7.4). In other words, the standard deviation defines the width of the normal distribution.

Knowing how the data is distributed is useful in two respects. First, it gives you useful information about your measurement instrument. If grades on an exam, for example, are skewed positively (the data is spread out more to the right of the mean and the peak of the curve is shifted to the left), this could mean that the assessment was too difficult and did not differentiate enough between students. On the other hand, if students are asked to rate their satisfaction with a particular learning activity on a Likert scale of 1–5, you would, as an instructor, likely be happy to see a distribution that was skewed due to more positive responses (called a negative skew, meaning the mean and majority of students are clustered in the top of the range). Second, knowing whether the data is normally distributed is necessary in order to conduct inferential statistics, i.e., choose a parametric or non-parametric test. The simplest way to check for normal distribution of any data set is just to plot the data using a histogram (see Chapter 13), calculate the standard deviation, and see if the data fits the normal curve. The equation for skewness could be used with minimal programming of a calculator or spreadsheet, or common tests such as Kolmogorov–Smirnov's

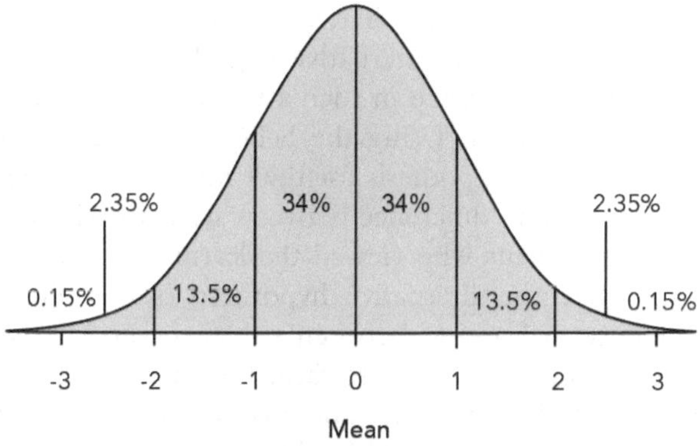

FIGURE 7.4 The normal curve, showing the percentages of a normally distributed data set which fall 1, 2, and 3 SDs away from the mean.

and Shapiro–Wilk's tests, which are available in freely available computer code or statistical packages.

Testing for Significance–Inferential Statistics

If your research question involves comparing at least two different groups or correlating two or more variables, you will need to conduct inferential statistics. These types of statistical tests determine whether there are any differences between groups, or any correlations between variables, and if they are statistically significant; that is, the difference is likely NOT caused by chance. In other words, they are also ways of estimating whether your data is a good estimate of the study context and target population, and therefore are always reported in terms of probability. A correlational analysis quantifies direction (positive or negative), form (linear or not) and strength of the relationship between variables. The correlation coefficient (r, usually reported as r^2) determines the proportion of change in one variable that can be explained by the second variable. Correlations can also be shown visually using scatter plots and correlation matrices (Chapter 13). For conducting and reporting inferential statistics, it is useful to use all three ways of estimating the population: hypothesis testing, the confidence interval, and the effect size.

Hypothesis Testing

Hypothesis testing checks whether the sample mean is a good estimate of the population mean. Since we can never absolutely prove that our sample is a good estimate of the broader population (because we haven't measured the entire population!), we test the "null hypothesis," which is written to state that there is no difference between groups if we are comparing groups, or there is no relationship between variables if we are looking for correlations. We also write the alternative hypothesis (the opposite of the null hypothesis), which is written in such a way as to indicate whether the probable direction is known. Using the Schönwetter et al. (2016) study described above, the null hypothesis for their first research question could be written as "There is no difference between students who received face-to-face lectures vs. students who viewed the learning tool in terms of student learning," while the alternative hypothesis is non-directional, that there is a difference in learning between students who viewed the video lecture vs. those who attended face-to-face. For the second research question, the null hypothesis would be "There is no difference in engagement between students who viewed the video lecture vs. students who attended face-to-face," whereas the alternative hypothesis is directional: "Students who attended the face-to-face lecture were more engaged than those who viewed the video lecture." Once these hypotheses have been written, we choose a significance level and select statistical test(s).

The significance, or alpha, level reflects the number of times you are willing to accept that your findings are due to chance. Statisticians will tell you that it is important to choose a significance level before doing the test, so that you are not distracted afterwards by results that show an *almost* significant result—it is often possible to find significant differences or relationships that have no practical meaning. For examples of what alpha level to choose, look for similar studies in a target dissemination venue; for educational (typically low-risk) research, significance level is often set at 0.05 (5% of times the result will be due to chance) or sometimes a more conservative 0.01 (1% of times it will be due to chance) (Creswell & Guetterman, 2019, p. 188).

A choice of statistical test will depend on four factors: whether the goal is to make comparisons between independent groups, make comparisons between repeated measures, to test for multiple factors, or to test for correlations between variables; whether each variable is measured using a continuous or categorical scale (see Chapter 4); whether the data for each variable is normally or non-normally distributed; and whether the alternative hypothesis is directional or non-directional. Common tests are listed in Table 7.1. For a directional alternative hypothesis, use a one-tailed test which has more power; if direction is not known, use a two-tailed test which is more conservative. We also recommend doing further reading on whatever test is chosen, to ensure that your data meets the requirements and assumptions for the test; for example, a t-test should only be used to compare groups with similar variances. Looking at studies which have measured and compared/correlated similar variables is another way to gain confidence in one's choice of test. Finally, for more complex data sets than what are shown below, we recommend consulting someone with additional statistics training.

Using the chosen test, calculate a p value (probability) or r value (correlation factor) in order to reject or fail to reject the null hypothesis. For tests looking for significant differences in means, statistical significance is when the p value is less than the alpha level, meaning we can reject the null hypothesis (i.e., there *is* a difference or a correlation). For correlation tests, 0.3 is considered a weak correlation, 0.5 a moderate correlation, and greater than 0.7 a strong correlation. A positive number indicates a positive, linear relationship and a negative number indicates a negative, linear relationship; that is, as one variable increases, the other decreases.

Finally, it is important to remember that significance is influenced by sample size and effect size. For example, a large sample size can result in significant differences even if the differences in means are small (not a meaningful difference); a too-small sample size can result in a not-significant

TABLE 7.1 Most Common Statistical Tests

Statistical test	*Number of independent variables*	*Number of dependent variables*	*Scale of independent variable*	*Scale of dependent variable*	*Distribution of scores of continuous variable(s)*
Group comparison tests (to make comparisons between independent groups)					
Independent sample t-test	1 variable with 2 categories	1	Categorical	Continuous	Normal distribution
Analysis of variance (ANOVA)	1 or more	1	Categorical	Continuous	Normal distribution
Mann–Whitney U test	1	1	Categorical	Continuous	Non-normal distribution
Chi-square	1	1	Categorical	Categorical	Non-normal distribution
Multiple factors group comparison (to test for additional factors that cause differences between groups)					
Factorial ANOVA	2 or more variables with 2 or more categories	1	Categorical	Continuous	Normal distribution
ANCOVA	2 or more variables with a continuous covariate	1	Categorical	Continuous	Normal distribution
Repeated measures tests (to make comparisons between, for example, pre-post or test-re-test)					
Paired samples t-test	1variable with two conditions	1 variable (measured twice)	Categorical	Continuous	Normal distribution
Paired samples ANOVA	1 variable, two or more conditions	1 variable, measured for each condition	Categorical	Continuous	Normal distribution
Variable correlation tests (to test for correlations between variables)					
Pearson correlation	1	1	Continuous	Continuous	Normal distribution
Spearman rank-order correlation	1	1 or more	Categorical	Categorical	Non-normal distribution
Point-biserial correlation	1	1	Categorical	Continuous	Non-normal distribution

Tests to choose based on variables, types, and distribution of data (adapted from Creswell and Guetterman, 2019).

difference even when there are differences between groups. For these reasons it is also very helpful to calculate and report the confidence interval and effect size.

Interpreting the Data

Confidence Intervals

While the hypothesis test tells us when the null hypothesis is rejected, confidence intervals tell us how sure we can be. When comparing groups, the confidence interval is the estimated upper and lower range of means that are likely to contain the actual population mean, a certain percentage of the time (usually 95%). If calculating correlations, the confidence interval tells us the estimated range of r values. Statistical packages will calculate confidence intervals automatically, but remember that confidence interval calculations assume there is a genuine random sample of the relevant population.

Effect Size

Effect size tells us the strength of the conclusions regarding the difference between two means or relation between two variables. There is a different coefficient for different statistical tests; for example, *Cohen's d* is calculated for t-tests, and *Pearson's* r^2 for correlational tests. All coefficients are reported in terms of standard deviation units, so a coefficient greater than 1 is a fairly large difference in a practical sense; the lower the coefficient, the weaker the difference or association. In summary, both statistical significance and practical effect size are important for understanding impact or correlation.

Common Problems Encountered When Analyzing and Interpreting Quantitative Data

Assuming that issues of measurement validity and reliability were addressed during instrument development and data-gathering, and decisions related to sampling and analysis methods followed the recommendations described above, the most common problem that novice SoTL researchers are likely to encounter is not providing enough contextual information for others to interpret or use their results. Typically, sampling information is most important in survey designs, and statistical interpretation is most important in experimental and correlational designs.

In a survey study, where the purpose is to learn about and describe trends in a population but not to test hypotheses, descriptive statistics are usually enough to answer the research question. However, the sampling strategy and response rate will affect the generalizability of the results. If the sampling strategy, response rate, and demographics of respondees are not reported, it will not be clear to your reader whether the findings are generalizable even *within the study context.* For example, perhaps only the most dissatisfied students responded to a survey, or perhaps only students with higher grades (*A*s and *B*s) agreed that their assignments be included in the study. By collecting and reporting some demographic information from participants, such as gender, age, cumulative GPA, and ethnicity (depending on which may be relevant to the research question), you should be able to provide evidence that your sample is fairly representative of your target population, as appropriate. Further, it can help give indication of how many students from underrepresented groups were included in the study, which is becoming more important as awareness of issues of equity, diversity, and inclusivity grows. In order for potential participants to give informed consent, a researcher should also explain why they are collecting such information, especially if it doesn't seem directly connected to the stated research questions.

In an experimental or correlational study, where the purpose is to test a hypothesis, SoTL researchers need to use inferential statistics in order to report findings that are not simply due to chance, and report enough information so that the reader can interpret the findings. In other words, in choosing data analysis methods, researchers should check and then report that their data aligns with the underlying assumptions associated with a particular statistical test (normal distribution, similar variances, ordinal vs. continuous data, etc.). Onwuegbuzie and Daniel (2003) classify not doing so as a type of data analysis error called "violated assumptions," and state, "when it is unknown whether assumptions have been met, data interpretation can be extremely misleading and invalid" (p. 8). Similarly, not reporting effect size is likely the most common interpretation error (Onwuegbuzie & Daniel, 2003), and results in the reader not having enough information to understand the magnitude of the statistically significant effect or relationship. Finally, even with a rigorous research design and significant findings, there is always a possibility that the result was caused by some unknown factor, i.e., an intervening or confounding variable. We encourage SoTL researchers to be cautious in the conclusions they make, to read widely, and discuss their research with both colleagues and students to consider what factors may have influenced their findings; there is always the possibility of addressing some of these limitations with the next study.

In summary, quantitative SoTL studies typically fall within post-positivist and critical realist paradigms and focus on understanding learning by testing theories and relationships between variables in various contexts. Quantitative research's strengths are that when variables are accurately controlled and/or measured, it can reveal and quantify patterns and relationships amongst variables and within populations. Further, quantitative findings may be more convincing to colleagues from quantitative disciplines. Because quantitative methodologies strive to minimize effects of bias and variability in the data, sampling strategies are important and descriptive and inferential statistics are necessary for data analysis. However, quantitative studies only measure what they set out to measure; despite efforts to collect and analyze data objectively, the choices of theoretical framing, what questions to ask, and what variables to measure are still highly influenced by the researcher. For this reason, it is becoming more common to include positionality statements in quantitative research articles, even by SoTL researchers from quantitative disciplines. Finally, although it can be tempting to use quantitative data because it's relatively easy to collect and quick to analyze, it is critical to remember that if we don't have an appropriate sample or statistical power, then the quantitative "findings" of a study such as differences between means and groups could be entirely due to random chance and therefore are not findings at all.

A checklist for evaluating quantitative research:

- Does the research question offer theoretical and practical value?
- Was the study design identified and assumptions articulated?
- Does the study define the variables and sampling strategy?
- Were the scores used valid and reliable?
- Were the appropriate statistical tests used?
- Do the descriptions of the methods and context provide enough detail for another researcher to repeat or modify the study?
- Were the interpretations and suggested implications reasonable?
- Were the limitations of the study and the authors' positionality stated?

Key Concepts

- Quantitative SoTL research requires large enough numbers to achieve statistical power (internal validity).
- Highly contextual studies can address external validity by comparing and contrasting findings with other studies, also helping to establish the generalizability of a theory.
- Sampling strategies will affect how representative the study sample is of the target population.
- Three common types of quantitative research designs are quasi-experimental, correlational, and survey designs.
- Choosing an appropriate statistical test depends not only on the type of research question but also the nature of the data.
- At a minimum, descriptive statistics should be reported, including measures of central tendency and variability, as well as a description of how representative the sample is thought to be of the population of interest.
- Inferential statistics take into account the variability in a data set and are necessary for correlational and quasi-experimental studies.

Further Reading

Bartsch, R. A. (2013). Designing SoTL studies—part I: Validity. *New Directions for Teaching and Learning*, 136, 17–33.

Bernstein, J. L. (2018). Unifying SoTL methodology: Internal and external validity. *Teaching & Learning Inquiry*, 6(2), 115–126. https://doi.org/10.20343/teachlearninqu.6.2.9.

de Leeuw *et al.* (2022). Generalizability, transferability, and the practice-to-practice gap. *Behavioral and Brain Sciences*, 45(11). https://doi.org/10.1017/S01450525X21000406.

Gurung, R. A. R., & Wilson, J. H. (Eds.). (2014). *Doing the scholarship of teaching and learning: Measuring systematic changes to teaching and improvements in learning*. Jossey-Bass.

Harpe, S. E. (2015). How to analyze Likert and other rating scale data. *Currents in Pharmacy Teaching and Learning*, 7(6), 836–850. https://doi.org/10.1016/j.cptl.2015.08.001.

Wilson-Doenges, G., & Gurung, R. A. R. (2013). Benchmarks for scholarly investigations of teaching and learning. *Australian Journal of Psychology*, 65(1), 63–70. https://doi.org/10.1111/ajpy.12011.

8

EMPIRICAL QUALITATIVE APPROACHES

This chapter will be a primer on conducting qualitative SoTL studies from post-positivist or critical realist perspectives. Here the researcher treats data as if the data is relatively transparent and reflects reality. We begin by introducing some empirical approaches used in SoTL. We then provide more detail about content analysis and empirical thematic analysis before describing coding basics and common issues.

When we work with new SoTL researchers, they are often unsure of how to begin the analysis process with what they have gathered. This chapter will outline some of the most common processes for analyzing qualitative data in SoTL studies, including a detailed explanation of coding data. But decisions about what to do with your data begin long before you gather anything. They begin with your assumptions about learning and knowledge that lead to your research question. As Saldana (2016) notes, "The nature of your central and related research questions—and thus the answers you seek—will influence the specific coding choice(s) you make" (p. 70). For many SoTL inquiries, this means using an empirical method, whether qualitative (as discussed in this chapter) or quantitative (as discussed in the previous chapter). Empirical, here, just means based on observations made by the researcher. As Miller-Young and Yeo (2015) note, the goal of qualitative empirical research "is to discover aspects of an observable reality, and it attempts to be as objective as possible in its approach" (p. 42). Note the emphasis on "an observable reality," suggesting a post-positivist or critical realist framework. Regardless of the type of data collected (whether think-alouds, interviews, or artifacts), the researcher treats that data through a relatively transparent lens as if it reflects reality. For example, if a majority of students report that problem-based learning increased their competence in a particular area (i.e.,

DOI: 10.4324/9781003447054-11

their confidence has increased), a post-positivist or critical realist researcher might suspect that problem-based learning was beneficial in this context. Self-reported confidence in itself is not empirical evidence of competence, and so these researchers would ideally examine something like artifacts or think-alouds, something that demonstrated student competence in this context. The researcher is less likely to examine the power structures underlying that context (a critical approach) or articulate what it is about problem-based learning that made students gain more confidence (an interpretive approach). For many SoTL researchers who seek to understand what is going on in a classroom and how students are learning, or not learning, a focus on qualitative data as empirical is appropriate.

Empirical Qualitative Research

Empirical qualitative research includes a wide range of analytical techniques, some of which are more tied to ideals of objectivity than others, but all involve treating qualitative data as if it reflects the world as it is. Much SoTL research is generic qualitative research. Caelli et al. (2003) describe generic qualitative studies as

> those that exhibit some or all of the characteristics of qualitative endeavor but rather than focusing the study through the lens of a known methodology they seek to do one of two things: either they combine several methodologies or approaches, or claim no particular methodological viewpoint at all. Generally, the focus of the study is on understanding an experience or an event.
>
> *(p. 2)*

Generic qualitative studies, then, either combine methodologies, hopefully in ways that are congruent with each other, or are silent about methodology, an option we discourage. So why would someone choose to use a generic qualitative approach rather than a more established approach like phenomenology? Percy et al. (2015) address the distinction between phenomenology and generic approaches as the distinction between experiencing and experiences:

> If your focus is outward—on the content of opinions, on the actual-world experiences and happenings, on the thoughtful description and reflection of historical occurrences in people's past—you might want to select generic qualitative inquiry as your methodological approach rather than phenomenology or one of the other approaches.
>
> *(p. 78)*

Much SoTL research, seeking to learn more about particular experiences of learning, fits Percy et al.'s (2015) description: "The core focus is external and real-world, as opposed to internal and psychological" (p. 79). Generic qualitative research also allows researchers more freedom to combine different analytical techniques, including thematic or content analysis. It's also suitable for what Braun and Clarke (2013) call, "small q" qualitative research, that is, qualitative data used in more post-positivist or critical realist studies, perhaps as a precursor to, or alongside, quantitative methods as in a mixed methods study (p. 5). Of course, because generic qualitative research has this flexibility, it is important to describe how the research was conducted and analyzed when disseminating the work. Caelli et al. (2003) note that often generic qualitative research studies "cannot invoke a known method in a few words. Enough detail about the study, the approach, and the methods needs to be included so that the reader can appropriately evaluate the research" (p. 4).

While quantitative research is usually deductive (that is, testing theory with specific data) and interpretive qualitative research is usually inductive (moving from specific data to theory), empirical qualitative research can be inductive, deductive, or a combination of the two. Your decision about whether to approach your data inductively or deductively should be consistent with the method you choose. Some empirical methods like template analysis and content analysis can involve inductive and/or deductive processes, while others like phenomenography or some forms of thematic analysis are more appropriate for inductive approaches. Before we address two of the most common approaches, content analysis and empirical thematic analysis, we will briefly outline two other empirical qualitative approaches that may be useful for SoTL researchers, depending on their inquiry. These approaches exist on a continuum from "small q" qualitative approaches to "Big Q" qualitative approaches.

Phenomenography

If you are primarily interested in variation from an empirical perspective, you might consider phenomenography. Phenomenography tries to map variation in how something is understood by participants: it is primarily interested in the content of the thinking rather than the process of conceptualization (Marton, 1986, p. 32); as such, it has been a fruitful approach for various SoTL researchers interested in how their participants perceive different topics, including everything from attitudes towards scholarly sources, problem-solving strategies in chemistry, and attitudes towards research-informed teaching (MacMillan, 2014; McCollum et al., 2016; Joseph-Richard & Jessop, 2020). Rather than emphasizing common patterns, researchers deliberately focus on the range of responses and then express logical or hierarchical relationships

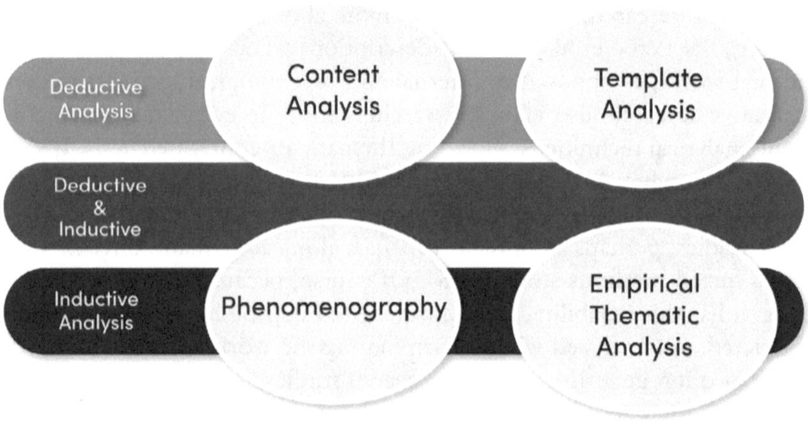

FIGURE 8.1 Qualitative approaches range from "small q" to "Big Q" (left to right), and analysis processes can be inductive, deductive, or a combination of both.

between responses in what's called an outcomes space (Åkerlind, 2005). This space is often represented as a matrix (see, for example, MacMillan, 2014). Phenomenography has also led to the development of the Variation Theory of Learning, an approach that tries to apply phenomenographic principles to curricular development (Åkerlind, 2015).

Template Analysis

If you are primarily interested in exploring how an existing conceptual framework fits your data, you might consider something like template analysis. As Brooks and King (2017) note, "Template Analysis evolved as a generic approach within the wider tradition of thematic analysis, specifically among approaches with a strong emphasis on research in real-world settings" (p. 2). As a generic approach, template analysis can be appropriate for a variety of methodological approaches, from post-positivist to critical, but often, especially in applied disciplines, there is an emphasis on reducing researcher subjectivity and providing quality checks during the coding process (p. 17). Often researchers will begin with a priori codes, that is, themes from existing literature or from earlier stages of a research project (Brooks et al., 2015). At the same time, however, researchers will want to pay attention to those places where the data does not fit the a priori codes. In template analysis, a subset of the data is examined deductively and inductively. Both a priori codes and inductive codes are combined into a template that, once refined and tested, can be applied to the rest of the data in a systematic way to generate hierarchical coding (Brooks et al., 2015). In a large-scale qualitative study, Snijders et al. (2021) use template analysis with a priori themes to explore student perceptions of relationships with academic staff; on a much smaller scale, Manarin and Abrahamson (2016) discuss faculty perceptions of SoTL using template analysis.

While phenomenography and template analysis are two specific approaches to qualitative data analysis, most often SoTL researchers seeking to analyze qualitative data through a relatively transparent lens will use either a version of content analysis or of empirical thematic analysis. The names themselves make the situation a little confusing because most (if not all) qualitative approaches are interested in the content of the data and most (if not all) qualitative approaches are interested in themes within and across the data. In what follows, we try to delineate each approach.

Content Analysis

Content analysis allows researchers to analyze and quantify messages, either in terms of their ideas or the relationships between ideas. Although content analysis was originally associated with the study of mass media, it is also used by researchers in many other fields interested in the manifest, or easily identifiable, content of textual or visual messages (White & Marsh, 2006; Margolis & Zunjarwad, 2018). Manifest content is sometimes contrasted with latent content, the underlying meaning that can be inferred from the message. If a researcher focuses on manifest content, the analysis is more likely to be replicable. For some research frameworks, that's important. Indeed, content analysis strives to be "objective, systematic and observational" (Margolis & Zunjarwad, 2018, p. 620). Researchers are concerned with reliability and validity, so they will include descriptions of how codes were defined and interrater reliability. After all, the idea is that someone else coding the data in the same way that you did would reach similar conclusions. Often content analysis involves quantifying the manifest content of qualitative data. Researchers may count the presence, absence, or frequency of particular elements in the data corpus, and report these numbers in their findings. As Vaismoradi et al. (2013) note, such quantification "cautiously may stand as a proxy for significance" (p. 404). Neuendorf (2017) notes that

> Content analysis is a summarizing, quantitative analysis of messages that follows the standards of the scientific method (including attention to objectivity-intersubjectivity, a priori design, reliability, generalizability, replicability, and hypothesis testing based on theory) and is not limited as to the types of variables that may be measured or the context in which the messages are created or presented.
>
> *(p. 17)*

Some of these elements are very attractive for SoTL researchers, especially those who come from disciplines with more post-positivist orientations. The approach is easily understood and described; it doesn't require an in-depth knowledge of particular theorists. On the other hand, content analysis is inherently reductive; it reduces complex texts into a few categories or concepts. It is also difficult to deal with latent or implicit content that could be interpreted in different ways by different people (Margolis & Zunjarwad, 2018).

Hsieh and Shannon (2005) identify three main types of content analysis: conventional (using an inductive approach to coding); directed (using a priori codes); and summative (using frequency counts of words, generated by hand or through computer-aided text analysis—CATA). Neuendorf (2017) notes that, because content analysis emulates the scientific method, it is important that the research design be carefully planned ahead of time, whether the coding is inductive or deductive; that is,

> All decisions on variables, their measurement, and coding rules must be made before the final measurement process begins. In the case of human coding, the codebook and coding form must be constructed in advance. In the case of computer coding in CATA, the dictionary or other coding protocol should be established a priori.
>
> *(p. 18)*

Content analysis then requires significant preparation.

Elo and Kyngäs (2008) argue that the preparation stage of content analysis is similar whether the researcher is using inductive or deductive coding. If the corpus is very large, the researcher may need to apply a sampling strategy that allows for a representative sample to be selected. The details of that strategy should be reported along with the findings. Elo and Kyngäs (2008) also note that the researcher must decide on the unit of analysis and become very familiar with the sample in order to make sense of the data as a whole. The unit of analysis here is connected to the research question. So, for example, if we want to learn more about our students' work in terms of Bloom's taxonomy, our students' work is the unit of analysis. If we have collected our students' work, then our students' work is also the unit of data collection or observation; however, if we are examining teachers' interviews about their students, we have different units of data collection but still the same unit of analysis. Neuendorf (2017) notes that

> In content analysis, a *unit* is an identifiable message or message component that (a) serves as the basis for identifying the population and drawing a sample, (b) is the component on which variables are measured, and/or (c) serves as the basis for reporting analyses.
>
> *(p. 70)*

The researcher using content analysis thus considers units of sampling, units of data collection, and units of analysis. In content analysis, the researcher decides what messages to collect to create a representative sample in order to answer the research question; then the researcher decides how to break up those messages consistently into components that can be analyzed. Neuendorf (2017) identifies etic and emic approaches to breaking up messages: "the general notion is one of etic referring to scientifically generated knowledge and emic denoting subjective knowledge or experience" (p. 71). She recommends considering both approaches: etic units are more consistent with the epistemological assumptions of content analysis, but emic units can be discovered by the researcher: "Through immersion in the message pool, the researcher may discover what units make sense within the world of those messages" (p. 71). The actual content analysis, however, does not begin until units have been decided.

After this preparation, the researcher undertaking content analysis will examine the units to begin to define categories and levels of abstraction, if undertaking inductive coding, or describe categories and levels of abstraction, if undertaking deductive coding. As Mayring (2000) notes, inductive coding in content analysis is an iterative process of category formation, definition, and revision with repeated checks for reliability. Deductive coding, on the other hand, involves applying theoretically informed codes to particular texts. Mayring (2000) notes that the researcher seeks "to give explicit definitions, examples and coding rules for each deductive category, determining exactly under what circumstances a text passage can be coded with a category. Those category definitions are putted [sic] together within a coding agenda." Again, the analysis involves multiple reliability checks at different points in the analysis process.

Both interrater reliability (the level of agreement between coders) and intrarater reliability (the consistency of a coder's decisions across time) are important when conducting a content analysis. Neuendorf (2017) argues that "at least two coders need to participate in any human-coding content analysis" (p. 166) in order to validate the coding scheme. Multiple coders also help lessen the workload since, once intercoder reliability is established, coding of the data set can be divided up among collaborators. However, SoTL researchers often work alone, investigating something that is happening in their own classes. For these solo researchers who want to do a content analysis, one workaround is to have a colleague or research assistant participate in a coding exercise even if they are not analyzing the complete data set. These interrater reliability exercises can uncover places where the coding scheme is unclear or there is confusion among the coders. Another possibility is to develop the research project in partnership with students who can participate in the coding, sharing their insights about the teaching and learning environment.

Training the coders will improve reliability. As Neuendorf (2017) notes, "coder training typically involves several sessions and practice codings to establish good initial reliability for the pilot test" (p. 170). The results of interrater reliability tests are often reported during dissemination, though how they are reported varies according to the norms of particular disciplines and publication venues. Sometimes, it is sufficient to provide a narrative about how issues of interrater reliability were addressed; other times, researchers will indicate how often they agreed in percentages; and in still other contexts, particular coefficients like Cohen's *kappa* (calculating reliability between two raters, or code-recode) or Fleiss's *kappa* (calculating reliability for any number of raters) are reported. Neuendorf (2017) offers a detailed explanation of when (and how) to use different coefficients for interrater reliability. Some software programs, like SPSS or Excel, will calculate this for you, but it's also possible to do a couple simple calculations by hand once you understand which test you need. Intrarater reliability, that is, assessing the stability of coding practice over time, is often given less attention in content analysis; however, it is good practice to revisit training protocols periodically during the coding to minimize coding drift. These practices increase the reliability of the content analysis, and so should be disclosed during dissemination.

Content analysis is one of the most quantitative of qualitative approaches. It strives to be objective and reliable, as demonstrated by its focus on a priori design and reliability. In both inductive and deductive content analysis, the interpretation of results is likely to include quantitative elements like frequency counts. There may even be charts or graphs demonstrating findings in summary form. For example, Manarin et al. (2021) present their findings about the foci of SoTL journals in a series of charts; they also describe their iterative coding processes and their attempts to account for rater variability. Gelbman (2011), on the other hand, demonstrates a more qualitative approach to content analysis, as she still relies heavily on the manifest content but provides a series of quotations to illustrate categories rather than reducing the material to a chart or data point. Although she describes her approach as ethnographic content analysis, it could also be described as empirical thematic analysis, demonstrating that these empirical approaches are on a continuum. Similarly, Acai et al. (2017) describe what they are doing as thematic analysis, but their structured approach to coding has much in common with content analysis.

Thematic Analysis

Thematic analysis is another common approach used with qualitative data. Indeed, Braun and Clarke's (2006) step-by-step description of how to do thematic analysis has over 120,400 citations, according to Google Scholar.

Since then, Braun et al. (2019) have refined their thinking about thematic analysis, dividing it into three categories that span very different epistemological and methodological assumptions: coding reliability approaches (which would be very similar to what we've described as content analysis or phenomenography, for example); codebook approaches (which can include what we've described as template analysis); and reflexive analysis (which we will discuss in Chapter 10). Braun et al. (2019) note that "the shared name 'TA' [thematic analysis] obscures divergence, both in terms of procedures, and, more importantly, in underlying philosophy and the conceptualization of key elements of the method (e.g., a theme, a code, or coding)" (p. 845). While coding reliability approaches are firmly anchored in "small q" assumptions about empiricism, and codebook approaches occupy an "in-between" space between "small q" and "Big Q" qualitative research, Braun and Clarke's later work is primarily focused on reflexive analysis, which emphasizes the "researcher's role in knowledge production" (Braun & Clarke, 2019, p. 594). Braun and Clarke (2013) describe thematic analysis, whether undertaken in an empirical or constructivist framework, as a "flexible, foundational method" (p. 174) that can be used to answer many different types of research questions and that is "relatively easy and quick to learn, and to do" (p. 180). When using thematic analysis with an empirical lens, the researcher codes the data as if it reflects the external world or the participants' experiences of the external world, which makes it an appropriate choice for many SoTL studies.

Coding

Coding is a very common way to make meaning in many types of qualitative analysis; it's not the only possibility for making meaning, and in some cases it may be inappropriate (Jackson & Mazzei, 2012; Saldana, 2016). St. Pierre and Jackson (2014) complain that coding has become synonymous with qualitative data analysis: "we teach analysis as coding because it is teachable" (p. 715). They claim that coding is inherently reductive as it decontextualizes data. Elliott (2018) conceptualizes coding as a decision-making process, arguing that decisions appropriate for one research project may not be appropriate for the next. Saldana (2016) describes coding as a heuristic: "a method of discovery that hopefully stimulates your *thinking* about the data you have been given and have collected" (emphasis in the original, p. 42). Recognizing that coding is one of many ways to encourage thinking, we provide some advice and examples of coding using thematic analysis in the remainder of this chapter.

Coding involves several processes: organizing data; labeling segments of data; grouping segments of data based on a characteristic; identifying patterns (and variations from pattern) in and across the groups; and suggesting an interpretation of, or way to explain, these patterns. Coding is a way to defamiliarize your data, so that you can see it differently and gain insights into meaning that you might otherwise miss. Coding, done well, is not mechanistic; it is a tool for thinking about data. Sometimes researchers talk about themes "emerging from the data" but

> an account of themes "emerging" or being "discovered" is a passive account of the process of analysis, and it denies the active role the researcher always plays in identifying patterns/themes, selecting which are of interest, and reporting them to the readers.
>
> *(Braun & Clarke, 2006, p. 80)*

Novice qualitative researchers often worry about the decisions they need to make in this active role. They may hesitate to begin coding because they worry about getting it "right" or believe that a computer-aided analysis program like N-Vivo will make decisions for them. Whether coding by hand or with a computer program, the researcher is still making the decisions, and there are likely to be false starts. They are not even false starts; they are necessary parts of the process of thinking. Recognize that your ideas about your data will change and evolve over time as the coding proceeds; indeed, coding is an iterative process, as elements that you first thought were important become less significant, and other ideas or relationships become more prominent in your thinking about the data. The important thing is to keep track of decisions and recognize that you can always make different decisions. You will often report these decisions during dissemination.

Pre-Coding. Regardless of the type of coding, researchers need to familiarize themselves with the data before coding, whether that is by listening to the audio of interviews, reading through transcripts, examining artifacts, or reading observational notes. You want to start thinking about the data. As Braun and Clarke (2013) note, "Familiarization is not a passive process of just understanding the words (or images); it is about starting to *read data as data*" (emphasis in the original, p. 205). By this, they mean reading critically and asking questions about the data and what it might mean. Keep track of your impressions when you first see the data, whether through analytic memos or annotations.

In this pre-coding phase, you will also decide how to organize the data and how to represent the different types of information you will be dealing with. Again there is no right or wrong way. Some people use different fonts, colors, or brackets to signal what a participant said, what they noticed, and what they thought later. You will also decide how to set up your data for coding. One common format is to use columns where raw data is in one column and preliminary codes in another; a variation involves three columns with raw data, preliminary codes, and revised codes (Saldana, 2016).

One of the first decisions you will make is deciding on the data to be coded. Will you focus on specific segments of the data (selective coding), or will you code all data that may be relevant to the research question (complete coding)? The benefit of paying attention to specific episodes is that researchers can give those segments of data more attention; the risk is that they will miss something important. Saldana (2016) recommends that novice researchers code more rather than less until they gain more experience with coding and analysis. You will also need to decide on the segment of data to be labeled. As Merriam and Tisdell (2016) note, the segment of data can vary dramatically in size, but should be meaningful; that is, it should "reveal information relevant to the study and stimulate the reader to think beyond that particular bit of information" (p. 203). Saldana (2016) describes coders as lumpers and splitters: a lumper may take a whole paragraph of an interview transcript and provide a holistic label; a splitter, on the other hand, will assign multiple labels as they work through the paragraph line by line. Again, each approach has its own advantages and disadvantages. Lumping is more efficient, but can be superficial. Splitting provides a more nuanced account but can be overwhelming as the researcher tries to analyze the material. As Saldana (2016) notes, "it is only from experience that you will discover which approach works best for you, your particular study, and your particular research goals" (p. 25). Don't be afraid to experiment with different approaches, recognizing that it is prudent to keep a clean copy of the data separate from the copy you will be using for your analysis (Merriam & Tisdell, 2016).

Initial Coding. Merriam and Tisdell (2016) describe coding as "*nothing more than assigning some sort of shorthand designation to various aspects of your data so that you can easily retrieve specific pieces of data*" (emphasis in the original, p. 199). A code is a label applied to a segment of data. It often seems more complicated than that for novice researchers because so many different aspects of data could be coded, depending on the research question. Saldana's *The Coding Manual for Qualitative Researchers* (2016) lists dozens of ways that data can be coded. Saldana distinguishes between first cycle coding methods, as the researcher begins to work with the raw data, and second cycle coding methods, where the researcher reorganizes the data in order to "develop a sense of the categorical, thematic, conceptual, and/or theoretical organization from your array of first cycle codes" (p. 234). First cycle coding may involve labeling segments based on structural elements (i.e., applying a content-based phrase); using descriptive or topic coding (similar to the use of hashtags (#) in social media); using gerunds to identify actions in process coding; or labeling segments according to emotions or values displayed (Saldana, 2016). For an empirical qualitative methodology, using a specific term when describing your coding is less important than describing what you did. Remember that coding is there to help the researcher analyze the data; it's not an end in itself. In what follows we will use thematic analysis as our example, but many of the principles remain the same when doing other types of coding.

In thematic analysis, segments of data are labeled and then organized based on what the researcher notices related to the research question. Braun and Clarke (2006) advise the researcher to "work systematically through the entire data set, giving full and *equal* attention to each data item, and identify interesting aspects in the data items that may form the basis of repeated patterns (themes) across the data set" (emphasis in the original, p. 89). So the researcher works through the data set labeling items that seem connected to the research question. Many qualitative researchers will use what's called the constant comparison method. Originally developed for grounded theory studies but used in many varieties of qualitative research now, the constant comparison method involves collecting and coding the first participant's data, keeping those codes in mind as the next participant's data are collected and analyzed, and so on. The codes change and evolve as the analysis proceeds. We commonly say that saturation is reached when the data can be described without additional codes, although saturation is actually more complex than this as different models of saturation focusing on data collection, analysis, and theory exist (see, for example, Saunders et al., 2018).

The specific codes or labels can be expressed in the participants' words (in vivo) or the researcher's words. These initial codes can be either data-derived codes that "provide a succinct summary of the explicit content of the data" or researcher-derived codes that "identify *implicit* meanings within the data" (emphasis in the original, Braun & Clarke, 2013, p. 207). Braun and Clarke (2013) note that novice researchers often rely heavily upon data-derived codes because "they are easier to identify, and rely less on having conceptual and theoretical knowledge through which to make sense of the data"; researcher-derived codes, on the other hand, "assist in developing an interpretative analysis which goes beyond the obvious" (p. 210).

Moving from Codes to Categories. Data-derived codes can be very interesting, but the researcher still needs to analyze them. That is, the researcher needs to "make sense of the patterning of responses" (Braun & Clarke, 2006, p. 94). To do this, the researcher begins to group different codes together into categories. Essentially, the researcher is moving from data-derived codes to researcher-derived categories. With researcher-derived codes, some of this work is already done, but the researcher will still want to identify patterns, and variations from patterns, in and across the groups. Merriam and Tisdell (2016) note that this process of moving from codes to categories is highly inductive and emphasize that "categories are abstractions derived from the data, not the data themselves" (p. 207). Braun and Clarke (2006) describe this process of category formation as searching for themes: "Essentially, you are starting to analyze your codes and consider how different codes may combine to form an overarching theme" (p. 89). They recommend using visual representations, like tables, mind maps, or sticky notes that can be organized in different ways, to help identify possible relationships between codes. Merriam and Tisdell (2016) argue that, ideally, categories should be responsive to the research question; exhaustive (all the codes fit somewhere); mutually exclusive (a particular piece of data fits into one category only); sensitive to the data (the name of the category should help people understand what's in in); and conceptually congruent (that is, at the same level of abstraction) (p. 213). Braun and Clarke (2006), on the other hand, argue that it is possible at this stage to have codes that don't fit anywhere and to put those codes in a category called miscellaneous. They note that researchers "end this phase with a collection of candidate themes, and sub-themes, and all extracts of data that have been coded in relation to them" (p. 90).

Reviewing Categories to Create a Thematic Map. Once segments of data have been coded and sorted into categories, the researcher needs to consider how these categories relate to each other. Braun and Clarke (2006) recommend returning to the data set. First, coded extracts are reread to see if they all fit within a category, or "candidate theme," and if the categories "form a coherent pattern" (p. 91). There is no set number of themes, but the themes need "to convey the richness and complexity of a central concept of your data" (Braun & Clarke, 2013, p. 232). Remember, too, that you might have different levels of themes—perhaps an overarching theme, themes, and subthemes. If the categories fit the data and seem to connect to each other, you can create a thematic map or model: "a visual presentation of how abstract concepts (categories) are related to one another" (Merriam & Tisdell, 2016, p. 216). Larsson et al. (2020), for example, use a chart to provide more nuanced dimensions of each theme.

If, on the other hand, the data doesn't fit into categories or the categories don't fit together to create a coherent pattern, you need to return to the data. As Braun and Clarke (2006) note,

> you will need to consider whether the theme itself is problematic, or whether some of the data extracts within it simply do not fit there—in which case, you would rework your theme, creating a new theme, finding a home for those extracts that do not currently work in an already-existing theme, or discarding them from the analysis.
>
> *(p. 91)*

Researchers may need to review their data multiple times before being satisfied with the categories and themes generated. Recognizing that it can be tempting to search for the perfect fit, Braun and Clarke (2013) recommend that "once you don't want to make any substantial changes to your thematic map, it's a good time to stop and move on" (p. 236).

Analyzing Themes. In thematic analysis, then, the researcher labels raw data with codes, groups those codes into categories, and thinks about how those categories relate to each other to create a thematic map. The process of analysis doesn't end there, however. Each of those themes still needs to be analyzed. In this analysis, the researcher will create a narrative, explaining what each theme is, what is interesting about the themes, and how the themes (and any sub-themes) relate to each other (Braun & Clarke, 2006, p. 92). When disseminating the analysis, specific extracts from the data are used to illustrate themes, but as Braun and Clarke note,

> Extracts need to be embedded within an analytic narrative that compellingly illustrates the story you are telling about your data, and your analytic narrative needs to go *beyond* description of the data, and make an *argument* in relation to the research question.
>
> *(emphasis in the original, p. 93)*

This overall argument may include an organizing principle of the themes. This path from codes to categories to themes may seem linear (see Figure 8.2a) but is much messier in real life as researchers move back and forth, continuing to revise their thinking as they work with the data (see Figure 8.2b).

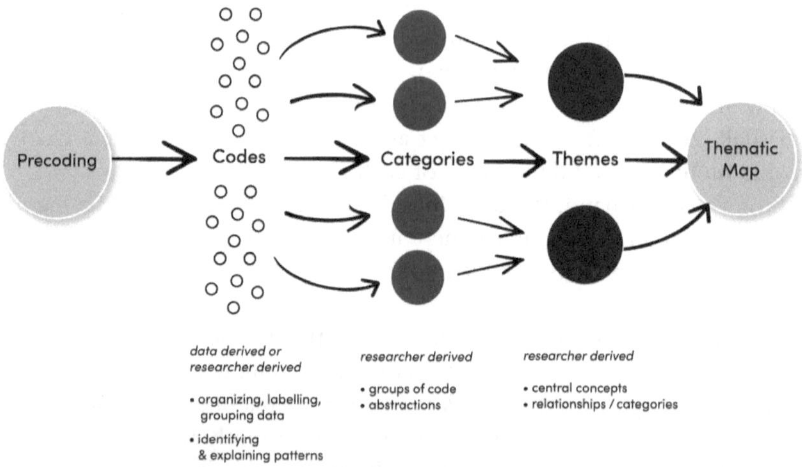

FIGURE 8.2A The qualitative data analysis process (as planned): ideally, the researcher moves from codes to categories to themes.

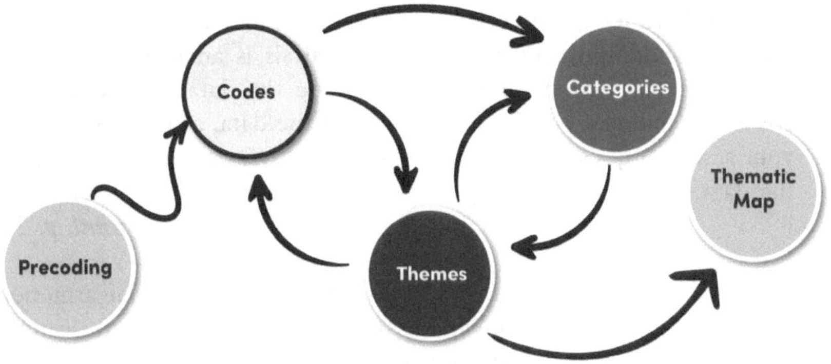

FIGURE 8.2B The qualitative data analysis process (as lived): the analysis process is not linear.

Common Problems Encountered When Using Empirical Qualitative Approaches

Too Many Codes, Categories, or Themes

Novice researchers may find that they are generating a lot of different codes/labels as they work through the data. This proliferation of codes can be overwhelming. To deal with this common issue, Saldana (2016) recommends coding as a lumper, using select codes repeatedly, subsuming codes into broader categories as you go (remembering to record your decisions), deciding whether you really need to code everything you've collected, and writing about the process as you go in analytic memos.

Novice researchers may also struggle with the number of categories. How many categories are too many? It really depends on the project. Braun and Clarke (2013) remind us that the number of categories or themes will vary depending on our goals. If we want to present an overview, we need to present the "*breadth* and *diversity* of patterns in the data;" one or two themes would oversimplify the data set (emphasis in the original, Braun & Clarke, 2013, p. 232). For an article-length study, five or six themes is an appropriate number in many cases (Creswell, 2007; Braun & Clarke, 2013; Merriam & Tisdell, 2016). Of course, if the study focuses on a particular aspect of the data set, it may be completely appropriate to have one or two themes with subthemes (Braun & Clarke, 2013). In general, researchers agree that "the fewer the categories, the greater the level of abstraction, and the greater the ease with which you can communicate your findings to others" (Merriam & Tisdell, 2016, 214).

Sometimes novice researchers generate too many codes, categories and themes because they are trying to account for all of the coded data within a single analysis. Braun and Clarke (2013) emphasize that

> Being able to let go of coded material (and indeed, candidate themes) that does not fit within your overall analysis is an important part of qualitative research. Your task in analysing the data is a *selective* one. It's about telling a *particular* story about the data, a story that answers your research question. It isn't to represent *everything* that was said in the data.
>
> *(emphasis in the original, p. 230)*

A convincing analysis provides a rich description of a particular argument; other arguments are likely possible with the same data set. Researchers will often use the same data set to explore different aspects of the research questions, generating multiple publications in the process.

Not Enough Analysis or Analysis That Is Inconsistent with Approach Taken

Another common problem is to rely too heavily upon extracts, description and paraphrase rather than analysis. For this reason, Braun and Clarke (2006) warn researchers against using the data collection questions as themes: "In such a case, no analytic work has been carried out to identify themes across the entire data set, or make sense of the patterning of responses" (p. 94). The researcher may begin but should not remain at the level of data-driven codes. Remember coding is a heuristic to help with the interpretation of the data (Saldana, 2016); rearranging the data is not sufficient on its own. For this reason, Saldana (2016) cautions novice coders against using descriptive coding (that is, hashtag topic-based nouns) as a default method for interpreting interview transcripts; he suggests that using in-vivo coding, emotion coding, or process coding to help move beyond paraphrasing (pp. 76–78). Remember qualitative analysis, of whatever type, involves analysis.

It's also important that the analysis remain consistent with the epistemological and methodological underpinnings of the approach. In this chapter, we have focused on empirical approaches, that is, the data is treated as if it reflects an observable reality, however imperfectly. If the analysis swings too far into interpretivist or transformative orientations, it may not seem credible.

Analysis Lacks Consistency and Credibility

As Merriam and Tisdell (2016) note, while quantitative research may focus on reliability (that is, the possibility of replication), qualitative researchers strive for consistency, that the findings are consistent with the data collected. One key way to demonstrate this consistency is to "demonstrate how data analysis has been conducted through recording, systematizing, and disclosing the methods of analysis with enough detail to enable the reader to determine whether the process is credible" (Nowell et al., 2017, p. 2). Strategies to enhance consistency and credibility for empirical qualitative approaches include triangulation of methods, data sources, investigators, or theories. For example, Hassel et al. (2011) support their analysis of patriarchy as a threshold concept by conducting thematic analysis of written work but also by analyzing student achievement based on rubrics. Thus, they achieve corroboration by triangulation, increasing the study's credibility. Other strategies to increase credibility include participants and peers providing feedback on preliminary findings; purposely looking for variation in the data; researcher self-reflexivity; creating an audit trail that records decisions along the way; and providing enough detail in the research product that readers can decide whether the findings are meaningful in their contexts (Merriam & Tisdell, 2016, p. 259). In qualitative research you cannot rely on statistical analysis to make your case; you will have to describe your methodology and your findings to your audience in more detail, so that they feel they can trust the choices you have made throughout the research process.

Much SoTL research involves looking at qualitative data through an empirical lens, that is, examining the data as if they reflect an external reality. These approaches exist on a continuum from "small q" to "Big Q" qualitative analysis, so we encourage novice SoTL researchers to consider how comfortable they are with subjectivity and ambiguity as they select an approach.

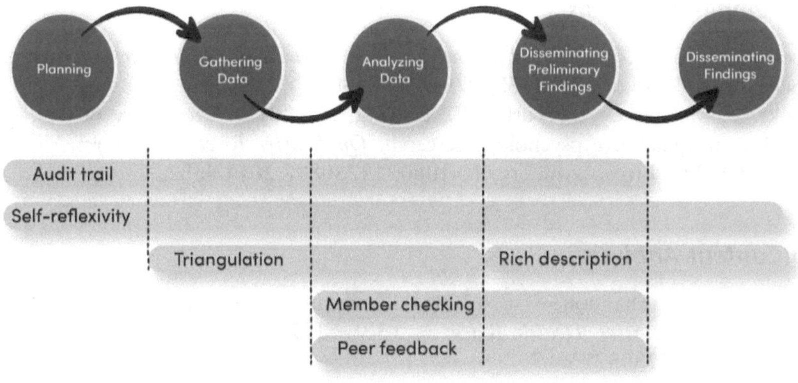

FIGURE 8.3 Qualitative researchers should use multiple strategies to enhance credibility throughout the research process.

Key Concepts

- Empirical approaches involve looking at data as if it reflects, however imperfectly, an observable reality.
- Researchers using phenomenography work inductively to focus on variation in participant responses.
- Researchers using template analysis use a combination of deductive and inductive processes to create hierarchical structures.
- Researchers using content analysis seek to summarize data in an objective fashion.
- Researchers using empirical thematic analysis strive to move beyond summary as the researchers' subjectivity begins to contribute to the analysis in the coding choices made.
- Coding is a tool that helps researchers think about the data.
- Coding involves labeling segments of data and then linking different segments across the data so that the researcher can identify patterns.
- There is no one correct way to code data, but decisions made while coding should be recorded.
- Researchers should consider issues of credibility throughout the research process.

Further Reading

On Phenomenography

Åkerlind, G. S. (2005). Variation and commonality in phenomenographic research methods. *Higher Education Research and Development*, 24(4), 321–334. https://doi.org/10.1080/07294360500284672.

Marton, F. (1986). Phenomenography—a research approach to investigating different understandings of reality. *Journal of Thought*, 21(3), 28–49.

On Template Analysis

Brooks, J., & King, N. (2017). *Template analysis for business and management students.* Sage. https://doi.org/10.4135/9781473983304.

Brooks, J., McCluskey, S., Turley, E., & King, N. (2015). The utility of template analysis in qualitative psychology research. *Qualitative Research in Psychology*, 12 (2), 202–222. https://doi.org/10.1080/14780887.2014.955224.

On Content Analysis

Hsieh, H.-F., & Shannon, S. E. (2005). Three approaches to qualitative content analysis. *Qualitative Health Research*, 15(9), 1277–1288. https://doi.org/10.1177/1049732305276687.

Neuendorf, K. (2017). *The content analysis guidebook* (2nd ed.). Sage. https://www-doi-org.libproxy.mtroyal.ca/10.4135/9781071802878.

White, M., & Marsh, E. (2006). Content analysis: A flexible methodology. *Library Trends*, 55(1), 22–45. https://doi.org/10.1353/lib.2006.0053.

On Empirical Thematic Analysis

Braun, V., & Clarke, V. (2006). Using thematic analysis in psychology. *Qualitative Research in Psychology*, 3(2), 77–101. https://doi.org/10.1191/1478088706qp063oa.

Braun V., Clarke V., Hayfield N., & Terry, G. (2019) Thematic analysis. In P. Liamputtong (Ed.), *Handbook of research methods in health social sciences.* Springer. https://doi-org.libproxy.mtroyal.ca/10.1007/978-981-10-5251-4_103.

Vaismoradi, M., Turunen, H., & Bondas, T. (2013). Content analysis and thematic analysis: Implications for conducting a qualitative descriptive study. *Nursing & Health Sciences*, 15(3), 398–405. https://doi.org/10.1111/nhs.12048.

On Coding

Elliott, V. (2018). Thinking about the coding process in qualitative data analysis. *The Qualitative Report*, 23(11), 2850–2861. https://doi.org/10.46743/2160-3715/2018.3560.

Saldana, J. (2016). *The coding manual for qualitative researchers.* Sage.

9

MIXED METHODS RESEARCH DESIGNS

This chapter will discuss mixed methods research designs. First, we briefly describe the development of this paradigm, and its defining features, which include the use of two methodologies, rather than simply two methods. We then describe the three common designs, along with their advantages and challenges, supplemented with examples and discussion of how mixed methods can be used for SoTL research.

Mixed methods research developed in the latter half of the 20th century, with initial studies using quantitative surveys and interviews to answer research questions (Merriam & Tisdell, 2016). This resulted in the perhaps unfortunate name of "mixed methods," whereas now it has evolved and is commonly understood to mean "mixed methodologies" despite the original title having staying power. Several useful sources describe the paradigm debates which occurred during the 1980s and 1990s, where the epistemological differences between scientific, interpretive, and transformative research were raised, and which are useful background for the current debates about mixed methods (e.g., Morgan, 2007; Creswell & Plano Clark, 2017). In short, some argue that quantitative and qualitative research should not be combined due to incompatibility of worldviews, while "pragmatists believe that multiple paradigms can be used to address research problems" (Creswell & Plano Clark, 2017, p. 26). Although these definitional and paradigmatic debates are ongoing, mixed methods research has become widely accepted and used, especially within applied disciplines (Timans et al., 2019), and continues to be further developed, with the commonly accepted description that this paradigm consists of both quantitative and qualitative methodologies.

DOI: 10.4324/9781003447054-12

We had difficulty, in situating mixed methods within this book, deciding whether to place it before or after interpretive approaches, since it has been developed as its own methodological orientation more recently. It fits well within a critical realist framework but can also be used in other paradigms. Ultimately, we came to embrace Creswell and Plano Clark's (2017) perspective that the worldview(s) of a mixed methods study must relate to the study context and type of mixed methods design, and that multiple paradigms may be used as long as the researchers are explicit about it. Citing Burke Johnson and Stefurak (2013), Creswell and Plano Clark describe this approach as having three key characteristics:

- researchers attend to different worldviews, theories, and stakeholders;
- researchers' and stakeholders' values guide the study;
- researchers collaborate with all stakeholders with fairness, justice, and equality.

However, we also acknowledge that researchers with experience or training in only one area will likely have difficulty combining methodologies from more than one paradigm, and that post-positivist, critical realist, and interpretive researchers may even have difficulty accepting each others' approaches as valid. We suggest mixed methods is worth exploring because it incorporates strengths from both quantitative and qualitative traditions. Because of the need to distinguish it from other paradigms, mixed methods researchers tend to be very explicit about their choice of methodology, data analysis procedures, and even how they choose to represent their procedures and data. For those with some level of comfort with either quantitative or "small q" qualitative SoTL research as we have described in the previous chapters, exploring mixed methods will help you generate interesting and creative new insights for doing your SoTL work as well as for communicating it effectively in the multidisciplinary SoTL space. Also, if one methodology is likely to be more convincing for your intended audience but the other type of methodology could better answer your research question, using mixed methods can help meet both these needs. We will explore these ideas further, as they relate to SoTL, by discussing some important considerations as well as three common mixed method research designs.

Key Considerations

Beyond simply analyzing two sets of data, using mixed methods requires researchers to be intentional and explicit about the integration of their multiple data sources, in order to meet the goals of this approach, which are to provide a more complete understanding of a complex situation than what can be gleaned from separate quantitative and qualitative results. Rather than relying on induction or deduction, mixed methods researchers describe a process of "abduction," or moving back and forth between both processes, ultimately generating both explanation and new knowledge (Mingers, 2014). As we discussed above, this requires expertise in multiple research methods as well as typically more time and resources. However, the potential to provide deeper understanding of complex situations and contexts is precisely the reason that we believe it can be very powerful for SoTL studies. It also provides open-minded SoTL researchers an opportunity to gain experience with new (to them) research paradigms by collaborating across disciplines and areas of methodological expertise.

Key to the mixed methods approach is the integration of data; data from one phase is used to confirm, explain, and/or inform data from the other phase. According to Creamer (2018), this results in a "meta-inference": an insight that would not have been possible unless quantitative and qualitative data had been combined with one another at some point in the design. In addition to integration, it is also critical that both qualitative and quantitative data are also analyzed rigorously in their respective phases of the study; in other words, the quantitative analysis should have statistical power and the qualitative analysis should be trustworthy. Because of the need for both rigor and integration, the need for data analysis software such as N-Vivo is much higher with mixed methods than with either quantitative or qualitative methodologies alone. For example, in purely quantitative research analysis can often be performed with commonly available spreadsheets, and for qualitative methodologies coding can be done by hand; however, data analysis software could easily allow the researcher to explicitly connect the quantitative to the qualitative data in order to sort both in multiple ways such as by a quantitative variable or a qualitative theme.

Because of the use of multiple methodologies in mixed methods, researchers have to be explicit about their assumptions as well as decisions made throughout the research process—a practice we recommend for all SoTL researchers. In addition to the usual considerations of quantitative and qualitative studies, mixed methods researchers also need to carefully and transparently decide on the timing of each phase of the study, the weighting of each data source in interpreting the findings, and what sampling strategies make sense in each phase. Communicating the timing and reasons for these decisions is also important in any dissemination. To address this need, mixed methods researchers have developed a notation system as well as procedural diagrams guidelines, which are commonly used in dissemination in order to help convey these complex details. Further, findings should be presented in an integrated way, in order to show how the two sets of data relate to and inform each other. Again, SoTL researchers using any paradigm may find these strategies useful. While we won't present all notations and dissemination formats in this chapter, we use them in our descriptions of the three most common designs which are described in the following section. For example, if the quantitative results take priority in the overall research findings, the QUANT phase is usually represented with capital letters, and the qual phase with lower-case letters. We recommend Creamer (2018) for descriptions of integration strategies, and Creswell and Plano Clark (2017) for more information on notation systems and integrated displays.

Designs

As with any other research design, it is important to explain why mixed methods were chosen as the methodology for addressing the research question(s). However, questions are not always entirely determined a priori, such as in the two sequential designs, explained below. Similarly, theory used from the outset can help to integrate the data, especially in sequential studies; however, sometimes a new theory needs to be used in order to interpret sequential findings.

Explanatory Sequential Design

This is the most common type of mixed methods design, where quantitative results are collected first and analyzed (quant phase); then qualitative data and analysis are conducted (qual phase) in order to provide explanation or clarification of any surprising or perplexing quantitative findings. However, this does not mean that qualitative data can make up for data from poorly designed quantitative instruments or a lack of statistical power. Rather, the emphasis of the qualitative data collection phase should be to probe into, and therefore explain, the surprising, significant, or outlier results from the quantitative phase. For this reason, a purposeful sample should be chosen from the quantitative participants, selecting participants who can best shed light on the results from the first phase (Figure 9.1). Further, the quantitative results will guide the analysis of the qualitative data set; for example, important factors identified in the quantitative phase may be used for codes in phase 2. For example, in Janice's mixed methods study of a first-year engineering class, a quantitative survey found significant differences in sense of belonging between genders and different ethnographic groups; interviews were then conducted with a purposeful sample of participants from the underrepresented groups; this helped explain some of the factors that affected underrepresented students' sense of belonging in engineering (Miller-Young et al., 2023). Using mixed method shorthand, this study could be described as QUAN -> QUAL, indicating that the quantitative phase was followed by the qualitative phase, and both phases were of equal priority in the interpretation of findings. Themes from the quantitative and qualitative phases were presented together in a table, along with the inferences derived from integrating the two, in an explanatory joint display.

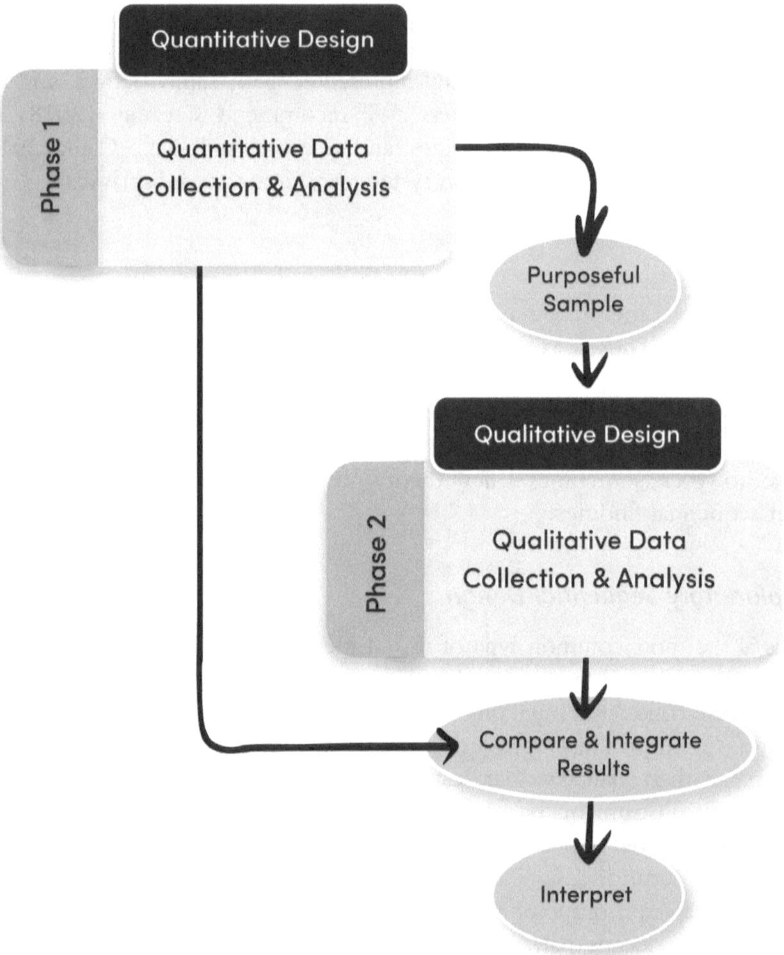

FIGURE 9.1 The phases of explanatory sequential studies, showing that quantitative analysis occurs before the design of the qualitative phase.

The explanatory sequential design may be most attractive to quantitatively oriented researchers who have predetermined variables in mind for the quantitative phase of the study. Other considerations include whether the researcher has the opportunity, capacity, and/or time to follow up with participants for the second phase of data collection. Note that although the example above and Figure 9.1 describe a linear process, it is also possible that qualitative findings may reveal the need for additional statistical examination of the quantitative data, which, in turn, may help better understand the qualitative results; researchers should keep close track of each step and could show an iterative process by having arrows going back from qualitative analysis to quantitative analysis in their procedural diagram.

Convergent Design

The intent of a convergent design is to obtain a more complete understanding of a research question by collecting quantitative and qualitative data at the same time. This means that parallel questions should be used in both aspects of data collection, and common themes should be reported from the analyses. To do so, the researcher analyzes both data sets separately, looks for common themes or concepts across the results, and then merges the two sets of results either by comparing the two data sets or by transforming one of the data sets (for example, using content analysis to convert qualitative data to quantitative data) and conducting further analysis. One example of a convergent study would be a SoTL researcher conducting a survey and focus groups over the same period of time, asking students the same questions in each. Note that Creswell and Plano Clark (2017) describe a study that uses a questionnaire that has both open- and closed-ended questions as a "questionnaire variant" of the convergent design, explaining that "because the qualitative items are an add-on to a quantitative instrument, the items generally do not result in a rigorous context-based qualitative data set" (p. 73).

We emphasize that the convergent design is different from a qualitative, empirical approach that may triangulate multiple sources of data, including quantitative data (multi method); the latter does not involve inferential statistics which check for the potential for bias in the quantitative data, so it is therefore essentially a qualitative approach. There's no perfect delineation here, but if someone is simply using descriptive statistics, without an appropriate attempt to address internal validity (Level I generalizability, see Chapter 7), then the quantitative strand does not fit with the ideals of quantitative research paradigm, and therefore also does not qualify something as a mixed methods study. Rather, the convergent mixed methods approach uses descriptive and inferential statistics to analyze the quantitative data and an appropriate qualitative approach to analyze the qualitative data, then merges the two sets of data by comparing, contrasting, and/or synthesizing the results (Figure 9.2).

In a highly relevant example from a methodologist and practitioner, Poth (2014) used a mixed methods design to study students' experiences in a graduate-level course about mixed methods research. The "quant strand" consisted of pre-post analysis of students' self-assessment of knowledge and skills, and the "QUAL strand" consisted of analysis of their long-answer responses on the pre-post questionnaire as well as a mid-course evaluation and an end-of-course focus group. In short, this quant+QUAL study found that a single course was inadequate for preparing students to conduct mixed

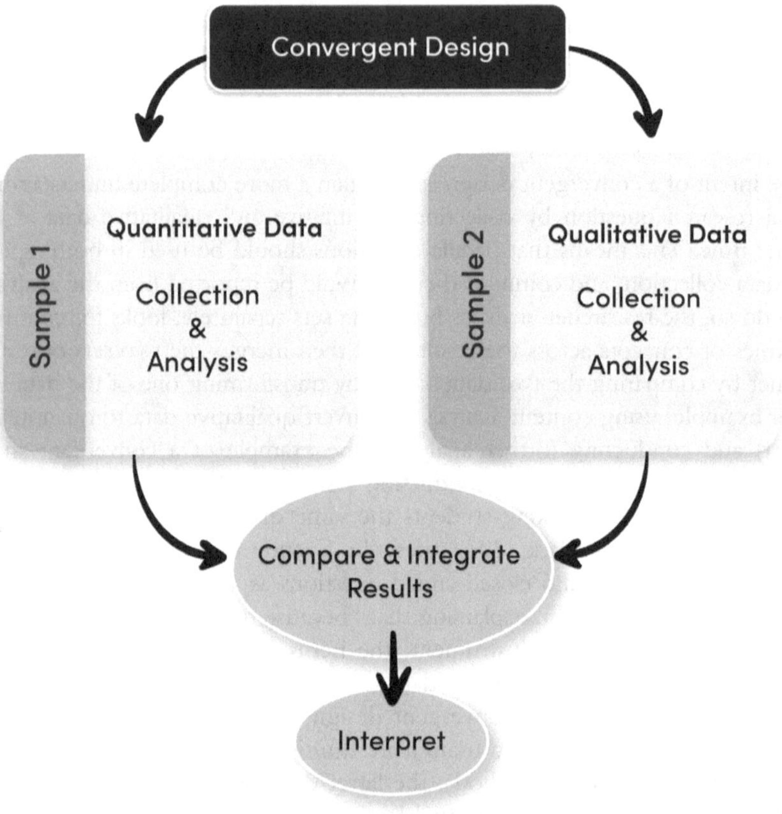

FIGURE 9.2 The phases of convergent design studies, where quantitative and qualitative data are collected and analyzed simultaneously, then integrated.

methods research, and the instructor's conclusion is aligned with one of our philosophies for this book: that there is a need for an integrated approach to learning research methodologies "whereby knowledge and skills of mixed methods research are taught alongside other more traditional approaches" (p. 85).

Because all the data is collected during one phase of the research but collected and analyzed separately, a convergent design may be more efficient from a time and collaboration perspective. However, a challenge could arise with what to do about findings that do not agree. Also, according to Creswell and Plano Clark (2017), for a truly convergent design both qualitative and quantitative results should substantially contribute to the findings, and therefore, it is usual to have similar quantitative and qualitative sample sizes, or if not, then a purposeful reason for different samples. To evaluate your analysis, ask yourself questions such as, "To what extent do each set of findings contribute to the results?" and, "To what extent do the quantitative and qualitative results converge or diverge?" Finally, to usefully present your findings, consider presenting side-by-side comparisons of the qualitative and quantitative results, or present both quantitative and qualitative results one theme at a time.

Exploratory Sequential Design

This type of sequential design begins with a qualitative phase, followed by a quantitative phase and then interpretation of findings (Figure 9.3). The intent of the qualitative phase, then, is typically to develop a deeper understanding of a context, in order to develop a quantitative instrument. This design has much potential for SoTL researchers because of the time and resources required to develop a valid questionnaire from scratch; instead, the exploratory sequential design could be used to modify or combine existing questionnaires by conducting a pre-test before full implementation of the quantitative phase of a study. Another possible use of this design would be to test whether the qualitative findings in Phase 1 are transferable to a different context or larger population.

In Chapter 4 we suggested conducting interviews or focus groups to provide feedback on a new or modified questionnaire; this step could certainly be incorporated into an exploratory sequential research design by ethically collecting, analyzing, and disseminating the qualitative data as phase 1 of the study. The goal of the qualitative phase would be to ensure participants have the same understanding of the questionnaire items as the researcher intends. Several questioning strategies are recommended in the literature, sometimes under the name cognitive interviews, and include asking students to paraphrase a question, i.e., "Can you repeat this question in your own words?", or asking them to interpret a question, i.e., "Can you explain what you think this question means?" Another strategy is called anchoring, which involves asking, "How does this question need to be worded so that you can answer it with a yes or no?" And finally, asking students to think aloud as they answer a question can be very revealing, for example, asking, "Please give examples of experiences that relate to what this question is asking and explain your answer" (e.g., Desimone & Le Floch, 2004; Deng et al., 2021). These kinds of questions may also help identify new variables to be included in the quantitative phase.

Since this design begins with a qualitative phase, the qualitative strand often has greater emphasis in the overall design (Creswell & Plano Clark, 2017). In one example study, Dorit et al. (2021) conducted a qualitative analysis of 1,312 entries in students' reflective journal writing to identify dimensions of reflective thinking, and then develop a questionnaire to measure 171 students' perceptions of their reflective writing experiences, as well

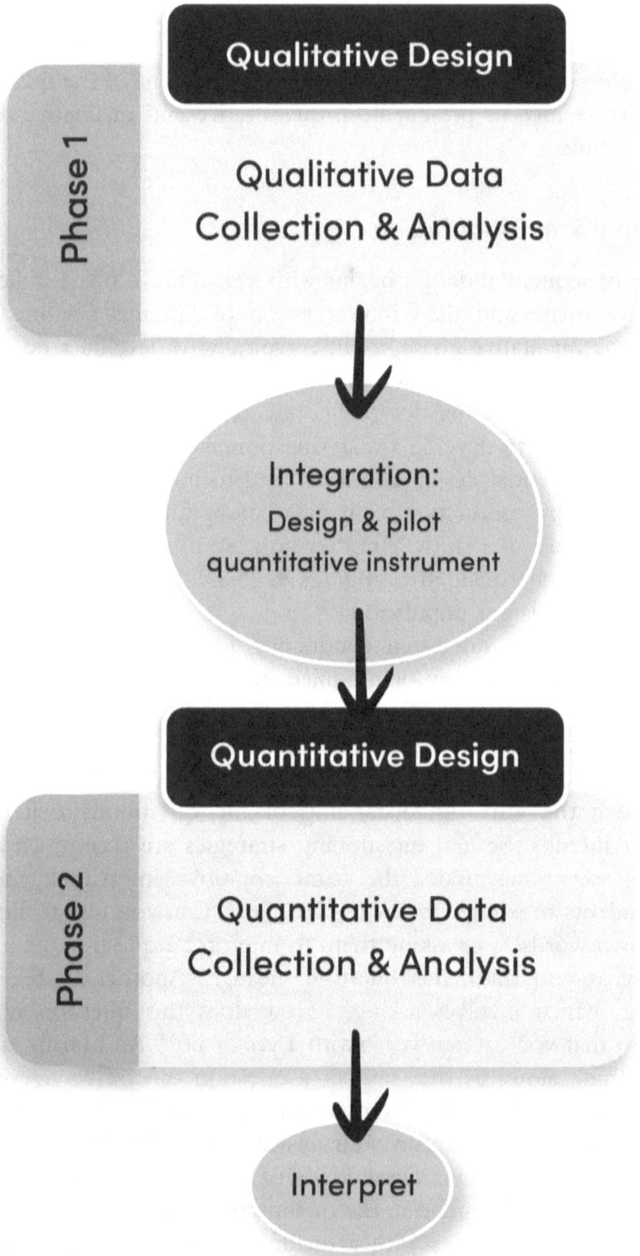

FIGURE 9.3 The phases of exploratory sequential studies, showing that qualitative analysis occurs before the design of the quantitative phase.

as their tendency to use reflective journals in their future careers and personal lives. As demonstrated in this study, the benefit of the exploratory sequential design is that it can be used when no instrument exists which provides measures the researcher is interested in. The main challenge of this design is the time and resources required to complete. However, as we state in Chapter 4, talking to students in advance of executing a quantitative phase of a study is never a bad idea. Finally, researchers should be aware that an ethics application might have to be reviewed in two phases, because the questions for the quantitative phase will not be known until the qualitative phase is completed. Usually an initial ethics application would describe the qualitative phase, and then a modification would be submitted for review once the quantitative design is finalized.

Evaluating Mixed Methods Research

Beyond conducting rigorous and appropriate quantitative and qualitative analysis, there are additional criteria for evaluating mixed methods studies. These include a strong rationale for the study and for the decision to use mixed methods, detailed explanations of the research design and (usually complex) decision-making process, and study limitations, and framing the process and procedures within theory (Creswell & Plano Clark, 2017). Further, there are well-established strategies for mixing and integrating data which researchers should either be explicit about using or provide a rationale for adapting, and a study may use more than one option (Creamer, 2018). Some examples include:

- Blending: a variable or theme emerging from one analysis is tested or further explored using another strand of data, which is common in sequential studies;
- Cross-case comparison: consolidating some data strands to construct profiles (usually of participants) that can then be compared and contrasted using other data strands;
- Extreme case sampling: selecting outlier cases at the ends of a distribution of a particular variable or data strand, and exploring the differences using another strand of data.

As described in Divan et al. (2017), the most common issue encountered in mixed methods research is not integrating the two (or more) sets of data. However, by following the considerations and guidelines above, SoTL researchers can realize the potential of this paradigm by drawing upon the strengths of both quantitative and qualitative approaches. We encourage novice SoTL researchers to reach out and build collaborations with colleagues with complementary expertise, in order to deepen their learning about their students as well as about research methodologies.

Key Concepts

- The benefits of mixed methods include more complete understanding of a research question than could be obtained from quantitative or qualitative methods alone.
- Mixed methods studies involve more than simply collecting two types of data.
- A mixed method study consists of a quantitative methodology phase and qualitative methodology phase, either sequentially or concurrently.
- Mixed methods is typically more time- and resource-intensive than a single-phase study.
- Integration of the qualitative and quantitative findings is a defining feature.
- Mixed methods requires both qualitative and quantitative expertise.

Further Reading

Desimone, L. M., & Le Floch, K. C. (2004). Are we asking the right questions? Using cognitive interviews to improve surveys in education research. *Educational Evaluation and Policy Analysis*, 26(1), 1–22. https://doi.org/10.3102/01623737026001001.

Gurung, R. A. R. (2014). Getting foxy: Invoking different magesteria in the scholarship of teaching and learning. *Teaching and Learning Inquiry*, 2(2), 109–114. https://doi.org/10.20343/teachlearninqu.2.2.109.

Morgan, D. L. (2007). Paradigms lost and pragmatism regained: Methodological implications of combining qualitative and quantitative methods. *Journal of mixed methods research*, 1(1), 48–76. https://doi.org/10.1177/2345678906292462.

Plano Clark, V. L., Garrett, A. L., & Leslie-Pelecky, D. L. (2010). Applying three strategies for integrating quantitative and qualitative databases in a mixed methods study of a nontraditional graduate education program. *Field Methods*, 22(2), 154–174. https://doi.org/10.1177/1525822X09357174.

10

INTERPRETIVE RESEARCH

This chapter describes six major types of "Big Q" qualitative, interpretive research methodologies. In alignment with the interpretive paradigm, we shift here from directives about data analysis to the philosophical underpinnings of each approach, and how that becomes a lens through which to interpret qualitative research data. Reflexive thematic analysis, ethnography, grounded theory, phenomenology, hermeneutics, and narrative inquiry are described and defined, along with examples of how this work is conducted more broadly in qualitative research as well as specific SoTL examples.

In this chapter, we delve into interpretive research methodologies, which we consider "Big Q" qualitative research, as referred to by Braun and Clarke (2013). As the reader will recall from Chapter 3, there is a distinction between research that seeks objectivity and that which prioritizes a subjective lens. Interpretive research is where we see the subjective viewpoint most fully embraced, where the researcher is usually seen as an additional participant. In the literature, interpretive approaches may also be termed constructionist (Kara, 2022) or constructivist, as explained by Merriam and Tisdell (2016):

> Interpretive research, which is the most common type of qualitative research, assumes that reality is socially constructed; that is, there is no single, observable reality. Rather, there are multiple realities, or interpretations, of a single event. Researchers do not "find" knowledge; they construct it. Constructivism is a term often used interchangeably with interpretivism.
>
> *(p. 9)*

DOI: 10.4324/9781003447054-13

In Kara's case, she is making a slight distinction between constructionism (multiple realities as constructed by individuals) and interpretivism (multiple realities as interpreted by individuals), but we are considering these under the same larger interpretivist umbrella. In the quote above, Mirriam and Tisdell note that interpretive research is the most common form of qualitative research across disciplines. At SoTL conferences and in journals dedicated to SoTL, we see more examples of qualitative empirical "small q" work (Braun & Clarke, 2013; see Chapter 8) than interpretive studies. However, interpretive approaches are becoming more common in SoTL, and we see potential for growth.

Interpretive Research as a Quest for Meaning

The focus in interpretive work is on meaning and understanding, and this is salient to scholarship of teaching and learning. In the Hutchings (2000) taxonomy, interpretive approaches might be fruitfully used for "what is" type questions, as the purpose, like in interpretive research, is to "achieve an understanding of how people make sense out of their lives, delineate the process (rather than the outcome or product) of meaning-making, and describe how people interpret what they experience" (Merriam & Tisdell, 2016, p. 15).

Thus in a SoTL study, interpretive work might be more interested in students' experience of the classroom, or their perception of their own learning or a learning intervention, rather than measuring or otherwise making a case for the actual effectiveness of it. Alternatively, it might seek insight into the experience of teaching, or the growth of a faculty member in a SoTL development program. The goal is rich description rather than measurement or categorization. In 1998, Schwandt asserted that in his view, for research about teaching and learning, interpretive work is the most appropriate stance. He wrote, "to understand what it means to educate (and what it means to do educational inquiry) is to participate in the cultivation and acquisition of practical wisdom. Therefore, as a process of this kind, education is interpretation" (p. 411).

As mentioned in Chapter 3, interpretive research contains an underlying critique of objectivist ideals, with the argument that in human contexts such as classrooms, the observer cannot and should not write themselves out. In this text, we intend to represent the broad range of possible approaches to SoTL without promoting one over another, but it is worth acknowledging that each approach contains within it, either explicitly or implicitly, a critique of the others. From the perspective of the positivist/post-positivist paradigm, interpretive research is overly subjective and individualized. From the perspective of the interpretive paradigm, positivism is oblivious to its own perspective; interpretivists argue that objectivity is not possible, because as humans we are in Heidegger's terms "always already" in a process of interpretation as we engage with the world (Moran, 2000), and that we can never truly observe, only perceive. While post-positivism and critical realism take a softened stance towards objectivity, believing that it can only be approached rather than achieved, interpretivism abandons the effort of objectivity entirely, suggesting that we can learn with insight and nuance about the social world through fully subjective and intersubjective viewpoints.

Our purpose here is not to settle this argument, but rather to be explicit about these perspectives so that the SoTL researcher can find the methodologies that best suit their worldview, their discipline, and their question. Unlike previous chapters, this chapter will not give direct instructions for data analysis, because it is less a question of "method" and more one of understanding the stance and way of "reading" the data. Approaches previously described, such as thematic analysis, can be applied in a general way, but it is the rich interpretation using the particular lens the researcher has identified that makes it an interpretive study. In interpretive research, interpretation does not take place outside the phenomenon being studied. Rather, there is a sense of inhabitation in the work. It requires a high level of sensitivity to the phenomena being studied, for the researcher to consider multiple possibilities and perspectives, always situating these socially and historically. This last statement is also true about critical realism, but instead of seeking the generative causation and the stratified realities important to critical realists (Kara, 2022), "interpretivists regard each context as unique, and so would not expect research to be replicable" (p. 24). It is a matter of recognizing "the centrality of the tradition from whence one speaks, set among and in between the fluid motion of the world" (Mayers, 2001, p. 6). In some interpretive writing—often in phenomenology, hermeneutics, and narrative inquiry—researchers write in a voice that leans on metaphor, poetic expression, and artful presentation.

Each research paradigm, as introduced in Chapter 3, rests on epistemological assumptions about how the world can be known. In the interpretive paradigm, philosophical traditions become very important to understanding and conducting the work. For example, Merriam and Tisdell (2016) note the importance of phenomenology and symbolic interactionism as foundational to interpretive research. Phenomenology, as a branch of philosophy, relates to both phenomenology and hermeneutics as research methods, which we will describe in this chapter. Symbolic interactionism is defined by Carter and Fuller (2016) as "a micro-level theoretical framework and perspective in sociology that addresses how society is created and maintained through repeated interactions among individuals" (p. 932). It is most influentially associated with the philosophy of George Herbert Mead, emerging in the mid-20th century as a response to prevailing models of the time—for example, structural functionalism—for how society operates. Carter and Fuller (2016) explain:

> These dominant, positivist approaches tended to examine society from the "top down," focusing on the impact of macro-level institutions and social structures and how they impose on and constrain individuals. Departing from this tradition, symbolic interactionism was developed to understand the operation of society from the "bottom up," shifting the focus to micro-level processes that emerge during face-to-face encounters in order to explain the operation of society.
>
> *(p. 932)*

Symbolic interactionism was influential in the practice of ethnography (see Rock, 2001), and subsequently on grounded theory (see Charmez et al., 2018). Throughout all interpretive research, the notion of stories as being a natural vehicle for human understanding is a theme, which is taken up by narrative inquiry (Clandinin & Rosiek, 2007).

Tracy (2010) outlines eight "big tent" criteria (using the same metaphor often used in SoTL) for excellent qualitative research—by which she is talking about "Big Q" interpretive work, which provide the counterpoint to the generalizability, validity, and reliability sought after in quantitative research. The criteria she identifies are:

1. worthy topic (relevant, timely);
2. rich rigor (using theoretical constructs and adequate and well-analyzed data);
3. sincerity (self-reflexive and transparent);
4. credibility (thick description, triangulation, and multi-vocal);
5. resonance (evocative and transferable);
6. significant contribution (whether conceptually or practically);
7. ethical (relational and procedural); and
8. demonstrates meaningful coherence (alignment between question and methods chosen, well connected and appropriate literature) (p. 840).

It is important to think of these criteria as goals to pursue, rather than black and white "yes" or "no" checkboxes. For example, it is easy to know whether a study has the required ethical review completed by a university ethics board, but attending to the relational ethics embedded throughout a SoTL study is a continuous process of self-examination on the part of the researcher. This ethical position should be pursued in any SoTL study, regardless of methodology.

Merriam and Tisdell (2016) outline some other key features of interpretive work, including the researcher as a primary instrument, the inductive process of the work, and presentation through rich description. They note that interpretive researchers need to be comfortable with ambiguity, and become attentive to the world and be willing to write about it in an insightful and even creative way. As Jardine (1998) describes, it often begins with a particular instance or incident:

> Rather than beginning with an ideal of clarity, distinctness, and methodological controllability and then rendering the given into the image of this ideal, it begins in the place where we actually start in being granted or given this incident in the first place. It begins (and *remains*) with the evocative, living familiarity that this tale evokes. The task of interpretation is to bring out this evocative given in all its tangled ambiguity to follow its evocations and the entrails of sense and significance that are wound up with it.
>
> *(p. 40)*

To some, interpretive work seems so ambiguous that it would be difficult to make any kind of claim. But importantly, the kind of truth that is sought is different—one not based on a notion of "the real" but rather one based on sincerity, resonance, and credibility (Tracy, 2010). In interpretive research, as Jardine describes, the incidents that address us and open a study "make a claim on us and open up and reveal something to us about our lives together. In this sense, our unanticipated, unmethodical being in the world, can, quite literally, in certain instances, make a claim to truth" (p. 40). For SoTL researchers, then, this kind of truth can lead to deeper insight about our students and their experience of learning. The goal becomes how to live well with one another in teaching and learning, rather than, necessarily, "improvement" of this or that technique.

Below, we outline six major types of interpretive research, each with its own philosophical underpinnings (although, as will be seen, these can overlap). What distinguishes them from one another is the focus of the work (see Table 10.1), which then guides how the data is analyzed and what the final product might look like. It is important to note that these six are not exhaustive—in fact, there is a huge range of methodologies that might be considered interpretive. However, these are six major types, and many of the

TABLE 10.1 The Focus of Different Interpretive Methodologies

Methodology	*Focus*
Reflexive thematic analysis	Reflection
Ethnography	Culture
Phenomenology	Essences (of human experience)
Hermeneutics	Dialogue and texts
Narrative inquiry	Story

others hold a "family resemblance" (Wittgenstein, 1953) to at least one of these types.

Reflexive Thematic Analysis and Basic Qualitative Research

Before discussing more philosophically oriented interpretive approaches, the first stop along the continuum is reflexive thematic analysis (TA), which might be undertaken within a basic qualitative study. Reflexive TA, in Braun and Clarke's 2019 clarification of their 2006 work, is a fully interpretive form of TA in contrast to the empirical forms of content analysis and TA described in Chapter 8. All three approaches involve looking at data for recurring concepts and coding, or labeling, segments of data; and all three can accommodate deductive or inductive coding, although the epistemological assumptions underlying the coding differ. Content analysis seeks to follow the standards of the scientific method, including objectivity, a priori design, and reliability. The empirical form of TA, as described in Chapter 8, follows the procedures of coding segments of data and building these up into themes; however, it approaches the data unproblematically with a relatively transparent lens, taking the words of interview participants, for example, at face value.

Reflexive thematic analysis, on the other hand, comes out of a qualitative paradigm and values researcher subjectivity and reflexivity (Braun & Clarke, 2013). Braun and Clarke's (2019) revisit of their previous work is a useful illustration of how research methodology continues to evolve and be refined. Reflexive thematic analysis allows for greater flexibility than content analysis during the data analysis process, as the study may shift in focus depending on the interpretation of the categories derived from the data. And, as Braun and Clarke (2013) note, "procedures such as calculating the 'inter-rater reliability' of qualitative coding are problematic (because of the assumption that coding can and *should* be objective)" (emphasis in the original, p. 279). In contrast, Braun and Clarke note that what makes reflexive TA distinct is that "the researcher's role in knowledge production is at the heart" of the approach (p. 594). They write,

> Reflexive TA needs to be implemented with theoretical knowingness and transparency; the researcher strives to be fully cognisant of the philosophical sensibility and theoretical assumptions informing their use of TA; and these are consistently, coherently and transparently enacted throughout the analytic process and reporting of the research … The coding process requires a continual bending back on oneself—questioning and querying the assumptions we are making in interpreting and coding the data.
>
> *(p. 594)*

Reflexive thematic analysis is compatible with what Merriam and Tisdell (2016) call basic qualitative research, also sometimes called generic qualitative. Merriam and Tisdell explain that in basic qualitative research,

> researchers … would be interested in 1) how people interpret their experiences, 2) how they construct their worlds, and 3) what meaning they attribute to their experiences. The overall purpose is to understand how people make sense of their lives and their experiences.
>
> *(p. 24)*

They identify this as a primarily constructivist and interpretive approach. They suggest that this is a good place to start for new qualitative, interpretive researchers. Other types of interpretive and critical research include these criteria but also involve additional elements, including specific philosophical assumptions, discussed in the below sections. In "Leadership, SoTL, and mentorship in a teaching scholars community of practice," Din et al. (2022) describe the experiences of a diverse group of international participants in a Teaching Scholars' Program and Community of Practice, aimed at developing educational leadership and SoTL capacity. One of the projects described explicitly uses reflexive thematic analysis as formulated by Braun and Clarke, but the paper as a whole reflects a reflexive viewpoint.

Ethnography—a Focus on Culture

Ethnography might be a recognizable term to those with even a passing familiarity with qualitative research. As a research method, ethnography has a history at least a century old, and within its expansive umbrella is a proliferation of approaches, with various schools, disciplines, and approaches that have developed and intersected over time. While traditional ethnography may not usually be conducted in SoTL, it is important to be familiar with the methodology as one that has had enormous impact on all qualitative research. Originally associated with anthropology and its study of culture, it is today utilized across the spectrum of qualitatively oriented disciplines. There are many kinds of ethnography, for example, institutional ethnography, focused ethnography, feminist ethnography, autoethnography (to name a few). But at its core, the *Handbook of Ethnography* defines ethnography by noting that ethnographic studies

> are grounded in a commitment to first-hand experience and exploration of a particular social or cultural setting on the basis of (though not exclusively by) participant observation. Observation and participation (according to circumstance and the analytic purpose at hand) remain the characteristic features of the ethnographic approach.
>
> *(Pinnegar & Daynes, 2007, pp. 4–5)*

Merriam and Tisdell point out that ethnography is both a method (as in, "anthropologists *do* ethnography") but it is also the final product—they write their findings up *as* an ethnography. They suggest that "the factor that unites all forms of ethnography is its focus on human society and culture" (p. 29). Culture can be variously defined, but generally these are the "beliefs, values, and attitudes that structure the behavior patterns of a specific group of people" (p. 29). Traditionally, the ethnographer immerses themselves within the culture for an extended period of time. Ethnographers will, in the process of their work, collect an enormous amount of observational data, interviews, and sometimes written artifacts. The researcher then needs to either use pre-existing schemes to make sense of this data, or else "organize their findings into schemes derived from the data themselves" (Merriam & Tisdell, 2016, p. 30). Regardless, the researcher must go beyond description to make sense of the "cultural meaning of the phenomena" (p. 30). Clifford Geertz (1973) wrote about ethnography that "what we call our data are really our own contractions of other people's constructions of what they and their compatriots are up to" (p. 9). James (2001) further points out that:

> This interpretive understanding evolves but slowly; through immersion in the lives of those we seek to understand, over a lengthy period of time, across a range of social contexts, and involving a variety of different kinds and levels of engagement between the researcher and his/her informants.
>
> *(p. 247)*

"Thick" description is absolutely central to ethnographic work (Geertz, 1973; Merriam & Tisdell, 2016), meaning that detailed, rich portraits are created. Thinking back to the "big tent" criteria (Tracy, 2010) for qualitative work listed earlier in this chapter, credibility is described as being composed of thick description, triangulation, and multi-vocal (p. 840). It is the first component that is emphasized in interpretive work, developed first perhaps in ethnography as an approach to doing research.

Within the SoTL context, an ethnographic approach might be fruitfully considered when trying to understand cultural elements of an institution—like a university—or group, such as students—being studied. For most SoTL researchers, a true longitudinal ethnography may be impracticable. Even when considering the tools of traditional ethnography, something like field notes can become problematic on an ethical level, because of classrooms that are private rather than public spaces, and all students in a given class may not have consented to participate in the study. There are different forms of ethnography, however, more applicable to the SoTL context. In one form called a focused ethnography, researchers might be already part of the context being studied, a university or a hospital, as two examples. Focused ethnographies will also be conducted over a shorter timespan—months, rather than the years of traditional ethnographic studies. According to Knoblauch (2005), in a focused ethnography, the researchers "hold an intimate knowledge of the fields to be studied" (p. 2) and "it focuses on small elements of one's own society" (p. 5). Focused ethnographies are similarly defined by Muecke (1994) as "time limited exploratory studies within a fairly discrete community or organization" (p. 199). Michelle, along with a research team, conducted a focused ethnography of the new faculty experience in an institution undergoing the transition from a college to a university (Yeo et al., 2015)—an institution of which they were an integral part. Because SoTL tends to take place within one's own context, and years- or decades-long timelines are often not practical, focused ethnographies can be a good consideration for the SoTL researcher.

In her book review article "Anthropologists, Education, and Autoethnography," Deborah Reed-Danahay (2009) explores four book-length autoethnographies (that include autobiographical elements in the account) conducted within educational institutions. One of these is a book that generated interest in teaching and learning centers for faculty development, called *My Freshman Year: What a Professor Learned by Becoming a Student* (2005). It is written by anthropologist Cathy Small, under the pseudonym Rebekah Nathan, which is the name she used to pose as an undergraduate living in residence and attending classes for an entire academic year at her own university. This raises many issues, practical and otherwise, but at the same time is a fascinating prospect as a university instructor. Reed-Danahay's review notes that "In writing about education … these books also deal with blending of the ethnographic and the autobiographical, including the issues of insider versus outsider perspectives, and the construction of the ethnographer as both participant and observer" (p. 29).

We are not aware currently of any longitudinal ethnographies that have been conducted directly in SoTL, which is a field that tends to work within shorter time horizons. However, there are shorter-term examples, particularly in the context of educational development (SoEd) where researchers are working towards applying the methodology (see Hardesty et al., 2018). Autoethnographies, wherein participant–researchers study themselves, seem to lend themselves to the SoEd context. See, for example, Bennett et al.'s (2016) autoethnography called "Being Chimaera: A Monstrous Identity for SoTL Academics" and Godbold et al.'s (2021) "The Courage to SoTL."

As stated above, it is important to think about ethnography, along with all of the methodologies that we will present in this chapter and Chapter 11, as families rather than absolute and clear categories. In interpretive research, the methodologies grouped here have certain things in common, mainly that objectivity is not sought, that reality is viewed as basically interpretable, and that the research is interested in how participants themselves understand the world. The work, then, makes interpretations about that understanding, but the participants themselves might not see the larger pattern of meaning—except in the case of narrative inquiry, in which the participant is active in the storying of their experience.

For the SoTL practitioner, if the focus of your question is cultural (understanding that term broadly to apply to any variety of groups, including students), and you are drawn to notions of participant–observation utilizing field notes that ultimately lead to a product emphasizing thick description, then ethnography might be for you. As explored above, doing a full ethnography in a classroom setting can be challenging, but as the borders of SoTL expand, so too do possibilities for utilizing ethnography and other interpretive approaches.

Grounded Theory—a Focus on Theory Building

Grounded theory was developed by sociologists Glaser and Strauss (1967) with the publication of their book *The Discovery of Grounded Theory* "at a time when qualitative research in sociology had become increasingly marginalized" (Charmez et al., 2018, p. 413), and was an innovation to the type of work that had come before. The emphasis on grounded theory is on building theory "from the ground up"—from the data itself, in an exclusively inductive process. Charmez et al. (2018) assert that grounded theory is a "flexible, systematic, comparative method of constructing theory from data that supports studying social and social psychological processes," (p. 411). The theory developed, however, is "usually 'substantive' rather than formal or 'grand' theory" (Merriam & Tisdell, 2016, p. 31), so is relevant to SoTL in the sense that it is interested in "specific, everyday-world situations such as the coping mechanisms of returning adult students" (p. 31). The work is not content to merely describe, but seeks to theorize in a highly specific way that is useful to practice. While there is a more empirical version of grounded theory, what seems most relevant to SoTL is the more current interpretive version. Charmez et al. (2018) describe:

> The constructivist version of grounded theory assumes that people construct both the studied phenomenon and the research process through their actions. This approach recognizes how historical, social, and situational conditions affect these actions and acknowledges the researchers' active role in shaping the data and analysis.
>
> *(p. 412)*

This process, in its original form, is quite structured and even strict—so much so that researchers were directed not to read the literature in advance of analyzing their data, so that it doesn't influence their analysis. However, in more recent interpretive developments the benefits of familiarity with the literature is recognized, as it can "enhance sensitivity to nuances in data, generate concepts of making comparisons with fresh data, stimulate analytical and critical questions and suggest areas for possible conceptual development" (Charmez et al., 2018, p. 419). Rich or thick description is important in grounded theory, but not emphasized (Merriam & Tisdell, 2016, p. 31) in contrast to the other forms of interpretive research outlined in this chapter. Indeed, originators Glaser and Strauss "chastised qualitative researchers for producing descriptive studies rather than theoretical analyses" (Charmez et al., 2018, p. 413). On the other hand, grounded theory overlaps with ethnography in the underlying influence of symbolic interactionism on the methodology. The relevance becomes apparent when we consider how symbolic interactionism maps the way people use language and symbols to understand their subjective experience and communicate with others (Carter & Fuller, 2016), with a focus on the meaning individuals make of their world and how this shapes their behavior (Merriam & Tisdell, 2016).

There is a highly structured process to use in formal grounded theory, involving *theoretical sampling* and *the constant comparative method.* Theoretical sampling means that data collection, coding, and analysis are not done in sequence, but rather the data is coded and analyzed as it is collected, which then helps the researcher to determine what data to collect next in order to develop an emergent theory (Glaser & Strauss, 1967, in Merriam & Tisdell, 2016). A process is conducted of initial coding and later, focused coding. Focused codes are more "directed, selective, and conceptual than most initial codes" (Charmez et al., 2018, p. 426). The constant comparative method means that each piece of data is constantly put beside other segments in order to determine similarities and differences, and then grouped together as appropriate. The goal is to find patterns in the data (Merriam & Tisdell, 2016). Researchers engage in a practice of *memo writing* where "grounded theorists raise new questions and form ideas about their data" (Charmez et al., 2018) as they collect, code, and analyze data.

These practices proved so useful as innovations to qualitative data analysis that they are now widely used in many forms of interpretive and even qualitative empirical work. This may account for the rather loose use of the term in many studies that claim to be conducting grounded theory, when really the researchers mean that they are using constant comparison or memo writing in their data analysis. Unless you are building substantive theory, along with Merriam and Tisdell (2016) we don't recommend that you say you are doing grounded theory. However, it is useful to be familiar with the term and the development of the methodology.

Phenomenology—a Focus on Essence

Phenomenology is a broad Western philosophical tradition that "sought to reinvigorate philosophy by returning it to the life of the living human subject" and "was seen as reviving our living contact with reality" (Moran, 2000, p. 5). But it has also been fruitfully applied as an interpretive research methodology. According to Henriksson and Friesen (2012), phenomenology "is the study of experience, particularly as it is lived and as it is structured through consciousness. 'Experience' in this context refers not so much to accumulated evidence or knowledge as something that we 'undergo'" (p. 1). Indeed, early phenomenology is often described as empirical, a term we usually associate with more objectively oriented research paradigms. But if we recall that empirical refers to that which is observable, phenomenology considered itself empirical in the sense that it was interested in the concrete particulars of life as it is actually lived as an alternative to previously abstract philosophy. It is particularly interested in embodied, lived experience (Van Manen, 2014). It attempts to uncover something essential and fundamentally human about the experience—how it manifests and lives in the world, and how, intersubjectively, we can commonly come to understand it (Yeo et al., 2018). Merriam and Tisdell (2016) explain that "the task of the phenomenologist then, is to depict the essence or basic structure of experience" (p. 26). Patton (2002) notes that the assumption of essence becomes the defining characteristic of a purely phenomenological study. It is a study of "people's conscious experience of their life-world" (Merriam & Tisdell, 2016, p. 26)—or indeed, as Van Manen describes, their "pre-reflective experience" (2014, p. 28). The studies tend to focus on "intense human experiences such as love, anger, betrayal"—or might focus on the essence of a particular aspect of experience and context, such as the physical remembrance of childhood (Smith, 1993), experiences of giving birth (Bergum, 1989), or in the SoTL context an example might be the experience of first-generation university students.

Phenomenology understands "the self" not to be separate from the world; rather, "being" is understood through the phenomena that present themselves to us. It is the "descriptive study of whatever appears to consciousness … Phenomenology is usually characterized as a *way of seeing* rather than a set of doctrines" (Moran, 2002, p. 1). Husserl's famous maxim, in describing phenomenology, further appropriated by Heidegger, is to "return to the things themselves" (Dastur, 2000, p. 180). This return, however, does not imply that we are satisfied to merely describe what exists, what is simply there. Neither does it mean turning toward complete abstraction (Dastur, 2000). Instead, phenomenology "seeks to restore the richness of the world as experienced; it wants to be present at the birth of the world for us" (Moran, 2002, p. 2). It asks that we become attentive to what appears in everyday life, its "modes of appearing and givenness" (Dastur, 2000, p. 180). It is a process that is "always already" occurring and that is never finished. This, then, is a phenomenology of being and becoming (Yeo et al., 2018, p. 18), or what Heidegger, who followed Husserl, conceptualizes as "Being-in-the-world" (Moran, 2000, p. 13).

Because phenomenology is interested in the essence of lived experience, the means to understanding this experience is mainly through the senses. Many phenomenologists, then, focus on the body as a way to understand how humans interact with the world, restoring "life to its original difficulty" through a re-coupling of what Descartes so famously and fundamentally split in our Western consciousness—the mind and the body. Patton (2002) asserts that Husserl's most basic philosophical assumption was that "we can only know what we experience by attending to perceptions and meanings that awaken our conscious awareness" (pp. 105–106). Existential phenomenologist Merleau-Ponty is associated with this intense interest in embodiment. He "explored the relation of consciousness to the body, arguing for the need to replace these categories with an account of embodied human being in the world" (Moran, 2000, p. 13). Merleau-Ponty (1945) explains:

> When I reflect on the essence of subjectivity, I find it bound up with that of the body and that of the world, this is because my existence as subjectivity [=consciousness] is merely one with my existence as a body and with the existence of the world, and because the subject that I am, when taken concretely, is inseparable from this body and this world.
>
> *(p. 475)*

In this research methodology, the phenomenological interview is the main method of collecting data (Merriam & Tisdell, 2016, p. 27). First, the researcher will need to explore their own experience of the phenomenon, both to uncover aspects of the experience that might be salient to the study, but also to identify potential biases and assumptions. The idea here is that they can then be set aside, to some extent, in a process phenomenologists term *bracketing* (Merriam & Tisdell, 2016, p. 27). It is admittedly not fully possible, and the phenomenologist is expected to be aware and explicit about their own positionality. Merriam and Tisdell note that this process has influenced all of qualitative research in that it is common practice for researchers to examine their relationship to and assumptions about the phenomenon of interest before embarking on a study.

Another strategy that utilizes a term familiar from quantitative research (but used in a different way) is the phenomenological "reduction" (Merriam & Tisdell, 2016, p. 27). This is the process of returning iteratively, again and again, to the "things themselves" in order to uncover the essence. A phenomenological study will have a feeling of traveling inward to the center of a spiral structure—closer and closer to the essence of an experience. Like other forms of qualitative work, themes will be identified, but these would always be inductively generated, and they go deeper than a surface reading of what is overtly said or described. There would be an "interweaving" of the individual, the conscious experience they describe, and the phenomenon itself.

Phenomenology involves activation of imagination. For example, in "Phenomenology of surprise in a SoTL scholars' program," we explored the instances of surprise expressed in interviews of participants in a SoTL scholars' program, and read these in the context of Dastur's philosophical work on surprise as a phenomenological event (Yeo et al., 2018). In this study, phenomenology is introduced (and provides an early version of some of the material in this chapter), and a presentation of Dastur's work is explored in order to provide a lens through which to understand the participants' lived experiences of surprise.

Genevieve Currie (2017), in her phenomenological account of a set of interviews with faculty members, demonstrates how disciplinary knowing is a kind of embodied knowledge that permeates the individual's way of experiencing the world. She writes of a participant: "Louisa highlighted how she cannot turn off the disciplinary knowledge of performing a nursing assessment and continues her ways of practicing in everyday activities of daily living—how she can't 'turn off' her ways of 'seeing' as a nurse" (p. 41).

It is important to distinguish a phenomenological perspective, which you might be aware of and refer to as informing an interpretive approach to your inquiry, with choosing phenomenology as a research method to follow. In most interpretive work, the roots of the worldview can be found in phenomenology as a philosophical tradition, interested in the human experience of living in the world. As a research method, phenomenology focuses on the lived experience of individuals in search of the essence of a shared human phenomenon, the way it presents itself to participants (Patton, 2002).

Hermeneutics—a Focus on Dialogue and Texts

Hermeneutics is a branch of philosophy closely related to phenomenology; it is "the art and science of interpretation and thus also of meaning" (Henriksson & Friesen, 2012, p. 1), or described by Moran (2002) as "the art of interpretation or understanding ... a conversation leading towards mutual understanding, a conversation, furthermore, where this very understanding comes as something genuinely experienced" (pp. 248–249). It builds on phenomenology, but is less interested in the very essence of a human experience, rather extending that interest to the interpretation and meaning we both make and share of it through language.

Hermeneutics asks us to be attentive to our being-in-the-world, and is thus oriented towards ontology. It is traced to Husserl's phenomenology (Caputo, 1987), in a way that recognizes "things just as the things which they are" (p. 57), but rather than resting with Husserl, it was further developed through the work of thinkers such as Heidegger and Gadamer (Moran, 2002). Heidegger took a critical appropriation of Husserl, finding his phenomenology too cognitive and abstract. Instead, he thinks the way to proceed is to "avoid philosophical systems and concentrate on the matters themselves" (Moran, 2000, p. 228)—on the "concrete particularity of a lived life" (p. 228). For this reason, to conduct hermeneutic research is to begin with a concrete instance, as described by Jardine (1998), but not as an "isolated incident"; rather, hermeneutics "does not wish to literally and univocally say what this instance *is*. Rather, it wishes to playfully explore what understandings this instance makes *possible*" (p. 41).

Gadamer (1999) saw the experience of understanding as a profoundly linguistic and dialogical event, as a conversation "between people and their transition—the common understandings which emerge in a dialogue and which go beyond the intentions of the speakers" (p. 249). While hermeneutics lives in the realm of philosophy, it also may be utilized as an interpretive research methodology to help think about and interpret the world; it wants to "describe the fix we are in" (Caputo, 1987, p. 3).

Gadamer follows Heidegger's *Being and Time* in seeing understanding as the central manner of human being-in-the-world:

> humans are essentially involved in the historically situated and finite task of understanding the world, a world encountered and inhabited in and through language. ... Philosophy, then, is a conversation leading towards mutual understanding, a conversation, furthermore, where this very understanding comes as something genuinely experienced.
>
> *(Moran, 2000, pp. 248–249)*

Gadamer (1999) sees this experience of understanding as a profoundly linguistic event, with the relationship between texts (broadly defined) and our lives, and additionally, between the old and what is new. Not only does the text have something to say about the decision we make today or the way we read or understand a situation, but this new situation then helps us recast the past and see the text anew. Gadamer writes, "so also it is universally true of texts that only in the process of understanding them is the dead trace of meaning transformed back into living meaning" (p. 164). This is known as the "hermeneutic circle." Thus, a particular understanding of experience is invoked. Experience becomes interpretable and a way of making meaning and creating insight:

> Insight is more than the knowledge of this or that situation. It always involves an escape from something that had deceived us and held us captive. Thus insight always involves an element of self-knowledge and constitutes a necessary side of what we called experience in the proper sense. Insight is something we come to.
>
> *(Gadamer, 1999, p. 356)*

Hermeneutics, at its heart, is about interpretation. In conducting the practice of hermeneutics as educational inquiry, Smith (1991) elucidates four aspects of what he calls the "hermeneutic imagination" as a means of proceeding:

1. *"A deep attentiveness to language itself, to notice how one uses it and how others use it"* (p. 199). This means becoming deeply immersed in language, becoming aware of its nuances and undercurrents. Becoming attuned to etymology, to words within words, is useful and necessary. Metaphor, analogy, symbol—all create and evoke a sense of our collective consciousness and even unconsciousness. The artistic expressiveness inherent in the writing that often gives interpretive work its distinctive, evocative style.
2. *"A second requirement for hermeneutical explorations of the human life–world is a deepening of one's sense of the basic interpretability of life itself"* (p. 199). Part of this is a belief that one can interpret what is happening, and also that grand narratives can be recognized and interrupted so that fresh interpretations of life as it is "actually lived" can be made, rather than continuing to see the world through the old lenses of, for example, patriarchy or materialism.
3. *"Hermeneutics is not really concerned with hermeneutics per se: that is, with its character as another self-defining imploding discourse within a universe of other discourses. Far more important is its overall interest which is the question of human meaning"* (p. 200). Hermeneutics asks larger questions and sees each of us in the middle of narrative, storied experiences. The hermeneutic imagination requires a deep rendering of significant topics; it is not content to scratch away at the surface.
4. *"A fourth aspect of hermeneutical inquiry implicit in all of the others suggested so far has to do with its inherent creativity. Hermeneutics is about creating meaning, not simply reporting on it"* (p. 201). As Henriksson and Friesen (2012) point out, it "is particularly open to literary and poetic qualities of language, and encourages aesthetically sensitized writing as both a process and product of research" (p. 1).

As a research methodology, the aim is always understanding and meaning, but never closure. Caputo (1987) remarks, "we do not aim at a conclusion, but an opening" (p. 294). Researchers may use interviews in this methodology, and very frequently will use text, whether this is text written by participants (such as reflective journals), and/or documents that relate to the topic at hand, for example, a curriculum document. In hermeneutics, the tradition works a little bit like case law (indeed, readers may have heard of legal and biblical hermeneutics as fields of study). The idea is to take the current iteration, the current case or event, and read it against past iterations. In the legal example, the current case is decided on the basis of previous cases, but then the current case becomes part of the law that helps to recast the original. In SoTL, a student might arrive with a question that breaks open an instructor's previous understanding of a topic, creating a generative space. Vicky Gunn and Leah Shopkow (2007), in their discussion-based article on "Doing SoTL in medieval history: A cross-Atlantic dialogue," describe practical hermeneutics as "a more inclusive 'interpretive encounter', where we explore not just our relationships with texts but also with one another" (p. 260). David Jardine illustrates how this reading and writing process works in his book *To Dwell With a Boundless Heart: Essays in Curriculum Theory, Hermeneutics, and the Ecological Imagination* (1998). As an example related to developing novice SoTL practitioners, with Cherie Woolmer, Michelle wrote about how for SoTL researchers the ethics review process can present itself as a mythical monster (Yeo & Woolmer, 2022).

Hermeneutic Phenomenology

As can be seen from the above, hermeneutics and phenomenology are tightly connected and overlapping, such that a piece of research may not be purely one or the other, and indeed methodologies such as hermeneutic phenomenology have arisen in educational research practice. This development recognizes the co-dependent nature of these two; "it is impossible to study experience without simultaneously inquiring into its meaning, and it is impossible to study meaning without experiential grounding" (Henriksson & Friesen, 2012, p. 3). For thinkers such as Paul Ricoeur, experience and language are co-emergent, "with language having not merely a descriptive function, but one that is expressive, and 'co-constitutive' of experience" (Henriksson & Friesen, 2012, p. 3). These are some of the fine distinctions that can be made—phenomenology might be more interested in the embodied, even pre-linguistic essence of an experience. Hermeneutics has an emphasis on the dialogical and linguistic, and focuses on a rich interpretation of texts—what the previous case might have to say about the new one, the recasting of my understanding based upon the concrete particulars of what faces me now. Hermeneutic phenomenology recognizes the potential interdependence of these two approaches.

Henriksson and Friesen (2012) make the point that this means of inquiry contains a natural affinity for the classroom, as it is inherently a place where theory and practice meet in a continual dance. They write:

> Framed by ethical considerations, it involves hand (acting), heart (feeling), and head (thinking) ... hermeneutic phenomenology embraces the thought that language and our world view are intertwined: language shapes our world and our world is shaped by language. Hermeneutic

> phenomenology writes and talks in a language, which … makes the world of pedagogical practice recognizable for teachers.
>
> *(p. 9)*

For an example in SoTL, see Michael Strawser's (2009) article "Assessing assessment: Toward a hermeneutic-phenomenological perspective," which demonstrates the in-depth philosophical consideration often associated with this approach. Henriksson and Friesen, noted above, are working in the field of education, and hermeneutic phenomenology has also gained traction in the field of nursing (see Van der Zalm & Bergum, 2000). As a similarly applied field that is interested in developing practical wisdom, SoTL researchers might also find the methodology of interest.

Narrative Inquiry—a Focus on Story

In the final iteration of interpretive research we will describe here, the focus turns to stories and story-making as a means of making sense of a phenomenon and our lives. While the emergency of this methodology is relatively recent—in the latter part of the 20th century—the process of storytelling as a means of making meaning seems as old as humanity itself. As Clandinin and Rosiek (2007) remark:

> Human beings have lived out and told stories about that living for as long as we could talk … These lived and told stories and the talk about the stories are one of the ways that we fill our world with meaning and enlist one another's assistance in building lives and communities. What feels new is the emergence of narrative methodologies in the field of social science research.
>
> *(p. 35)*

As with all other methodologies, narrative inquiry has its own history, forms, debates, and evolution. However, for our purposes there are elements that we can identify as clearly part of what Pinnegar and Daynes (2007) call the narrative turn, and they describe "those who most fully embrace narrative inquiry" as those researchers who "simultaneously embrace narrative as a method for research and narrative as the phenomenon of study. For narrative inquirers both the stories and the humans are continuously visible in the study" (p. 7). This aspect of interpretive research should begin to sound familiar—all of the types we have described have contained this notion of the way and the thing (Caputo, 1987)—where the means of inquiry, the phenomenon being described, and what is ultimately written up contain a relationship and coherence. In narrative inquiry, story is "the thing."

Like hermeneutics, narrative inquiry is interested in concrete particulars, but finds the meaning in the individual's story of their own experience rather than reading it "against" what has come before. Unlike phenomenology, narrative inquiry is not seeking an essence of experience. Rather, the interest is in how participants "story" their experiences as a way of making meaning. Participants can be described as seeking the plotline of their own lives (Clandinin & Huber, 2002, p. 164). A strong interest in metaphor emerges, and again the artistic and aesthetic dimensions seen in hermeneutics and hermeneutic phenomenology. Narrative inquiries, in their final form, are "composed" rather than reported.

In educational research, narrative inquiry has proven particularly fruitful to describe teachers' experiences through the work of researchers such as Clandinin and Connolly (2000). The practice can involve both narrative interviews and reflective writing on the part of participants, which then undergo an iterative interpretive process of analysis. It also might collect visual, digital, or other artifacts (Kim, 2016)—but the focus is always a search for story. The participant continues the engagement with the process for a period of time, and is invited to make sense of the work alongside the researcher. In this way, the narrative is meant to represent how the participant stories their lives, rather than the way the researcher or researcher alone makes sense of it. The narratives are then composed in a write-up that reveals a narrative arc. Clandinin and Huber (2002) describe how through many years of conducting narrative inquiry they came to develop a "metaphor of a three dimensional narrative inquiry space" (p. 163). The three dimensions are temporality (thinking about past, present, and future), "they focus on the personal and the social in a balance appropriate to the inquiry; and they occur in specific places or sequences of places" (Clandinin & Connelly, 2000, p. 50). Jeong-Hee Kim's text, *Understanding Narrative Inquiry* (2016), provides useful examples of narrative inquiries that have been conducted in educational settings more broadly. Some DBER journals embrace narrative inquiry; for example, in a 2017 editorial for *Journal of Biological Education*, Ian Kinchin encouraged submission of "a rich diversity of methodological approaches" explicitly including narrative inquiry. Marie Vander Kloet et al. (2017) take a narrative inquiry approach in what they call a collaborative writing inquiry about the experiences of contingent faculty in pursuing SoTL. Laura Ng and Mary Carney (2017) advocate using "Scholarly personal narrative in the SoTL big tent" in their article by that name.

Worth noting here are more examples of cross-over. Autoethnography, discussed above and which by its name categorizes it as a form of ethnography, in many ways might also be considered a form of narrative inquiry, with its focus on story and the researcher (or researchers) making sense of their experience through narratives. Self-study is another term applied to such approaches, described by Samaras and Freese (2009) as a research methodology that emerged in the work of teacher educators to question, reflect upon, and improve their practice, and which Jennifer Boman and Michelle Yeo (2020) adapted to SoEd as one example. We do see development of such work in SoTL, and it seems particularly salient to educational developers making sense of their work.

Critiques

We have already discussed the critique that would come from a positivist/post-positivist perspective, namely, that research in an interpretive paradigm would be perceived as subjective and biased, and possibly not seen as research at all. But this type of work can be critiqued from a different angle. Interpretive work, while intrinsically appealing to many non-positivist researchers, to others seems overly accepting of the world as it is. Because the focus is mainly on meaning, understanding, and insight, the work seems to do little to transform practice. The interpretivist might argue that transformation must start with insight; however, the transformative approaches of the next chapter seek more disruption and change. But it is also fully possible for these approaches to be combined—post-structural approaches to narrative inquiry (Kim, 2016), a radical hermeneutics (see Caputo, 1987), feminist phenomenology (Shabot & Landry, 2018) are all examples—conceptually one lens can be used to recast previous versions, opening new possibilities.

Finally, it is important to recognize the way in which all of these interpretive approaches rest on a foundation of Western philosophical tradition and anthropological efforts, all of which have contributed to colonialism. Indigenous perspectives in their practice, however, are not incompatible with research that seeks meaning and story. Because of the interest in transformation, we have placed it in the next chapter, when we turn our focus to transformative approaches.

Key Concepts

- The focus in interpretive work is on meaning and understanding, and it is the paradigm where we see the subjective viewpoint most fully embraced.
- Key features of interpretive work are that the researcher is a primary instrument of data collection and seen as an additional participant, the research process is inductive, and presentation includes rich description.
- Criteria for good interpretive work include sincerity (reflexive and transparent), credibility (multi-vocal), and resonance (evocative and transferable).
- Reflexive thematic coding focuses on self-reflection in the research process, ethnography focuses on culture, grounded theory on theory building, phenomenology on essences, hermeneutics on dialogue and texts, and narrative inquiry on story.
- Critiques of the interpretive paradigm include that it is an overly subjective view, and that it does little to address inequity.

Further Reading

Braun, V., & Clarke, V. (2013). *Successful qualitative research: A practical guide for beginners.* Sage.

Braun, V., & Clarke, V. (2019). Reflecting on reflexive thematic analysis. *Qualitative Research in Sport, Exercise and Health*, 11(4), 589–597. https://doi.org/10.1080/2159676X.2019.1628806.

Carter, M. J., & Fuller, C. (2016). Symbols, meaning, and action: The past, present, and future of symbolic interactionism. *Current Sociology*, 64(6), 931–961. https://doi.org/10.1177/0011392116638396.

Clandinin, D. J., & Huber, J. (2002). Narrative inquiry: Toward understanding life's artistry. *Curriculum Inquiry*, 32(2), 161–169.

Reed-Danahay, D. (2009). Anthropologists, education, and autoethnography. *Reviews in Anthropology*, 38(1), 28–47. https://doi.org/10.1080/00938150802672931.

Smith, D. (1991). Hermeneutic inquiry: The hermeneutic imagination and the pedagogic text. In E. C. Short (Ed.), *Forms of curriculum inquiry* (pp. 187–207). State University of New York Press.

Tracy, S. J. (2010). Qualitative quality: Eight "big-tent" criteria for excellent qualitative research. *Qualitative Inquiry*, 16(10), 837–851. doi:10.1177/1077800410383121.

Van Manen, M. (2014). *Phenomenology of practice: Meaning giving methods in phenomenological research and writing.* Left Coast Press.

11

TRANSFORMATIVE METHODOLOGIES

This chapter discusses a collection of research paradigms that have in common an interest in transformation, conceptualized differently. We include here critical, postmodern, and Indigenous research methodologies, as well as Students-as-Partners (within critical research). Similar to the interpretive paradigm, the philosophical and theoretical underpinnings of each approach are key, and include interests in emancipation, disruption, restoration, authenticity, and partnership, depending on the paradigm.

In this chapter, we turn to transformational approaches to inquiry, which seek not only to understand, but to alter. Transformative approaches share with interpretive research the intersubjective worldview, agreeing that "knowledge is socially constructed and takes form in the eyes of the knower" (Kilgore, 2001, p. 53). However, transformative perspectives critique the interpretive stance as too satisfied with an unjust world as it now stands. Creswell and Poth (2018) explain that researchers may want to pursue a transformative framework because, from their perspective, "the postpostivists impose structural laws and theories that do not fit marginalized individuals or groups and the constructivists do not go far enough in advocating action to help individuals" (p. 25). Transformative approaches, as suggested by the umbrella term we used in this chapter, are interested in change—in empowerment, disruption, restoration, and authentic partnership. As mentioned in Chapter 3, Indigenous research methodologies share some of these goals, but also resist categorization within Western knowledge systems. This will be discussed in more depth later in the chapter.

Transformative researchers attempt to expose power imbalances and bring marginalized groups to the center of the conversation, rather than continuing to reproduce inequitable, taken-for-granted structures, known as hegemony. As

DOI: 10.4324/9781003447054-14

Creswell and Poth (2018) explain, "the basic tenet of this transformative framework is that knowledge is not neutral and it reflects the power and social relationships within society" (p. 25). These researchers may critique Western knowledge systems, whether that is social class, patriarchy, heteronormativity, white supremacy, or colonialism as some examples. In an educational framework, learning is seen as never neutral, but rather as "a process of receiving and creating communicative messages or 'discourses' about the social world" (Kilgore, 2001, p. 54).

In this chapter, we describe four different transformative lenses: critical, post-modern/post-structural, Indigenous, and finally Students-as-Partners (SaP). It is important to note that the transformative lens should not be considered a single research paradigm; rather, it is a collection of multiple research paradigms that share an interest in transformation as a goal. But even here, the nature of that transformation will vary significantly. In critical research, as Merriam and Tisdell (2016) note, the goal is "to critique and challenge, to transform, and to analyze power relations" (p. 59). Examples of critical approaches include feminist theory and critical race theory. Postmodern/post-structural approaches are focused on the disruption of grand narratives—these may be the very same grand narratives of patriarchy or colonialism, but informed by such philosophers as Derrida and Lyotard, they are less explicitly about empowerment and more about introducing a continuous sense of unpacking, transgression, and even playfulness (see Lincoln et al., 2018, p. 141). Indigenous approaches to research contain these disruptive elements, but are also restorative—interested in an approach to research that is relationally oriented and land-based, and that explicitly empowers Indigenous communities with "socially just relevancy" (Kovach, 2018, p. 215). All of these approaches are currently less common in SoTL, but they do exist, and certainly are evident in higher education research more broadly.

The Student Voice movement originated in K–12 education (see work from scholars like Alison Cook-Sather, Michael Fielding, and Jean Rudduck). The principles from that work, and ideas of "radical collegiality" (Fielding, 1999) have informed the SaP movement in post-secondary education. SaP makes an authentic effort to unravel the power dynamic between academic faculty and students, bringing students fully into the research process, from conception to publication/dissemination. Like Participatory Action Research, SaP in SoTL is a way of conceptualizing *and* doing SoTL research, research with rather than researching on students. SaP as a concept is founded on the idea that students are legitimate knowers in post-secondary contexts and are key stakeholders in the educational experience. Engaging students as partners in SoTL—inviting them to shape, deliver, and disseminate SoTL—is an enactment of the concept in practice.

All of the approaches we outline will explicitly (but differently) apply a theoretical, if not philosophical, lens throughout the research, particularly in the data analysis phase. In transformative research, the theoretical framework comes to the forefront of the methodology, and informs every aspect of the study. Taken together, all of the forms described are focused on transformation—and in the case of SoTL, specifically in the transformation of the academy, although all four paradigms described have a vested interest in education. All attend, differently, to issues of power, location, and knowledge in the research process.

Critical Approaches: A Focus on Power

Critical theorists and researchers are interested in critiquing and transforming existing power structures in society. Building initially on philosophical work such as Marx's analysis of socioeconomic conditions, Habermas's emancipatory knowledge, and educational theorists such as Paulo Friere, critical approaches to research are explicitly ideological (Merriam & Tisdell, 2016). In an educational context, the work is often to expose existing power structures in academic institutions, and work towards disrupting those structures and empowering marginalized groups. Kincheloe et al. (2018) say that "inquiry that aspires to be 'critical' must be connected to an attempt to confront structures of oppression" (p. 237). Creswell and Poth (2018) suggest that within a critical framework, the inquiry should

> contain an action agenda for reform that may change the lives of participants, the institutions in which they live and work, or even the researchers' lives. The issues facing these marginalized groups are of paramount importance to the study—issues such as oppression, domination, suppression, alienation, and hegemony.
>
> *(p. 25)*

In this approach, the relationship of the researcher and the participants is paramount, because it is understood that historically research has acted as a technology of oppression. Consider, for example, the historical exclusion of women from medical research, or the colonial anthropological project of Western researchers working in Indigenous communities. In a SoTL context, this might look like investigating pedagogical methods within disciplines that explicitly hold a critical worldview, such as women's studies. For example, Hassel and Launius's (2017) research analyzes student writing for evidence of threshold concepts in women's studies. This study demonstrates a critical stance, congruent with the discipline, and uses a critical approach to data analysis—researchers use an analysis of metaphor in student writing to help them understand how students come to know key concepts in the discipline which they identified as "the social construction of gender, privilege and oppression, intersectionality, and feminist praxis" (p. 31). In this way, the critical lens at all levels of the inquiry is visible. Another example from the field of student affairs is a grounded theory by Claire Robbins (2016), "White women, racial identity, and learning about racism in graduate preparation programs." This study is explicitly situated as a grounded theory for social justice (Charmez, 2005, in Robbins, 2016), which "interrogates structural inequities" (p. 258).

Merriam and Tisdell (2016) point out that critical research is not a *type* of qualitative research in the same sense that something like narrative inquiry or phenomenology (here, meaning the methodology rather than the philosophy as a whole). They suggest that instead, "critical research is about a worldview, and this worldview and the tools of analysis from this perspective can be applied to many types of qualitative research" (p. 59). It is more like a lens—the researcher views all aspects of the study through the lens of power relationships. Kincheloe et al. (2018) explain that "in its more recent conceptualization, critical theorists take apart normalized notions of democracy, freedom, opportunity structures, and social justice to denounce systems of power and domination" (p. 236).

Thus, critical research tends to be less interested in individuals; rather, the focus is on how individuals will be marginalized or empowered as a result of belonging to this or that group. Critical theorists argue, according to Kilgore (2001), that these "structures of privilege and oppression based on categories like race or ethnicity, gender, class, sexual orientation ... are reinforced because the logic that maintains those structures becomes a commonsense lens through which people view and interpret their everyday experiences" (p. 55).

As introduced earlier, these structures with their reinforcing logic of reproduction are referred to as *hegemony*, accepted as common sense by both the advantaged and disadvantaged. But it is the advantaged who determine and present "their definition of reality in such a way that it is accepted by other classes as common sense even though it serves the interest of the dominant classes alone" (Giroux, 1997, in Kilgore, 2001, p. 55). In a now classic study from the K–12 educational literature, Jean Anyon (1981) examined the implementation of an identical social studies curriculum in four schools, differentiated by social class, and found an entirely different implementation and accompanying narrative, with a "hidden curriculum" aimed at reproducing social class. For example, students in the lowest socio-economic class were not asked to think critically and creatively; rather, a "basic skills" narrative was expressed by the teachers and administration at the school. This is an example of how hegemony works: the teachers involved were not intentionally reproducing social class, yet they were key players in its enactment.

When critical theory is applied to research inquiry, Kincheloe et al. (2018) identify *bricolage* as one means of conducting the work—this term refers to the French word *bricoleur*, "a handyman or handywoman who makes use of the tools available to complete a task" (p. 244). In critical inquiry, the researcher might draw on a wide range of methodologies such as ethnography, textual and discourse analysis, phenomenology, hermeneutics, or psychoanalysis to understand how power functions in the context they study. This type of work is understood to be emergent as needs arise throughout the study—Kincheloe et al. use the term *tinkering* to describe "a high-level cognitive process involving construction and reconstruction, contextual diagnosis, negotiation, and re-adjustment" (p. 245). Ultimately, regardless of the tools used, social justice is the goal. An example of a study that explicitly uses bricolage as a methodology along with critical social theory is Cartmel et al.'s (2013) "Looking to the future: Producing trans-disciplinary professionals for leadership in early childhood settings." The authors drew from a number of complex data sets in order to create what they call a patchwork, using a quilting metaphor. They write:

> Producing the bricolage patchwork is not merely a matter of bringing together unrelated or antithetical theory and literature in order to make an argument or analyse data. Bricolage entails piecing together information from different data-sets and then applying epistemologically coherent theory and literature to the analysis of the data … bricolage fosters and encourages the use of multiple perspectives. This means that researchers are not necessarily restricted to following one line of enquiry endorsed by one particular approach.
>
> *(pp. 400–401)*

Students-as-Partners

The Student-as-Partners (SaP) movement has arisen in the last decade as a transformative moment in post-secondary education, with both research and pedagogical aspects (Healey et al., 2014). Foundational to this approach is a commitment to see and work with students as legitimate knowers in the teaching and learning process and, as noted earlier, is a way of conceptualizing as well as doing SoTL research. Alison Cook-Sather, Catherine Bovill, and Peter Felten's (2014) book *Engaging Students as Partners in Learning and Teaching: A Guide for Faculty* established a theoretical framework for this movement, suggesting principles of respect, reciprocity, and responsibility as the fundamental values that underpin partnership practice. They observe that respect "calls for willingness to consider experiences or perspectives that are different from our own, and it often requires a withholding of judgment" (p. 2). Reciprocity is a key feature in Indigenous methodologies, and it appears again here as "the mutual exchange that is key to student-faculty partnerships" (pp. 3–4). Importantly, Cook-Sather et al. note that it does not mean that students and faculty give and receive the same thing in the partnership; rather, that "partnerships invite faculty and students to share differing experiences and perspectives;

those differences are part of what can make partnerships so rich and diverse" (p. 4). But it is not only about sharing perspectives; it is also about a flexible positionality—"students taking on some responsibility for teaching and faculty re-envisaging themselves … as learners alongside their students" (p. 4). Finally, by responsibility, Cook-Sather et al. note the result of partnership becoming a more communal and collaborative approach, with both partners "equally invested in the common effort to engage in, and support, learning" (pp. 5–6).

While education has always ostensibly been "for" the benefit of students, it has historically excluded them from meaningful decision making in the process. Transformative methodologies, as discussed throughout this chapter, are interested in transforming power relationships and challenging unjust and/or exclusionary systems. SaP is no exception, with a goal of transforming the traditional relationship between teachers and students, where teachers hold all the power with the intention to achieve more equitable and socially just institutions. The SaP movement works explicitly against two forces—1) the consumerist model so prevalent in post-secondary education (Molesworth et al., 2009), where students are seen as "customers" paying for a "product"—with improvement tools such as student evaluations conceptualized as satisfaction surveys by the university, and 2) the transmission model of education, critiqued by educational theorists such as Paulo Freire (1970) in what he called the "banking concept" of education, or as it is often referred to in higher education, the "sage-on-the-stage" model of teaching (Morrison, 2014). Freire writes, "education thus becomes an act of depositing, in which the students are the depositories and the teacher is the depositor. Instead of communicating, the teacher issues communiques and makes deposits which the students patiently receive, memorize, and repeat" (p. 72).

Cook-Sather et al. (2014) note at the beginning of their book that "Faculty think a lot about teaching" but then ask: "how often and how carefully do we listen to students and respond to their ideas? How often do we collaborate and work alongside students to enhance learning?" (p. ix). In the SaP approach they outline, students become authentic contributors to the planning, implementation, and SoTL aspects of their education. They suggest the question then becomes, "how can we, together, deepen student learning in this course?" (p. x). In a SoTL context, this process is furthered by asking, how can we, together, inquire into and empower student learning through becoming research co-inquirers with our students? Woolmer et al. (2020) argue student–faculty partnerships in teaching and learning are important because:

- They provide opportunities for new kinds of conversations about teaching and learning outside of formal committee structures and institutional feedback processes.

- They offer a space to examine an issue from multiple perspectives and experiences, giving opportunity to be inclusive of different voices.
- The process for identifying and finding solutions is co-owned, shifting from an often consumerist and transactional approach.
- In their most radical forms, partnerships can disrupt traditional hierarchies and help develop more egalitarian learning communities (p. 81).

While SaP has arisen within the postsecondary context, with direct ties to SoTL, it has roots in the work of theorists such as Paulo Freire (see Giroux, 2010), but also in teacher education and K–12 work done on student voice (Cook-Sather, 2018). Educational models, such as the early childhood model of the Reggio Emilia Schools in Italy, prioritize student co-creation of curriculum for preschool-aged children (Edwards et al., 1998), which is known as one of the most innovative systems of early childhood education in the world. In these schools, children are seen as having rights, as researchers, as active constructors of knowledge, as social beings. Teachers are seen as collaborators, co-learners, guides, facilitators, researchers, and as reflective practitioners. These models are inherently generative and creative, and disrupt the assumption that the teacher/expert knows best how to proceed with learning, and assumes instead that students learn best and are most engaged when they are able to follow their own motivations and curiosities, and sees students as fully capable partners in the learning environment. As an alternative to transmission pedagogies, in Freire's words,

> apart from inquiry, apart from the praxis, individuals cannot be truly human. Knowledge emerges only through invention and re-invention, through the restless, impatient, continuing, hopeful inquiry human beings pursue in the world, with the world, and with each other.
>
> *(p. 72)*

In a research context, Students-as-Partners within SoTL has its roots in such methodologies as Action Research, specifically Participatory Action Research (PAR). Merriam and Tisdell (2016) note that Action Research

> is a form of practitioner research. It not only seeks to understand how participants make meaning or interpret a particular phenomenon or problem in their workplace, community, or practice, but it also usually seeks to engage participants at some level in the process in order to solve a particular problem.
>
> *(p. 49)*

As we have noted throughout this book, SoTL itself is a form of practitioner research. When students are engaged as authentic partners in the process, rather than as merely "participants," when the questions asked and choices made in the research are collaboratively developed with students, when students are co-researchers rather than research assistants, and when they share and even lead authorship in dissemination activities, it becomes participatory. Furthermore, it is co-owned through a process of shared responsibility.

Merriam and Tisdell (2016) identify some principles of Action Research salient to SaP and SoTL, including that it focuses on a "problematic situation" in practice, that the design of the study is emergent, and that researchers engage participants as co-investigators. Indeed, the example they give for Action Research is a classic description of SoTL: "teacher researchers, for example, typically conduct research with students in their own classes to improve some aspect of their teaching" (p. 52). One form of Action Research, Critical Action Research, contains the critical theoretical elements discussed earlier in this chapter, and is "specifically about attempting to challenge power relations based on societal structures of race, gender, class, sexual orientation, or religion" (p. 56). In Participatory Action Research, "the participants in the study act to a great degree as co-researchers" (p. 56). SaP is, by definition, participatory, has a relationship to critical theory, and aims to improve teaching and learning in this framework. One study that illuminates how a critical framework might be used within an SaP model in SoTL is Ada Jaarsma, Kyle Kinaschuk, and Lin Xing's (2016) "Kierkegaard, despair and the possibility of education: Teaching existentialism existentially," a philosophical exploration of how existentialism is taught in undergraduate philosophy classrooms, a partnership between Jaarsma and two undergraduate students. They ask, "Are there approaches to the classroom that emulate the commitments of existentialists to the transformative nature of subjectivity, passion and freedom?" (p. 446).

Alison Cook-Sather's extensive work in the SaLT (Students as Learners and Teachers) program at the Teaching and Learning Institute at Bryn Mawr College in the United States involves semester-long partnerships between faculty and students, where "these partners explore questions of classroom practice" (Cook-Sather et al., 2014, p. 73). The goals of the project are to not only improve classroom practice, but also to "foster open, critical, and constructive dialogue," as well as to "change the culture on campus to one in which dialogue about teaching and learning among faculty and students is a common desire, and desirable practice." These partnerships are further described by Cook-Sather and Abbot (2016) in an Action Research study on this project, using narrative analysis in "Translating partnerships: How faculty-student collaboration in explorations of teaching and learning can transform perceptions, terms, and selves" in which they explore the benefits to both students and faculty members of ongoing, deep conversations of teaching and learning. They write:

> The faculty members and student consultants we quote here are representative of the hundreds who are engaged in profound forms of translation through their collaboration. The new ways of naming and enacting powerful pedagogical practices that they develop together remind us that collaboration between faculty and students supports the ongoing processes of clarification and revision—of perceptions, terms, and selves—that can produce reflective practice, confidence and trust, thoughtful communication, student-centered teaching, and an enduring sense of capacity.
>
> *(p. 11)*

As the SaP movement has developed, it has become increasingly concerned with the exacerbated power disparities experienced in particular by both students and faculty from equity-seeking groups (see, for example, de Bie et al., 2022; Marquis et al., 2021). The critical theory underpinnings of SaP create an imperative for those working to establish respectful, reciprocal, and responsible collaborative relationships with students to examine the social locations of all involved.

The Postmodern Turn: Deconstruction

Postmodern and post-structural theories are closely related to critical theory; indeed, in many qualitative methodology texts, they will be placed together under the larger umbrella of "critical" perspectives. Kilgore (2001) suggests that "theorists from both perspectives are also interested in power as a factor in determining what and how we come to know about certain things and not others, and have certain ideas while not others" (p. 53). However, there are some important differences—the postmodern attempts to dismantle and deconstruct the categories that are so significant in critical theory. Queer studies, as one example, is interested in breaking down inherited categories of gender and sexuality, arguing that not of these categories are natural, but rather created by the society and language. According to Kilgore (2001), "postmodernists believe that since knowledge emerges from a particular context or event, it can shift as quickly as the context shifts, the perspective of the knower shifts, or as events overtake us" (p. 56). Merriam and Tisdell (2016) describe the postmodern world as one "where the rationality, scientific method, and certainty of the modern world no longer hold" (p. 11). Postmodern theory sees knowledge as "tentative, fragmented, multifaceted, and not necessarily rational" (Kilgore, 2001, p. 54).

Power is still important in the postmodern worldview, but seen as not held by groups, but rather, in the dynamics between people and groups. As Kilgore (2001) observes, "anyone can exercise power but no one can possess it" (p. 56). While these two terms—postmodern and post-structuralism—are tightly connected, they are not quite interchangeable. The term post-structuralism is used more commonly in literary studies, whereas when we say postmodern, we are really talking about a worldview that is disruptive and distrustful of any absolutes or understanding of concrete reality as a given.

Philosophers such as Derrida, Lyotard, and Foucault are foundational in postmodern theory, although Foucault resisted being categorized at all. Pierre Bourdieu in the latter part of the 20th century described the relationship between the individual and the social as the "tension between the individual and the social with his interrelated concepts of field and *habitus.* The field is analogous to a game, with both explicit and tacit rules of play" (Kilgore, 2001, p. 58). Habitus is how each of us internalize appropriate ways to act within various contexts, for example, within a classroom. Kilgore (2001) gives an example of a study (Baudelot, 1994) that demonstrates how the degree to which habitus is internalized determines success or failure in educational settings:

> Baudelot (1994) finds that one can distinguish "good" university student essays from "poor" ones without looking at the content at all but rather by looking at other characteristics of the papers. Those that receive higher marks tend to have longer sentences and a wealth of vocabulary, among other attributes.
>
> *(p. 58)*

Deconstruction is a common approach to analyzing data for the postmodern researcher. Texts or interviews are "unpacked" with a view to "identify and discredit the false binaries that structure a communication or 'discourse'" (Kilgore, 2001, p. 56). In SoTL, a researcher might take a set of interviews, but rather than simply look for themes where the perspective of the participant is "believed," rather, would "challenge the assertions of what is to be included or excluded as normal, right, or good" (p. 56). For example, a postmodern researcher might challenge narratives through their analysis in faculty transcripts about assessment practices where interviewees expressed a viewpoint that some students are just not capable of university-level work. Discourse analysis might be used to pay particular attention to how language is used to create ***grand narratives*** that can be disrupted, such as colonialism.

The postmodern analysis can also be inherently playful, staying as Caputo (2000) puts it, "in play with the play" (p. 46). Alecia Jackson and Lisa Mazzei (2011) take such an approach in their book *Thinking With Theory in Qualitative Research*, with analytic readings of two transcripts about first-generation female academics, considering them from the perspectives of six different postmodern theorists (Derrida, Spivak, Foucault, Butler, Deleuze, and Barad). Of this book Kara (2022) writes, "Their writing is not intended as definitive; rather, it is joyfully exploratory" (p. 36). Merriam and Tisdell (2016) say that "postmodern research is highly experimental, playful, and

TABLE 11.1 Comparison of Critical and Postmodern Perspectives and Aims of Inquiry

Critical Theory	*Postmodernism*
Knowledge is rationally produced in a society based on a struggle for power	Knowledge is tentative, multifaceted, not necessarily rational
Power is repressive and possessed by individuals/groups to greater or lesser degrees depending on their social location, has the function of maintaining and reproducing social structures	Power is expressed but not held by individuals or groups, productive rather than reproductive. "Anyone can exercise power but no one can possess it" (Kilgore, 2001, p. 57)
Knowledge frees individuals from power structures	Knowledge is an expression of power, truth claims are subject to question
Learning is achieved through critical reflection, consciousness raising	Learning is achieved through deconstruction, play, eclecticism, and transgression
Inquiry aimed at exposing structures of privilege and oppression as well as critique, emancipation, and social change	Inquiry aimed at deconstruction of prevailing grand narratives and false binaries through multi-vocal expression; the deconstruction process is never finished

Adapted from Kilgore (2001) and Lincoln et al. (2018).

creative, and no two postmodern studies look alike" (p. 11). Thus, alternative forms of writing up the work, including visual, poetic, and arts-based forms, might be pursued.

An example of a postmodern perspective on SoTL is Hewson and Easton's (2022) deconstruction of a grand narrative visible in SoTL, "Packing up the big tent: Que(e)rying and decolonizing SoTL." In it, they examine the "underside" of the big tent, inviting the possibilities of queer theory in "an effort to conceptualize a meaningful, ethical hospitality: a communion that acknowledges and is revivified by the differential of difference as opposed to its flattening or erasure" (p70). While critical and postmodern paradigms have in common an interest in deconstructing power and in transformation, as can be seen they are different in many fundamental and important ways. The above table summarizes some of the key differences in worldviews between the two paradigms, as well as comparing the aims of inquiry in a research context.

Indigenous Research Methodologies with Gabrielle Weasel Head

> My experience with this methodology is that it asks more. In asking more, Indigenous methodologies require exploration of identity, an ability to be vulnerable, a desire for restitution, and an opening to awakenings.
>
> *(Kovach, 2018, p. 217)*

While Indigenous research methodologies resist categorization and should not be conflated with Western research paradigms, it is helpful for those new to Indigenous perspectives in research to conceptualize Indigenous research methodologies in terms of parallels with Western research approaches. Increasingly, Indigenous researchers are pushing back against categorizing the Indigenous research paradigm and the methodologies that flow from it under the auspices of Western research approaches, arguing that to do so leads to the further erasure of Indigeneity (Ford et. al, 2018; Held, 2019). We respectfully acknowledge this tension and understand that while Indigenous research methodologies are inherently transformative, they are also connected to critical theory and postmodern lenses, but emerge from a wholly distinct paradigm that is characterized by its deviation from the Western paradigm. Given the holistic nature of Indigenous research paradigm, there are some parallels with critical realism (systems thinking, layered realities, phenomenon across levels). Indigenous research can also refute the subjective and objective in the sense that individual realities are never separated from a collective and relational universe so there is always a metacognitive component where the objective lens is turned toward self to ensure that reciprocity is always part of the research process.

In Canada, where we reside, the relationship of society to Indigenous communities has been a source of intense focus in recent years. The publication of the report of the Truth and Reconciliation Commission in 2015, documenting the experience of Indigenous children at Indian residential schools over multiple generations, resulted in 94 Calls to Action. Many of these include directives for education, attempting to interrupt the institutional racism built into the system, and the work of decolonization and reconciliation is a serious and fraught endeavor at post-secondary institutions across the country. While we intend this book to be relevant internationally, many other countries are also involved in similar discussions, in particular countries such as South Africa, New Zealand, and Australia. Because of the ongoing tensions related to epistemic exclusion of Indigenous ways of knowing in academic research, we feel the inclusion of Indigenous research methodologies here is important as it not only provides an alternative viewpoint to Western knowledge systems, but also helps us to envision an emancipatory path in SoTL research that others such as Kreber (2013) rigorously advance.

Looking back to Hutchings's heuristic presented in Chapter 2, Indigenous methodologies in SoTL research begin with possibilities. This section invites readers to reflect on "what might be possible" if reflexive relationality constantly guided SoTL researchers through which processes of teaching and learning are extended beyond the confines of the post-secondary classroom. As lead authors, we are not Indigenous, and therefore have respectfully invited Dr. Gabrielle Weasel Head, a Blackfoot colleague, to contribute to this component of the book, which is an approach that is respectful of a broader conversation happening in Indigenous communities wherein Indigenous academics, professionals, students, and researchers are rightfully challenging the pattern of exclusion and demanding from their non-Indigenous counterparts "nothing about us, without us." In this way, we offer our contribution on Indigenous research based upon voices of Indigenous academics, scholarship of Indigenous theorists, and the advice that any scholar further interested in these processes consult with local Indigenous communities and scholars.

In this context, an important question is: who can conduct Indigenous research? Historically, Indigenous research meant the anthropological project of white settler scholars doing exploitative research "on" Indigenous communities, often without appropriate consent, reciprocal relationships, or benefit to the community. We use the term settler here deliberately, meaning white Europeans and their descendants who colonized land where Indigenous peoples had been in residence for centuries (Wolfe, 2006). It is helpful to think of Indigenous research as existing along a spectrum. On one end, there is research that is conducted by Indigenous researchers from an Indigenous paradigm within which are embedded culturally distinct ontological, epistemological and axiological assumptions. The midpoint along the spectrum might include research that is conducted by non-Indigenous researchers in partnership with Indigenous researchers. At the opposite end is research that is done by non-Indigenous researchers with informed and explicit consent from Indigenous collaborators and participants with attempts on the part of the researchers to maintain reciprocity and respectful relationships with Indigenous communities.

Indigenous peoples in Canada are diverse, with complex worldviews; therefore, it is imperative that we push back against taking a pan-Indigenous approach, as though all Indigenous cultures are the same—Indigenous research must be positioned within a distinct cultural context that is geographically located. As such, we look at this question from a multifaceted, inter-nation Indigenous lens. As Cree scholar Margaret Kovach (2018) explains, the question of "who" can do Indigenous research is complex:

> it is more complicated than "if you're Indigenous you can and if you're not Indigenous you can't." I don't want to discount lineage and identity, but to me it is about an ongoing, mutual relationship with Indigenous peoples. It gets back to knowing the community and investing in that relationship … Indigenous methodologies are relational.
>
> *(p. 224)*

Kovach (2009) describes the development of a tribal methodology, based on a specific Indigenous epistemology and ontology, but including a decolonizing lens (more aligned with the critical methodologies described above) (p. 80). In her case, she creates a research framework based on Plains Cree knowledges, with tenets also "shared by other tribal groups as identified in the literature by Indigenous scholars" (p. 44). The elements of this methodology include: "(a) holistic epistemology, (b) story, (c) purpose, (d) experiential, (e) tribal ethics, (f) tribal ways of gaining knowledge, and (g) an overall consideration of the colonial relationship" (p. 44). Depending on the positionality of the researcher, they might pursue a wholly tribal methodology, most appropriate for Indigenous researchers in contexts where "there is a critical mass of Indigenous academics and where resistance to holistic epistemologies is not as great" (p. 80); they might use an approach with "decolonizing theory as its centring epistemology, thus becoming easily associated with transformative research" (p. 80); or they might pursue a third path as she has done, which centers tribal methodology but includes "a decolonizing lens as an integral component within the methodological design, but not as its epistemic basis" (p. 81).

Anishnaabe scholar Kathy Absolon's (2011) vision of Indigenous "re-search" is an example of research that Kovach refers to as a wholly tribal methodology, which is more concerned about the epistemological processes of coming to know as grounded in ontological responsibilities and assumptions that are distinct to Indigenous peoples. For Absolon, Indigenous re-search is a decolonizing journey through which processes of reclamation require approaches that are

> guided by Indigenous worldviews, beliefs, values, principles, processes and contexts. Indigenous methodologies are wholistic, relational, inter-relational and interdependent with Indigenous philosophies, beliefs and ways of life. The methods are determined by understanding the nature of our existence, of how we come to know, of how knowledge is produced and of where knowledge comes from.
>
> *(p. 22)*

Thus, Indigenous research is undertaken by Indigenous peoples using approaches that align with Indigenous ontological, epistemological, and axiological assumptions and Indigenous values transparently shape the methodology and associated methods. This is in contrast to Western research approaches that are, according to Absolon, "guided by colonialist beliefs and values, even though they claim, sometimes vehemently, that they are 'value neutral!'" (p. 22). Absolon's perspective offers an example of not only how Indigenous research pushes back against Western research paradigms but situates Indigenous research as distinct to and emerging from Indigenous lived experiences. Evans et al.'s exploration of "Toward a fusion of Indigenous methodologies, Participatory Action Research, and white studies in an urban Aboriginal research agenda" towards a method for decolonizing institutions (2009) offers an example of how researchers have attempted to co-locate critical epistemological traditions with Indigenous methodologies.

A key element in Indigenous research is the practice of researcher self-location, which underscores reflexivity as a key component (Russell-Mundine, 2012). Botswanan Indigenous scholar Begel Chilisa (2020) advances an Indigenous research paradigm as constructed by interdependent and interrelated concepts: relationality, which is about building relationships in research; responsibility, which is about conducting socially just research that resists Western domination and contributes to Indigenous communities and collective healing; reverence, which recognizes the role of spirituality in research and "values it as an important contribution to ways of knowing" (p. 10); respect, which ensures research processes are conducted with Indigenous communities in ways that are relevant and beneficial to communities; and reflexivity, which is a process of ongoing critical self-reflection on a researcher's socio-cultural positioning within existing power relations. Reflexivity is embodied through self-location/self-positioning statements. Thus, Indigenous research often begins with a deep and personal introduction to the researcher, where they come from, the land they are connected to, and an introduction to their families. Often included is a description of the researcher's journey through the research. In their book chapter detailing their research surrounding the embodiment of Indigenous resilience, Lindstrom, Baptiste and Shade (2021) each provide positioning statements through which they locate their identities in the contexts of their Indigenous tribal identities, connections to their lands and their responsibilities in conducting the research.

Kovach (2009) also describes her journey into tribal methodology. She began in her work with phenomenology, because of its narrative component, and later tried to weave in critical theory because of its transformative potential. Both of these still rested on Western epistemologies, however, and she eventually brought her own history and identity into her work. She writes:

> Once I understood I was privileging Plains Cree knowledges, a research framework began to form and give meaning to what I had been doing (or at least attempting to do) but as yet could not name. This was an attempt to honour the tribal knowledge that emerged from a social encounter with my world. In my case, Plains Cree knowledge offered guidance in research choices that reflected values, standards, ethics, and ways of Indigenous peoples generally and Cree specifically, and it demanded that I "write knowledge differently" than I had been instructed to do within previous Western research training. Once this tribal epistemology was visible, then all research choices were considered

> against it. My methodology world became, while not easier, certainly clearer.
>
> *(p. 43)*

Kovach's reflections on her research journey exemplify a set of Indigenous ontological responsibilities (Bastien, 2004) that give rise to a distinct epistemology that is positioned within the context of her Cree tribal identity. Ontological responsibilities are unique to each Indigenous nation and are the embodiment of Indigenous people's relationship with the sacred, the unseen, and transformational energies of the universe, through which Indigenous identities are constructed and affirmed. In the context of Blackfoot epistemology, Bastien (2004) asserts that

> the responsibility of seeking knowledge is fundamental to the identity of Niitsitapi. Knowledge is generated for the purpose of maintaining the relationships that strengthen and protect the health and well being of individuals and of the collective in a cosmic universe. In this respect, seeking knowledge is a fundamental responsibility for contributing to the collective good.
>
> *(p. 2)*

Seeking knowledge is at the heart of why we do research. In this way, research has always been a part of Indigenous ways of knowing (Wilson & Restoule, 2010), although the purpose of knowledges, how they are thought about, how they are generated, how they are used, and the relationship that individual researchers have to knowledge are what distinguishes an Indigenous research paradigm from Western research. Wilson and Hughes (2019) assert that within an Indigenous paradigm, "knowledge is alive, it has agency, it moves. Therefore, knowledge can't be discovered or owned but instead, it reveals itself, is experienced, is shared" (p. 9). According to Kovach (2018), Indigenous epistemology can be understood through these statements:

- Knowledge is holistic and implies empirical, experiential, sensory, and metaphysical possibilities.
- Knowledge arises from interconnectivity and interdependency.
- Knowledge is animate and fluid.
- Knowledge arises from a multiplicity of sources, including nonhuman sources (p. 218).

Moreover, an Indigenous research paradigm is constructed on a "belief that knowledge is relational. Knowledge is shared with all of creation [and] goes beyond the individual's knowledge to the concept of relational knowledge … You are answerable to all your relations when you are doing research" (Wilson, 2008, p. 56). This relational orientation demands an ethical rigor that ensures relational accountability on the part of researchers.

As we've discussed elsewhere in this book, conducting SoTL research ethically is important regardless of methodology. However, ethics is particularly critical when working with Indigenous communities because of the history of colonization, and the pattern of unethical and exploitative research that often typifies Western researchers' engagement in Indigenous communities. But what does this look like? In many ways, it means going beyond the expectations of an ethics review board, and "relying heavily on concrete actions most often known as, but not limited to, storytelling, ceremony, and protocols to communicate an Indigenous belief system" (Kovach, 2018, p. 224). According to Kovach, it further means demonstrating:

- evidence of respect for Indigenous knowledges;
- inclusion of multiple Indigenous voices (particularly in urban contexts);
- agreement with appropriate representatives on matters such as ownership and control of data;
- agreement on co authorship; and
- evidence of reciprocity (abbreviated list quoted from p. 225).

In doing research with Indigenous communities, there is a recognition of the importance of protocol that is set by the specific community, for example, the offering of tobacco to an Elder when requesting sharing of knowledge. The ethics and protocols attached to Indigenous research ensure the maintenance of balance and harmony within a complex web of relational alliances. This complexity is compounded when one considers the impacts of a long history of colonial Western research practices and both Indigenous and non-Indigenous researchers must learn to navigate this complexity in ways informed by their distinct socio-cultural positioning. For example, Cormier and Ray (2018) write that "ceremony is the purest form of Indigenous methodology" (p. 120) as they describe their research as a ceremony, using the structure of a traditional fast they both participated in. The ontological assumption in Indigenous research is that the universe is kind and the giver of gifts, imbued with transformative energies, and it is our responsibility to seek knowledges that ensure balance and harmony in a collectively held and understood reality. The axiology of research must reflect this kindness; thus researchers must act in-kind—this is where protocols come in. Thoughts matter, actions matter. Part of the axiology of Indigenous research could include daily smudge before beginning writing, asking knowledge-keepers to pray and hold ceremony on behalf of research participants, engaging in a sweat ceremony to seek knowledge about the direction of the research, and holding a pipe ceremony to start the research process in a good way. This is part of ethical research. Others such as George et al. (2020) advance ethics as part of the broader movement of Indigenous self-determination in research. The authors state that

> making space for Indigenous sovereignty within research is now a global phenomenon. Such a global surge in Indigenous research—and research ethics—speaks to all the exciting and innovative possibilities that flow from research in which Indigenous peoples reclaim their past, present and future.
>
> *(p. 3)*

As the statement above exemplifies, Indigenous research methodologies are complex and nuanced and often characterized by their distance from the Western research paradigm. While they hold much in common with other transformative methodologies, they are uniquely "research by and for indigenous peoples, using techniques and methods drawn from the traditions of those peoples" (Evans et al., 2009, p. 894). While commonalities can be identified, Indigenous methodologies resist homogenization. As Kovach writes, "Still there are tensions. Because so much of Indigenous ways of knowing is internal, personal, and experiential, creating one standardized, externalized framework for Indigenous research is nearly impossible, and inevitably heartbreaking for Indigenous people" (p. 43). As Indigenous scholars begin to work within the field of SoTL, enriching the movement, settler and other non-Indigenous SoTL scholars interested in these methodologies are encouraged to seek out both Indigenous colleagues and communities, and to read further from Indigenous scholars to understand more deeply the principles involved.

While some forms of transformative research explored in this chapter are currently less common in SoTL, such as that from a postmodern lens, the impulse of transformation and tradition of participatory and Action Research is highly compatible with the aims of SoTL. There is certainly room for more critical, postmodern, and Indigenous methodologies in the field. Within the transformative paradigms, SaP is the most well-developed transformative stream of SoTL, providing an exciting avenue to fundamentally shift traditional structures within post-secondary institutions.

Key Concepts

- Transformative approaches are interested in dynamics and goals such as empowerment, disruption, restoration, and authentic partnership, depending on the specific paradigm.
- The transformative category includes critical, postmodern, and Indigenous approaches, although the Indigenous paradigm also resists categorization in Western knowledge systems.
- Transformative researchers attempt to expose power imbalances and bring marginalized groups to the center of the conversation, rather than continuing to reproduce inequitable, taken-for-granted structures, known as *hegemony*.
- The transformative lens should not be considered a single research paradigm, but rather a collection of different paradigms with transformative goals (conceptualized differently).
- Students-as-Partners (SaP) is an important critical movement within SoTL, which involves students throughout each stage of the research process as knowledge producers.

Further Reading

Cook-Sather, A., Bovill, C., & Felten, P. (2014). *Engaging students as partners in learning and teaching: A guide for faculty*. John Wiley & Sons.

Evans, M., Hole, R., Berg, L. D., Hutchinson, P., & Sookraj, D. (2009). Common insights, differing methodologies: Toward a fusion of Indigenous methodologies, Participatory Action Research, and white studies in an urban Aboriginal research agenda. *Qualitative Inquiry*, 15(5), 893–910. https://doi.org/10.1177/1077800409333392.

Freire, P. (1970). *Pedagogy of the oppressed*. Herder & Herder.

Kincheloe, J. L., McLaren, P., Steinberg, S. R., & Monzó, L. D. (2018). Critical pedagogy and qualitative research: Advancing the bricolage. In N. K. Denzin & Y. S. Lincoln (Eds.), *The Sage handbook of qualitative research* (5th ed.) (pp. 235–260). Sage.

Kilgore, D. W. (2001). Critical and postmodern perspectives on adult learning. *New directions for adult and continuing education*, 89, 53–61.

Kovach, M. (2018). Doing Indigenous methodologies: A letter to a research class. In N. K. Denzin & Y. S. Lincoln (Eds.), *The Sage handbook of qualitative research* (5th ed.) (pp. 214–234). Sage.

McGregor, D., Restoule, J. P., & Johnston, R. (Eds.) (2018). *Indigenous research: Theories, practices, and relationships*. Canadian Scholars.

Woolmer, C. (n.d.). *SoTL as co-inquiry with students: Opportunities for partnership?* Worksheet on Mokakiiks Centre for SoTL website. https://drive.google.com/file/d/1XezA02b7EiMZgdMiV1mbs6G21J0gl-r8/view.

Woolmer, C., Marquis, E., Aspenlieder, E., & Goff, L. (2020). Student partnerships in higher education. In S. Marshall (Ed.), *Handbook on teaching and learning: Enhancing academic practice* (5th ed.) (pp. 81–94). Routledge.

PART IV

Disseminating SoTL

12

ACADEMIC GENRES

> In this chapter, we offer some advice for people who wish to disseminate their SoTL findings in academic genres. Many new SoTL scholars may find it difficult to begin, in part because of disciplinary identities and lack of confidence in a new academic area. To help people get started, we consider two common contexts for academic genres: conferences and publications.

For the purposes of this chapter, we assume that you have learned something about teaching and learning that you want to share with others by publishing in one of the traditional academic forms; this is not the only way you can share your insights, and indeed Chapter 14 takes a closer look at communicating with different stakeholders about your research, what is sometimes called knowledge translation or knowledge mobilization. Here, however, we focus on two common contexts for academic writing about teaching and learning: academic conferences and scholarly publications.

Most academics are all too familiar with the idea of "publish or perish"—the pressure to disseminate research in accepted scholarly formats or risk career stagnation. Publishing SoTL work in respected academic fora can positively impact careers; however, there are also more idealistic motives in sharing what we have learned through our SoTL projects. SoTL's emphasis on "going public" stems from a desire to create a culture where we learn from each other in order to improve the teaching and learning environment. See, for example, Shulman (1993) and Huber and Hutchings (2005). In their excellent open-access book on writing about teaching and learning, Mick Healey, Kelly Matthews, and Alison Cook-Sather (2020) describe "writing about learning and teaching as creating and contributing to scholarly conversations" (p. 25). They are not, of course, the first to use the conversation metaphor; Kenneth Burke (1941) famously described scholarship as an

DOI: 10.4324/9781003447054-16

unending conversation, where we enter a room in which a heated conversation is already going on, we listen for a while, join in, and eventually leave, with the conversation still going on behind us. This metaphor is powerful because it emphasizes the communicative nature of scholarship: it is a social activity involving specific rhetorical situations. Before we describe some common genres we use to communicate in these situations, we explore some of the issues involved in academic writing more broadly.

Why Is It Difficult for New SoTL Scholars to Disseminate?

While there are important reasons to disseminate our findings, many new SoTL scholars find it difficult to begin. Part of this difficulty is endemic in the academy. Academics have multiple conflicting demands on their time, many of which are more immediate than writing for publication. Plus, writing is hard, time-consuming, not as much fun as planning the next study, and not as immediately rewarding as working with students. Thus, there is a whole industry around providing advice for academics who wish to write more. From routines of daily writing (Boice, 1990) to writing retreats (Grant, 2008), from advice tailored specifically for graduate students or those writing in their non-native tongue (Roberts & Hyatt, 2018; Bailey, 2014) to advice for specific disciplines (Becker, 2007; Goldbort, 2006; Greene, 2013; Hayot, 2014) and advice on style (Sword, 2012; Harris, 2006), there are many sources available. We recommend Helen Sword's *Air & Light & Time & Space: How Successful Academics Write* (2017), not only because it pays explicit attention to the behavioral, artisanal, social, and emotional habits of writing—what Sword calls the BASE cornerstones (p. 5)—but because it is itself an example of a SoTL research project. Sword surveyed over 1,200 academics and interviewed 100 academic authors and editors, seeking to find out what works for successful academic authors. She illustrates the immense variety of successful approaches with interesting quotations from academics across the disciplines and provides suggestions for further reading, should some of these approaches catch the reader's eye.

Of course, some approaches may feel more comfortable than others, not only because of individual differences, but because we are socialized by our disciplines to think about writing in very different ways. Some approach writing as a specific stage in the research process that occurs after all the analysis has been completed; they might talk about "writing up" the project as if the writing process itself doesn't change the findings. You'll notice some of the post-positivist assumptions involved in this view of writing. Other disciplines embrace the idea that the process of writing clarifies, reshapes, or even creates the writer's understanding of what is being written about, views of writing that involve constructivist assumptions. When we consider writing as a communicative act, we want to communicate something to someone in a particular context, we also bring in assumptions about what is and isn't acceptable in that particular context. Swales (1990, 2017) discusses the role of academic discourse communities in determining not only what is disseminated, but also how it is disseminated. Many academics are socialized into the norms of their particular disciplinary community through the long process of postgraduate study. As Elliot-Johns (2011) notes, "our disciplinary training prepares us to think of academic writing in particular ways, and to also see ourselves as writers in the academy in particular ways." While this process may help us succeed within our disciplines, it does not necessarily help us write for other communities, including the SoTL community.

If, as Brett (1991) argues, "University academics do not write to persuade but to impress and gain approval within a hierarchy. They are trained to write for approval" (p. 520), what happens to academics when they suddenly find themselves as novices again in the scholarship of teaching and learning? Examining the emotional habits of successful writers, Sword (2017) identifies self-doubt as one of the most serious challenges. Scholars writing in a new context, perhaps engaging in a different type of scholarship or writing for readers outside of their discipline, may not have the confidence to share their work. Our earlier work indicates many novice SoTL scholars experience discomfort, and exhilaration, as they move beyond disciplinary boundaries to engage with SoTL (Miller-Young et al., 2018; Yeo et al., 2018). Webb (2019) identifies the "imposter syndrome" as one of the key constraints to conducting and disseminating SoTL. So part of writing for SoTL involves building confidence. Confidence can be built through supportive communities, for example, discussing what you've learned about teaching and learning with a trusted colleague, participating in a writing group that regularly meets to help each other with their writing goals, or taking advantage of opportunities to present works-in-progress at your own institution or at some teaching and learning conferences. Some institutions and organizations have created SoTL development initiatives to mentor people interested in pursuing this type of scholarship.

But we are also aware that some individuals may be doing this sort of work in relative isolation without easy access to advice about writing about teaching and learning. This chapter then examines some academic genres of SoTL more carefully. In what follows, we do not address graduate-level assignments or dissertations explicitly because these forms of writing will be shaped by the norms of the specific institution and students mentored by instructors or supervisors. Similarly, applications for teaching awards or for promotion are very context-dependent, although Healey et al. (2020) do offer some guiding questions for scholars putting their narratives together. We also do not address peer review of syllabi, teaching portfolios, and learning objects, although creating and sharing these types of artifacts is another way to go public with what we have learned about teaching and learning. For more information on these genres, please see Bernstein et al. (2006). Instead, we are going to focus on common academic genres seen at conferences and in publications.

Of course, this isn't the only way we could have organized our thoughts about the academic genres of SoTL. Maryellen Weimer (2006), for example, divides scholarly work on teaching and learning into Wisdom of Practice scholarship (including personal accounts of change, recommended practices reports, recommended content reports, and personal narratives) and Research scholarship (including quantitative, qualitative, and descriptive approaches). Different conference and publication venues may emphasize one of these approaches over the other. However, we believe that strong SoTL work often brings together elements of Wisdom of Practice, particularly self-reflexivity, and Research. Part of this self-reflexivity involves thinking about why we present findings and make arguments in particular ways. We offer the following observations about the academic genres, not only because explicit discussion of norms can help build confidence, but also because naming these assumptions and norms can allow us to bring other genres and other voices into the conversation (Manarin, 2017).

Conferences

If we are talking about scholarship as conversation, the obvious place to begin is the academic conference. At its best, an academic conference, whether in person, online, or hybrid, offers us an opportunity to share what we have learned with others and be inspired by what they have learned. Academic conferences allow us to try out ideas and get feedback; to learn about new methodologies, theories, and issues; and to make significant intellectual connections with an academic community. At its worst, an academic conference may be overwhelming, frustrating, and isolating. Some conferences may be so large that it's difficult for a newcomer to easily find any sort of community. They may reflect particular hierarchies in the discipline, or only welcome particular types of scholarship and particular types of scholars. Luckily, teaching and learning conferences, particularly those that are multidisciplinary, tend to welcome a variety of approaches and participants. The International Society for the Scholarship of Teaching and Learning, for example, emphasizes the values of collegiality, inclusivity, diversity, engagement, and scholarship in its conference pedagogy statement (Chick et al., 2017).

So why attend a conference (virtually or in person)? Jennifer Meta Robinson (2018) describes it this way:

> Academic conferences are places of teaching and learning. They are also, like all social sites of learning, places to practice identities, relations to

> knowledge, and positions to others present or absent. I can read a published article, sure, but I also value being close to the people who have expertise, to follow close up the moves their minds make, to see what I can about who they are. I want to hear their voices, where they speak with certainty and when they pause. I go to fill up on ideas.
>
> *(p. 144)*

Tobin (2021) offers a lot of helpful advice on how to plan for and enjoy an academic conference, including thinking about what you'd like to learn, taking time to recharge, and focusing on connection rather than transactional networking. If you are more introverted, you might want to attend the same conference multiple years in a row, or volunteer for a conference. Either way you will make personal connections that will enhance your conference experience.

Teaching and learning conferences can be roughly divided into those that focus on teaching and learning in a specific discipline, for example, engineering education, and those that are multidisciplinary. This distinction is important because it shapes with whom, and therefore how, we want to communicate. For example, Janice might present findings from the same teaching and learning inquiry at an engineering education conference and a SoTL conference, but how she frames the work, how she presents, and the details she focuses on will differ. In what follows, we offer a few observations about the common academic genres that you'll see at multidisciplinary teaching and learning conferences because the norms might be different from conferences in your home discipline. The most common genres are oral presentations or panels and conference posters; however, some conferences are experimenting with other genres as well. In each case, the presentation types will be described in the call for proposals along with the instructions for the proposal. Often conference organizers will want an extended abstract that they can send out to reviewers. If the conference doesn't require an abstract, or if it promises an extremely quick turnaround time, or even guaranteed acceptance, it may be a predatory conference (Pecorari, 2021). Quite often teaching and learning conferences will also indicate how these proposals will be adjudicated. For example, will the reviewer be looking for details about the methodology? Is a bibliography required? How will the presenters engage the audience? It makes sense to pay specific attention to those elements when submitting a proposal.

Oral Presentation

One of the biggest differences between oral presentations at teaching and learning conferences and those in some disciplines is the level of engagement expected between presenters and attendees. Karen comes from a discipline (English) where attending a conference presentation involves listening to a paper being read for 20 minutes followed by a few minutes for questions, or even listening to a series of three papers being read followed by a longer question period. In contrast, teaching and learning conferences tend to have much more interactive presentations. As Chick et al. (2017) note, "We may have some slides (or a poster), prepare handouts to capture our main points, and read aloud an occasional excerpt, but our presentation styles—regardless of session type—encourage conversation, facilitate interaction (or even active learning), solicit feedback, and of course invite questions." Depending on the conference, reviewers may even be instructed to score a proposal's interactive elements. Participants may be asked to do a short activity during the session, or at the very least have the opportunity to respond in a more robust discussion period.

Conference Poster

Many teaching and learning conferences will include a poster session where scholars stand near their posters and are prepared to discuss their research with participants. This is a type of presentation common in science and technology fields, and uncommon in the humanities. Advice is available online about how to create a legible and informative poster, for example, using an appropriate font size, paying attention to white space, and organizing material so that viewers can easily understand the project. We offer some suggestions about using visuals in the next chapter. It's important to check with the particular conference organizers about the size and material expected. Posters can be printed on paper or fabric; some will be laminated. Some posters at teaching and learning conferences will involve interactive elements and may depart from the traditional science poster template.

Other Genres

While the most common genres seen at teaching and learning conferences are the oral presentation and the poster, you may also find panel presentations, workshops, calls for collaboration, deeper discussion groups, and roundtable sessions where participants move from table to table to interact with different presenters. Again, there is an explicit emphasis on participant engagement in these different forms of presentation. For more information about teaching and learning conference presentations, we recommend Healey et al. (2020); as they note, "you should think as much about how you are going to communicate effectively with your audience and how they are going to respond as about what you are going to say" (p. 180).

Publications

In many cases, presenting at a conference, or presenting at multiple conferences, can provide you with important information as you decide what, where, and how to publish your teaching and learning research. A conference presentation, for the most part, will only be able to illuminate one aspect of your project—a publication will allow you to go into more detail, though again it's important to remember that you won't be able to say everything you want to say about a subject in a single article-length publication. For example, the material that eventually wound up in *Critical Reading in Higher Education: Academic Goals and Social Engagement* (Manarin et al., 2015) was presented at five different teaching and learning conferences over the course of two years. Different conference presentations became the backbone of different chapters in the book. It was a way for the research team to organize a lot of information, receive formative feedback from audiences, and keep motivated in a long-term project.

Experienced researchers will often have multiple publications from a single research project, each one addressing a different aspect of the project or a different audience. Together we have published three different articles based on one set of interviews of faculty members engaging in a SoTL development program; each article explored a different aspect of the data, and for each, we used a different approach to examine the data (Miller-Young et al., 2016; Miller-Young et al., 2018; Yeo et al., 2018). This work also influenced our thinking about new projects; that's how research programs develop. The process of writing for publication often generates other ideas that can be explored, perhaps with the existing data set, perhaps with additional data. When writing, we find it useful to keep a "parking lot" for ideas that we might want to explore later.

Deciding What and Where to Publish

Before we begin writing, however, we have an idea of what we would like to say to whom. Writing is a communicative act—we want to say something to someone. Deciding on a key focus and target audience before beginning the writing process provides the writer with a place to start, both in terms of where to publish—where are members of that target audience likely to see the work—and how to make an argument that is convincing, or at least intriguing, to that audience. After all, different target audiences read different publications and may expect different types of evidence and argumentation; publication venues have particular parameters, not only in terms of things like length of article or citation style, but also in terms of the types of work they are likely to publish. It makes sense to read the mission statement and aims of a journal or book series before submitting your work there to see if what you have to say fits within the scope. We have also used the following brief questionnaire about journal publication with novice SoTL scholars (Table 12.1); the questions could be easily adapted for book series.

Answering these questions can suggest whether the journal is a good fit for what you want to do, and can provide important information about how

TABLE 12.1 Questions About the Target Journal

Name of Target Journal:
Look at the aims and scope of the target journal. (This info will be on the journal's website or cover.) Write a one- or two-sentence summary of the journal's mission.
What formal instructions are you given in terms of length and documentation format?
In the past three years, has the journal published SoTL work (whether or not they call it that)? Look for whether they have published articles based on classroom data; look at the sample sizes; look at whether the author is the instructor. What type of studies do they usually publish?
Find at least two recent articles from the target journal that have a similar structure to what you want to do. The content doesn't matter. Consider the following aspects: a Point of View: Do the articles use first-person or third-person point of view? b Formality: How conversational are the articles? What makes you say that? What type of language can you point to in the articles? c Structure: Do the articles use the same structure (for example, subheadings in a particular order), or are they different? Does the journal encourage a particular structure? d What are the proportions of the articles? How many pages is each article? How many of those pages are devoted to literature review? How many to describing method and methodology? How many to data analysis or discussion? e What type of evidence do the articles provide? If it is quantitative, how do they present and discuss it? For example, do they use figures to help explain the data? If it is qualitative, how do they present and discuss it? For example, do they integrate each quotation into a sentence and then discuss it? Do they group quotations together under themes and then discuss them later?
Why do you think this journal would be a good fit for your project? What do readers expect from this journal? Can you provide that?

to write the article. The questionnaire can also be a helpful tool in writing residencies where people are providing peer-review feedback on drafts, as it helps the reviewers tailor their feedback to the target publication. Sometimes people are nervous about showing their work to colleagues, but contemporary scholarship is built upon the idea of peer review.

Peer Review

Peer review is the primary quality assurance process for academic publishing. Work that isn't peer-reviewed, for example work that is self-published, tends to be considered differently in tenure and promotion decisions. When work, whether article-length or book-length, is submitted to an academic publisher, it is typically sent out to multiple experts in the field for their opinions about the quality of the work. They examine the work carefully and decide whether it should be published in the target venue. Decisions range from outright acceptance (which honestly we've never experienced) to outright rejection (which, sadly, we have occasionally experienced). Most often reviewers will point out areas where the work could be strengthened and recommend that the piece be revised. Then the authors decide whether they want to make these changes and resubmit for another round of peer review. Authors don't have to make all the changes the reviewers suggest, but they should provide an explanation for their choices. It's important not to see revise and resubmit requests as rejection, even though it might feel that way at first. As Healey et al. (2020) note, "Because writing is entangled with our identities as scholars, the inherently judgmental nature of peer review can contribute to our professional growth but can also be emotionally taxing" (p. 301). They offer some helpful strategies for dealing with peer review productively. It's important to remember that most peer reviewers are volunteering their time and energy as service to the profession. It can be very useful for researchers new to SoTL to look for opportunities to serve as peer reviewers, perhaps for conference proposals, as this is an excellent way to learn how peer review works and how to improve their own submissions. Before we provide some observations about common article-length and book-length forms specifically, we want to address two issues that may cause confusion among novice SoTL scholars: open access and predatory publishing.

Open Access

Over the past two decades, as electronic publication has become more widespread, there has been a growing movement to increase access to scholarship by reducing barriers to access including subscription costs. Suber (2012) defines open access (OA) literature as "digital, online, free of charge, and free of most copyright and licensing restrictions" (p. 4). Suber discusses variations of OA; debunks some myths about OA, including the myths that OA work is less rigorous or involves less authorial control than traditional publication; and addresses why researchers might choose to disseminate their work through legitimate OA publishers. Many researchers believe in the philosophy of OA, that knowledge should be disseminated with as few barriers as possible, especially from a social justice perspective, but that's not the only reason.

Proponents of OA argue that "Open practices accelerate the dissemination of scholars' work and improve its quality, impact, and reach" (Association of Research Libraries, 2022). Works published OA are more frequently downloaded and cited (Piwowar et al., 2018). And, increasingly, public funding agencies require that researchers publish their findings in OA formats (see, for example, NIH, 2014; Tri-Agency Open Access Policy on Publications, 2016), which has led many for-profit publishers to offer OA options. Of course, someone has to pay for such work, and the price of making an article OA in some publications can be steep. Researchers with large grants will often build these costs into their budgets; individual institutions may have funding sources available for researchers who wish to make work published in traditional journals OA. In some cases, OA pre-publication versions may be placed in data repositories or uploaded on to OA platforms. But there is another type of OA that may be relevant for some SoTL scholars.

A number of well-respected teaching and learning journals are OA; they are typically sponsored by teaching and learning organizations or institutions. For example, the *Asian Journal of the Scholarship of Teaching and Learning* is associated with the National University of Singapore, *Teaching and Learning Inquiry* with the International Society for the Scholarship of Teaching and Learning, the *International Journal for Students as Partners* with McMaster University, the *International Journal for the Scholarship of Teaching and Learning* with Georgia Southern University, the *Canadian Journal for the Scholarship of Teaching and Learning* with the Society for Teaching and Learning in Higher Education, the *Journal of the Scholarship of Teaching and Learning* with Indiana University, and so on. Each of these journals publishes quality submissions at no cost to the authors; each has a rigorous peer-review process.

Predatory Publishing

A rigorous peer review process distinguishes these reputable OA journals from what are sometimes called predatory publishers. These are "entities that prioritize self-interest at the expense of scholarship and are characterized by false or misleading information, deviation from best editorial and publication practices, a lack of transparency, and/or the use of aggressive and indiscriminate solicitation practices" (Grudniewicz et al., 2019). Some journals operate on a pay-to-publish model without rigorous peer review. One marker is the promise of a very fast turnaround time (perhaps only a month or two) between initial submission and publication; after all, peer review requires significant time and effort. Another marker is an unsolicited email that invites you to submit to the journal because they have read [insert title of other work you've published here] and "believe you to be an expert in the field." Like predatory conferences, the journal title may be unusually broad or only tangentially related to your field. Beall (2015) offers a list of things to watch for when selecting a publication venue, but of course, you have to use your own judgment. For example, he provides *Journal of Education* as an example of an overly broad title, but the *Journal of Education* is in fact one of the oldest educational journals in North America, and is now associated with Sage publishers.

When you are considering whether to submit to a particular venue, do some research if you're not familiar with the journal/book series. What other types of things have they published? Are you familiar with the authors' names, or the names of people on the editorial board? Is it associated with a well-known organization or institution or publisher? After all, you don't want to throw away good work on a bad journal. Your work will not reach your target audience, who are unlikely to read and even less likely to cite a predatory publisher. Tenure and promotion committees may discount such work; they may also view you as at best naive, at worst duplicitous. Any short-term gain by the author is outweighed by the potential longer-term consequences (McLeod et al., 2018).

Article-Length Publication

Once you've decided what and where to publish, you will want to consider the form. We divide our discussion here into two main sections based upon length. Most novice SoTL researchers will begin with article-length publications, whether published in journals or as chapters in an edited book. Within that larger category there are many variations, from empirical research articles, to conceptual essays, standalone literature reviews, scholarly personal narratives, reflective writing, wisdom of practice pieces, case studies, and so on. In fact, there is a dizzying array of genres and stylistic choices possible, but all genres and styles are not possible for all publication venues, which is why we recommend beginning with an idea of where the piece might wind up. Some SoTL journals are more open to various forms than others, while a call for proposals for an edited collection will usually indicate the types of work the editors will consider. If you're not sure if what you want to do fits within the scope of the journal or edited collection, a quick query to the editor is a good idea. In what follows, we offer some suggestions for three main types of article-length publication. Depending on your disciplinary background, these distinctions may seem more or less obvious.

Research Articles

The majority of articles published in SoTL journals are research articles. For example, examining articles published over five years in three generalist OA SoTL journals, Manarin et al. (2021) found that 74% reported some sort of data about teaching and learning, as opposed to purely theoretical or conceptual essays. These research articles, however, demonstrate a wide range of methodologies and a wide range of stylistic choices. As is the case throughout the research process, it's important to consider alignment between the methodology and the article form chosen. For example, labeling sections of the article Introduction, Methods, Results, and Discussion (IMRaD) may work for quantitative or empirical qualitative studies, but it is less likely to be used with an interpretive study where the findings (rather than results) are often discussed as they are presented, i.e., a quotation illustrating a key finding is immediately followed by the researcher's interpretation. Regardless of the specific organizational structure used, Healey et al. (2020) argue that

> An empirical research article, whether published in a journal or as a book chapter, should provide a clear rationale for the study and its contribution to the existing literature, justification for the research methodology used, an analysis of findings, and a discussion of those findings and their implications for the field of study.
>
> *(p. 118)*

How these pieces fit together depends upon the researcher who wishes to reach a particular audience through a particular target publication.

IMRaD. One way to structure these articles is Introduction, Methods, Results and Discussion (IMRaD), a common pattern in some science and social science disciplines. Indeed, some people assume that this is a natural way to structure articles, although the IMRaD pattern for scholarly articles is relatively recent, only becoming prominent in the 1970s (Sollaci & Pereira, 2004). Often those specific words are used as subheadings because they allow readers to scan for information quickly. The overall flow of the article can be described as a wine glass or hourglass, as it begins with the broader context and narrows the scope through the literature review. The literature review describes similar studies in other contexts as well as theoretical or conceptual frameworks. The narrowest focus would be on the specific study methods and results before broadening out again in the discussion and (if available) concluding sections. Often authors will write different parts of the IMRaD article as time and energy allow; it's not necessary, or even very common, to write it by beginning with the introduction and moving through to the end. One of the benefits of the IMRaD structure is that the constraints provide clarity about what should be included where. Indeed, there are a number of resources available that will lead researchers through the different sections (see, for example, Braun & Clarke, 2013; Healey et al., 2019; Healey et al., 2020).

Variations. One of the most common variations on the IMRaD structure involves combining the Results and Discussion sections into one, and calling it something like Analysis and Discussion or Key Themes. As mentioned earlier, this variation may be more palatable for researchers who find it methodologically incongruent to present their findings as if they stand alone without interpretation. Another variation involves using content-specific subheadings, but still following the same basic pattern. Still other researchers, particularly those from the arts and humanities, have argued that science or social science models like IMRaD are not the only way to write research articles about teaching and learning (see, for example, Bloch-Schulman et al., 2016). Transformative methodologies also often seek to disrupt academic norms of publishing (Pathak, 2010; Denzin, 2016), sometimes in very playful ways. Helen Sword (2019) plays with academic conventions as she discusses her research about voice in scholarly articles.

Conceptual Article

Many disciplines separate conceptual articles from empirical ones; others blend the two together. Some SoTL journals will offer separate categories for submission; for example, the *International Journal for SoTL* has separate sections for essays on SoTL and research articles while other journals like *Teaching and Learning Inquiry* try to welcome different disciplines by encouraging many different types of submissions within the single category of article. Distinguishing between empirical and conceptual articles, Healey et al. (2020) argue that a theoretical or conceptual article "Draws on literature and theories (without presenting new data) to provoke, deepen, or expand thinking about a particular concept or practice" (p. 109). They note that "The argument of a theoretical or conceptual article is speculative, not empirical, hence you build your argument through noting connections, contradictions, gaps, complexities, or other patterns, putting ideas into dialogue with one another, highlighting previously unnoted phenomena" (p. 131). As with empirical research articles, authors will draw on the existing literature selectively to foreground a particular argument or train of thought. That's one of the key differences between a conceptual article and a systematic literature review, where all the literature must be categorized (Healey et al., 2020).

Conceptual articles do not follow a prescribed structure; instead, the authors have to create a logical structure based on the specific argument or idea that the authors are exploring. This can make them more difficult to write as the authors have to provide enough signposts for the reader to be able to follow the steps of the argument. Unlike IMRaD articles where the sections perform specific functions and can easily be written or read in different order, most conceptual articles are designed to be read from beginning to end. Jaakkola (2020) discusses four common types of conceptual articles: theory synthesis, theory adaptation, typology, and model; although these are not the only possibilities, Jaakkola's work can help people think through some of the requirements for this type of writing.

Scholarly Reflections

Aspects of reflective writing are increasingly common in writing about teaching and learning. For example, many pieces will include statements of positionality, where the authors explain how their personal experience has shaped their research. The distinction between experience and objectivity that Weimer (2006) highlighted is, we believe, breaking down, at least so far as research about something as value-laden as education goes. However, some pieces will deliberately foreground scholarly reflection, though what these pieces are called may vary. Ng and Carney (2017) argue that the scholarly personal narrative (SPN) "challenges researchers to apply theoretical concepts to personal and professional experiences" (p. 143). Rather than a discrete part of a larger article, the personal reflection here is the article. As Nash (2019) explains, "SPN puts the self of the scholar front and center" (p.18). Healey et al. (2020) prefer the term reflective essay, "a personal, contemplative, critical analysis based on lived experience but not necessarily grounded in your own data or others' research" (pp. 193–194). They see these essays as opportunities to explore ideas and emotions, and argue that reflective writing is often more accessible to a broad audience than some other academic genres (p. 196).

But this accessibility has led some to discount scholarly reflection as scholarship, to fear that these articles won't "count" for much during tenure and promotion applications, or to argue that only those academics who have already "made it" can afford to take such risks (Nash, 2019, p. 42). As Cook-Sather et al. (2019) note, reflective writing is sometimes subject to "dysfunctional illusions of rigor" (p. 24). They argue that "the time has come to both legitimate critical reflection as a form of scholarly writing about teaching and learning, and also to make *all* SoTL writing more explicitly reflective" (p. 23). Some teaching and learning journals are more welcoming of this type of work than others, which is why it's important to consider publication venue early on in the writing process. Healey et al. (2020) offer some guiding questions for those interested in writing, and learning from the writing of, reflective essays.

In this section we provided some observations about three common article-length genres: research articles, conceptual articles, and scholarly reflections. Of course, these are not the only options available. Depending on your project and inclinations, you might want to write case studies, systematic literature reviews, opinion pieces, and stories about teaching and learning. You can find out more information by researching each of these genres. Healey et al. (2020) is a good place to start.

Books and Edited Collections

We will conclude this chapter with a few brief words about scholarly books and edited collections, recognizing that there are whole books written about writing books. As Healey et al. (2020) note, "the conceptualization and review processes are different, and a book project can create a new conversation often containing a greater number and diversity of voices, which is more challenging to accomplish in the other genres" (p. 165). Usually a book-length project begins with a query to a series editor at a press to see if they would be interested in publishing something on that particular topic. The initial contact, if successful, may lead to a proposal including a prospectus that lays out the structure of the proposed work. Publishers will have their own requirements for what they want to see in a proposal. Proposals will describe the target audience for the work, outline the contribution it could make to scholarship, and provide information about the authors' experience and expertise. Sometimes publishers will want to see a completed chapter or two at this stage. Most publishers will not want to review an entire manuscript before signing off on a proposal. At this point, some publishers will offer a contract subject to successful completion of a manuscript; others will want to see the entire work before committing to a contract.

Editing a book-length collection involves an additional stage, probably between the initial query and proposal, where the editor lines up the chapter authors. Sometimes, that can happen through direct invitation; other times, the editor will put out a call for proposals, and potential authors will submit an abstract along with biographical information. The editor has to try to balance types of proposals in terms of content, but also in terms of contributors—ideally, an edited collection brings a variety of voices together in a coherent conversation. It is the editor's responsibility to keep contributors to the timelines, provide constructive feedback along the way, and prepare the manuscript for peer review.

Like article-length pieces, scholarly book-length projects, whether monographs or edited collections, are sent to experts for peer review. So, essentially, you have to convince two different groups of the importance of your work: the acquisitions editors of a press who are primarily concerned with who might be interested in reading the work and the subject matter experts who are primarily concerned with the content and how it is presented. The first type of review is not anonymous; the second usually is. Once the reviews are back, authors will revise and resubmit—leading, hopefully, to the next steps of copyediting, indexing, and production.

All of this takes more time and energy than you would expect. Indeed, it's common for a book-length project to take years to come to completion. And depending on your disciplinary norms and where you are in your career, that may or may not be a good use of your time. In particular, pre-tenure academics are often advised not to edit a collection (Kelsky, 2012; Chapnick & Kukucha, 2016). However, the process of writing a book or editing a book-length collection affords a tremendous opportunity to delve deeply into a particular area and to contribute to important conversations. We have learned so much in the process of writing this book, not only about SoTL methods and methodologies but about ourselves and our underlying assumptions about scholarship.

Key Concepts

- Attitudes towards writing are shaped in part by our disciplinary identities.
- Teaching and Learning conferences are an important way to disseminate what we have learned and can provide feedback we use when writing for publication.
- When writing for publication, consider what genre you are interested in and where you might publish it.
- Common article-length genres include research articles, conceptual essays, and scholarly reflections. These genres can be published in journals or as chapters in edited collections, but not all publication venues will accept all genres.
- Books and edited collections allow for more in-depth exploration, but require sustained engagement.

Further Reading

Healey, M. *et al.* (2020). *Writing about teaching and learning in higher education: Creating and contributing to scholarly conversations across a range of genres.* Elon University Center for Engaged Learning. https://www.centerforengagedlearning.org/books/writing-about-learning/.

Jaakkola. E. (2020). Designing conceptual articles: Four approaches. *AMS Review*, 10(1–2), 18–26. https://doi.org/10.1007/s13162-020-00161-0.

Suber, P. (2012). *Open access.* The MIT Press. https://library.oapen.org/handle/20.500.12657/26065.

Sword, H. (2012). *Stylish academic writing.* Harvard University Press.

Sword, H. (2017). *Air & light & time & space: How successful academics write.* Harvard University Press.

13

COMMUNICATING VISUALLY

Ideas and Data

This chapter continues the discussion about dissemination and presentation of SoTL research, with a focus on displaying ideas and data visually. We discuss how visuals and data can and should be presented differently in different venues, while still maintaining alignment with the underlying philosophical assumptions and goals of the research.

The goal of any visual representation is to be clear, useful, and memorable, and visual representations can make a message more memorable than simply communicating it by text alone (Baddeley, 1999). Using visual strategies to communicate information is relatively common in the STEM and social science fields, likely due to their traditional use of figures to display data. That said, scholars from all disciplines are likely to be presenting their work at conferences on slides and posters, and online venues that require more attention to visual details. As with all other steps in the research process, the underlying assumptions of a chosen methodology will influence how a researcher presents their ideas and findings to an academic audience. The needs and expectations of the audience in terms of style and detail will also differ depending on the form of dissemination. Below, we describe different ways visuals can be used to portray key ideas of a study such as procedures and structures, and common ways of visually presenting quantitative, qualitative, and mixed methods data.

Presenting Ideas Visually

As we have tried to show throughout this book, diagrams can be useful to visually portray complex concepts such as processes and structures. Infographics, visual abstracts, and video abstracts can also help make your work more easily found in online searches, and journals are starting to encourage them as

DOI: 10.4324/9781003447054-17

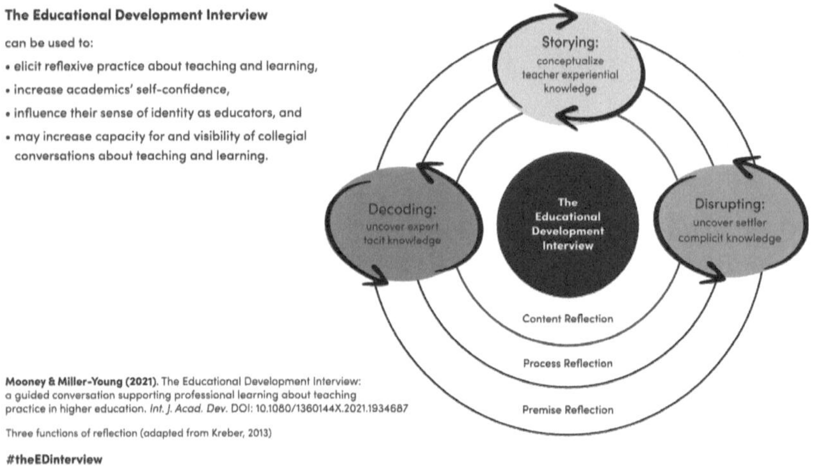

FIGURE 13.1 A visual abstract created to accompany an article, as requested by the journal, including a brief textual summary of purpose, graphic of the conceptual framework, and abbreviated citation.

supplementary materials (Figure 13.1). The field of data visualization is relatively new, and there is an ever-expanding set of resources online with recommendations for making effective visuals; we encourage scholars to explore them. In this section we will focus on portraying processes and concepts visually, with key considerations based on your chosen methodology and audience.

Flow Diagrams

Research processes and theories of change can be represented by flow diagrams and sometimes this is quite necessary. For example, the logic model developed for a self-study of a Center for Teaching and Learning was so complex that it could not be easily explained in words (Miller-Young & Poth, 2021). In this book, we have used flow diagrams to show both linear and iterative quantitative and qualitative data analysis processes (Chapters 7 and 8), as well as the main steps in three common mixed method research designs (Chapter 9). Another example from a published, quantitative SoTL study is Schönwetter et al. (2016), which provides a flowchart to show the order and procedures of the study, including the random assignment of students into groups, the intervention, and several phases of data collection. In a qualitative study by von der Heidt (2015), a decision tree was used to show the scoring protocol in a multi-researcher analysis of concept maps. For researchers considering using a diagram to communicate a process, review online resources and published examples for inspiration, and consider whether the process you want to represent is linear, circular or iterative, convergent or divergent, or multidirectional.

Structural Diagrams

Portraying relevant frameworks and structural connections between concepts can also be done visually and these are quite common in the SoTL literature. For example, theoretical and conceptual frameworks can be used to graphically show the main factors or variables in a study, and their presumed interrelationships. In a study of the effects of prior knowledge on text comprehension, McCarthy and McNamara (2021) display their framework, which identifies four key dimensions of knowledge that are relevant for comprehension, as a modified Venn diagram. They also display levels of specificity as a hierarchical tree, and conceptually as a three-dimensional cone, narrowing from general knowledge to topic knowledge. Concept maps are another common example that visually communicate someone's understanding of complex ideas and can therefore be used as a teaching, assessment, research, and/or communication tool (e.g., Kinchin et al., 2010). Finally, Venn diagrams, such as the one we presented in the Preface of this book, show how concepts or populations may overlap, highlighting differences and commonalities. Again, review many examples and also consider what kind of connectedness you want to portray—is your concept or structure best represented by a hierarchical tree, a hub with spokes, a linked chain, a ladder, a braid, layers, clusters, a web, a network, or a rhizome?

In summary, diagrams can be used as part of the research process, and as an effective communication tool. They can help portray complex ideas and need not be overly reductionist; they can be simple or elaborate, descriptive or causal. Focus on using them for the key messages you want to convey.

Presenting Quantitative Data

In quantitative research, researchers present comprehensive summaries of the data, rather than raw data, using tabular and graphical displays. These formats allow researchers to concisely portray as much information as possible about the data as a whole. A general rule is to portray the information only once; for example, do not use a table and a graph that show the same information, and do not write accompanying text for a figure that communicates all the same information as the figure. Rather, the text should typically include a descriptive summary of the figure or table and then go beyond that to offer explanations and interpretations. However, as Moore (2018) suggests, "If we are trying to make a complex research finding accessible to our international, multidisciplinary audience, we might present our results in multiple ways, such as written text, tables, and figures" (p. 122). The descriptions of types of tables and figures below are intended to help researchers choose the right format for what they want to portray; examples are provided using the same studies as described in Chapter 7.

Summarizing with Tables

Often, a table is the most useful for summarizing statistical results because it can portray a large amount of information. Typically, descriptive statistics would be presented in one table, and there would be an additional table for each inferential test conducted. For example, Schönwetter et al. (2016) present their one-way ANOVA results comparing traditional online vs. lecture delivery in one table, and the ANOVA results for pre-post assessments of recall and recognition in two additional tables. Each variable has its own column in a table. Table titles provide as complete a description as possible, and should contain any additional information that is not in the table, such as sample size or significance levels. In order to get a sense of the level of detail expected, look up some examples in your target journal and consult the relevant citation style guide.

Visualizing with Figures

Typically, figures such as graphs and charts don't portray as much information as a table; however, they are more useful for conveying trends and relationships amongst variables. Note that, because quantitative researchers are typically expected to be as objective as possible in their data collection, analysis, and presentation, figures for scholarly articles typically convey only essential facts without any distracting details. Figures should be used intentionally based on variables and types of scales used, and the type of relationship or trend you want to portray.

Percentages and Frequencies (for Data from Categorical Scales)

Examples of categorical data include the demographics of participants and responses to Likert scale questions. Both can be expressed as percentages if the latter is reported as a relative frequency. Both pie charts and bar charts are useful to report percentages.

- Pie charts and ring charts are better for showing large differences in percentages because too many categories can make them difficult to read (Figure 13.2a);
- Bar charts convey the information more precisely because the relative size of each category can more easily be determined by the viewer (e.g., Barrett et al., 2021), and can be particularly useful for larger data sets. Stacked bar charts can be used to convey even more information in one figure, if necessary (Figure 13.2b and c).

Descriptive Statistics

As discussed in Chapter 7, simply presenting averages for different variables and or groups is meaningless unless your audience knows something about the distribution of the data. Common ways of showing information about distribution are histograms, standard deviation bars, and box and whisker plots.

- Histograms are bar charts used to show distribution of a variable in a data set. This could include categorical data as well as continuous data which is put into "bins" by creating researcher-specified ranges. The variable is typically presented on the y-axis and categories or ranges on the x-axis. As discussed in Chapter 7, histograms are a simple way to determine and/or show whether your data is normally distributed.
- At a minimum, standard deviation (SD) bars should be used when presenting continuous data to give a sense of the distribution of the data (Figure 13.2b).
- Box and whisker plots include much more information about the spread and centers of a variable in a data set. As described in Chapter 7, measures of central tendency (such as the mean) are meaningless without providing some information about the distribution of the data. Therefore, a plot usually contains five pieces of information: the minimum, median, and maximum score in a data set (shown with "whiskers"), with the box ranging from the first to the third quartile (Figure 13.2d). In their study of students' interactions with online material in a blended delivery course, Watson et al. (2020) used three different box whisker plots to portray the multiple differences between mean and distribution measures of students' course grades, number of online objects accessed, and total number of online actions taken over five consecutive offerings of a course.

Trends and Relationships between Variables (Data from Continuous Scales)

- Line graphs are used to show change in a variable(s) over time, with time on the horizontal axis (Figure 13.2e).
- Scatter plots are used to show relationships between two variables, with data points represented as dots; the line of best fit is also typically shown, and correlation coefficients, confidence intervals, and other relevant statistical information provided in the figure caption (Figure 13.2f). Watson et al. (2020) also used scatter plots to portray distribution and correlations between students' grade in a course and year in their program.

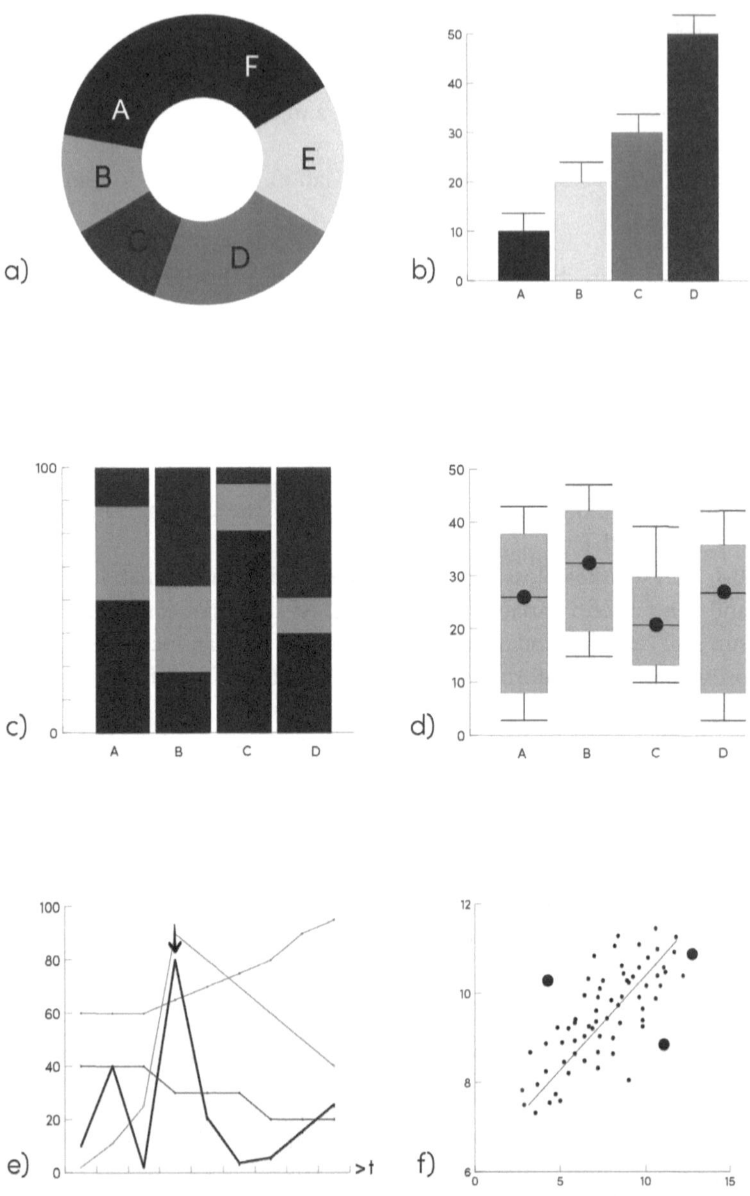

FIGURE 13.2 Examples of different types of figures, also showing strategies to emphasize an aspect of the data: a) ring chart with one category emphasized using color/hash lines; b) bar chart, showing SDs and emphasizing one category using color/hash lines; c) stacked bar chart; d) box and whisker plot with median indicated using bold dot; e) line graph with bold line emphasizing one data set, and arrow emphasizing peak; f) scatter plot with outliers emphasized in bold.

Focusing Attention Visually

In writing up quantitative research, the explanatory text is used to draw the reader's attention to the most important or surprising findings, but the tables and figures should be simple in order portray the data without any subjective interpretation. However, the opposite is the case in slide presentations, posters, and other venues where the accompanying text is not presented. In these cases, the purpose is usually not to summarize all the data, but to communicate conclusions and important insights. Therefore, think carefully about the main message(s) you want to convey, and don't be as concerned about being comprehensive. Because of their visual nature, figures are usually more appropriate than tables. Additionally, it can be useful to highlight important findings using color, arrows, and bold lines and fonts (Figure 13.2). If you expect your audience may want further information, provide them with a link to a website or a handout with supplementary information, or offer to follow up by email.

Presenting Qualitative Data

Unlike quantitative research, where it is relatively easy to present summaries of the data, qualitative data is not easy to "see" as a whole and therefore requires systematic distillation of the full data set into an arrangement which communicates your research process and findings in a credible and trustworthy way. From our experience, a quick scan of any SoTL journal is likely to show that the most common way of presenting qualitative data is to organize them by theme, with representative raw data such as quotes or artifacts of student work, as well as accompanying text that offers explanations of what the data demonstrates and how it informs the theme. In this section, we go beyond this common strategy to describe three visual formats for presenting qualitative data.

Thematic Maps

Thematic maps are discussed in Chapter 8 as an outcome of qualitative empirical analysis, where conceptually the researcher moves from coding, to categorizing, to theming and developing a thematic map of the data. These maps look similar to structural diagrams but are meant to show connections more than structures such as hierarchies (Figure 13.3). It is common to discuss this process, and the resulting themes, but less common to show them visually, although we're not sure why. It may be a lack of confidence on the part of SoTL researchers new to this approach, or that researchers doing thematic analysis tend to be more text-focused. One SoTL study on student perceptions of academic feedback shows a worked example of the

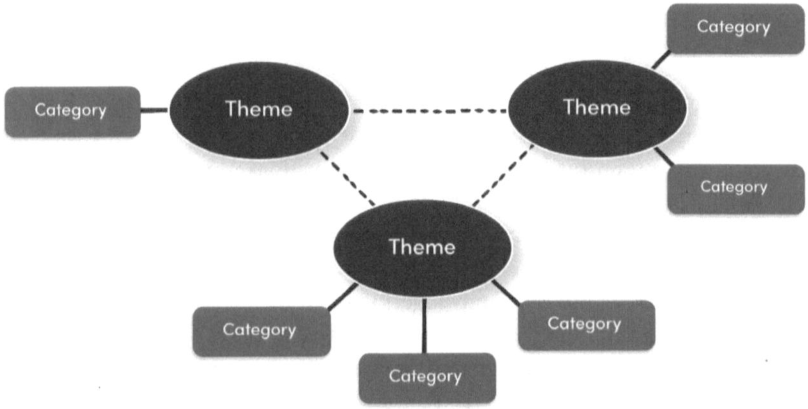

FIGURE 13.3 A thematic map showing connections between categories and themes.

coding process as well as a final thematic map that illustrates the relationships between themes (Maguire & Delahunt, 2017). Several other articles about the process of thematic analysis show initial and final versions of thematic maps, which SoTL researchers may find useful (see Braun & Clarke, 2006; Byrne, 2022). Note that Software such as N-Vivo will create a map automatically that then can be tweaked and adjusted by the researcher, although software is certainly not necessary.

Matrices

A matrix is essentially a table, with rows and columns, although the former term is more common in qualitative research (likely because "matrix" has a different and specific meaning in mathematics). The format and content of the matrix will depend on what you are trying to portray, but the rows and columns are likely to include participants, groups, and/or data sources, as well as the variables, codes, categories, or themes from the analysis, while the cells could include quotes, phrases, descriptions, explanations, or inferential remarks (Miles et al., 2014). This can be a useful way to communicate that the conclusions are drawn from the full data set, in other words the full range of participants and data sources. Creswell and Poth (2018) recommend no more than five or six rows and columns; if this is not enough then create groups or multiple displays if necessary.

Networks

Networks are similar to the thematic and concept maps we described above, except that they are more broad in their scope; they can be used to display complex interrelationships between events, processes, and variables, thus telling a narrative in a visual form (Miles et al., 2014). Networks consist of a collection of nodes, representing variables and events, connected by lines or arrows, to signify directionality and interactive effects. A network diagram might also be called a model. Although not commonly used in SoTL, we encourage researchers to experiment with network diagrams to help understand and explain the complex nature of teaching and learning.

Focusing Attention Visually

Methodologically, most visual formats transform qualitative data into quantifiable categories—an approach that can be opposite to the goals of many qualitative researchers. However, we encourage SoTL researchers to experiment with visual formats, especially in posters and presentations. Similar to presenting quantitative research in these formats, the emphasis should be on key messages rather than comprehensive descriptions of processes and findings, with the balance between narrative and visuals depending on the researcher, the study, and the audience. Integrating process and structural diagrams, as discussed above, with representative data such as quotes offer a rich array of possibilities. Other options include using icons to accompany themes, and the use of visual metaphors (Verdinelli & Scagnoli, 2013).

Word clouds are an interesting way to mix qualitative and quantitative approaches to presenting data. A qualitative source of data can be converted to quantitative data by categorizing the data and analyzing frequencies of categories; a word cloud then shows frequencies through the relative size of the words. Word clouds can be very effective in slide and poster presentations. We know of at least one SoTL researcher who tried to use a word cloud in a scholarly publication, to show frequency of use of certain terms in a systematic literature review. Reviewers felt the format was not precise enough for presenting the results. Perhaps this is because, similar to the issues with a pie chart, it can be difficult to interpret visually if there are too many categories. Or perhaps it was the reviewers' disciplinary biases. A word cloud might be very appropriate if there are not too many categories and if there are large enough differences in frequencies; a legend, color, or labels could also be included in order to provide additional information about quantitative differences if that is important for answering the research question. Again, we encourage SoTL researchers to think carefully about what findings are most important to portray, and to experiment and push boundaries while staying true to their methodological goals. As Miles et al. (2014) write, "**Think display.** Adapt and invent formats that will serve you best" (emphasis in original, p. 114).

Presenting Mixed Method Findings

As we alluded to in Chapter 9, mixed methods researchers have developed research designs and data analysis procedures that involve multiple phases and sources of data, as well as methods for integrating both quantitative and qualitative findings (Creswell & Plano Clark, 2017). Because of this additional complexity and emphasis on integration, new forms of "integrated joint displays" have also been developed which bring both the quantitative findings and qualitative findings together in one visual. The goal is not only to present the findings, but to visually demonstrate the integration of the data and how the integration led to new insights above and beyond what would have emerged from either quantitative or qualitative methodologies separately. We believe these formats could also be useful for, and adapted by, SoTL researchers conducting mixed methods as well as other types of complex studies, such as qualitative empirical studies and case studies, which often triangulate multiple sources of data. For more inspiration, we recommend Creswell and Plano Clark (2017) as a resource as well as dedicated journals such as the *Journal of Mixed Methods Research.*

Complex concepts and relationships, research processes, and data can all be displayed visually. How researchers do so will depend on their methodology, message, intended audience, and dissemination venue. While there are general guidelines and common practices for quantitative, qualitative, and mixed methods research, we encourage SoTL researchers to experiment with new strategies, especially when presenting their work in conference and online venues where effective visual representations can be especially valuable.

Key Concepts

- Consider both research methodology and venue when deciding how to present concepts and data.
- Accompanying text should expand upon the visual representation, not repeat it.
- Flow charts and structural charts are useful for portraying processes and frameworks, respectively.
- Quantitative data can be comprehensively summarized in tables and figures.
- Choice of figure will depend on the type of quantitative data (categorical or continuous) as well as the key message.
- Visual presentation of qualitative processes and data can support trustworthiness of the findings, for example by showing a coding process or the triangulation of multiple data sources.
- Mixed methods findings are presented using integrated joint displays.

Further Reading

Clarke, V. (2022). Navigating the messy swamp of qualitative research: Are generic reporting standards the answer? *Qualitative Research in Psychology*, 19(4), 1004–1012. https://doi.org/10.1080/14780887.2021.1995555.

Knaflic, C. (2015). *Storytelling with data: A data visualization guide for business professionals.* John Wiley & Sons.

Guetterman, T. C., Fetters, M. D., & Creswell, J. W. (2015). Integrating quantitative and qualitative results in health science mixed methods research through joint displays. *The Annals of Family Medicine*, 13(6), 554–561.

Levitt, H. M., Bamberg, M., Creswell, J. W., Frost, D. M., Josselson, R., & Suárez-Orozco, C. (2018). Journal article reporting standards for qualitative primary, qualitative meta-analytic, and mixed methods research in psychology: The APA Publications and Communications Board task force report. *American Psychologist*, 73(1), 26–46. http://dx.doi.org/10.1037/amp0000151.

Verdinelli, S., & Scagnoli, N. I. (2013). Data display in qualitative research. *International Journal of Qualitative Methods*, 12(1), 359–381. https://doi.org/10.1177/160940691301200117.

14

AMPLIFYING YOUR RESEARCH

> An important part of scholarship is not only adding to knowledge, but also contributing to change beyond our own practice. We want others to know about, use, and build upon our work. In this chapter we assume the SoTL researcher has conducted and disseminated a study through a traditional scholarly venue that involves peer review. This chapter will address how they can broaden the impact of their work through non-traditional forms of dissemination.

SoTL researchers are interested in advancing teaching through better understanding of student learning. Aligning with the goals of the various types of studies we present in this book as well as Booth and Woollacott's (2018) analysis of the current domains of SoTL, we suggest that the act of inquiry itself can have multiple benefits such as improving or affecting teaching and learning locally, contributing to knowledge, improving or transforming relationships between various stakeholders, and addressing issues of power, ethics, and inequalities. In our work with SoTL practitioners, we have also witnessed it reinvigorate teaching. But how can we go beyond improving local practice to make an impact beyond our own context?

Chick (2022) recommends thinking about impact from three different audience's perspectives: teachers and scholars, students and other stakeholders within higher education, and broader society. This is not an easy problem to tackle because the focus of our work has to be relevant to a particular audience, and we need to know how to frame our message in a way that the audience will take it up. This chapter will explore the why, who, and how of amplifying the results of your inquiries, but from the perspective of engaging in dissemination beyond the academic genres discussed in Chapter 12. We will share some simple strategies we have found helpful for

DOI: 10.4324/9781003447054-18

getting the results and products of one's research into the hands of others who will benefit, with colleagues and students as primary audiences, but also considering the broader public when appropriate. These strategies are also about engaging in the larger teaching commons as described in Chapter 1.

Why Amplify?

There are three important reasons to amplify your work. The first is to build recognition of your contributions as a scholar, so that others seek out your conference presentations and published work. Of course it is strategic to increase the visibility of your work for your own career development, but from the point of view of the development of the field, you have important insights to share that you've put a lot of time, effort, and potentially funding into gaining. It becomes, then, a responsibility not only to disseminate, but to share in less formal venues with your academic colleagues. Second, as a form of applied research, there are many stakeholders who can benefit from your insights who are unlikely to attend teaching and learning conferences or read scholarly articles, whether these are students, instructors who are not (for now) SoTL engaged, or where relevant, people in the community. Third, expanding our relationships and networks is part of how we as professionals learn, and knowing that our work has an impact is in itself rewarding; as O'Meara et al. (2008) conceptualize these aspects of faculty work, they are "synergistic and self-reinforcing" (p. 32).

Getting our scholarship into the hands of others who will benefit from it is commonly called "knowledge translation" in the health sciences and "knowledge mobilization" in the social sciences and professions (e.g., Nowell & Friberg, 2022). Traditionally, these models conceptualize the "stakeholders" as being separate communities from those involved in the research itself. This may or may not be the case depending on the nature of your SoTL work. As we will explore below, stakeholders, or possible audiences as we call them, could include academic audiences, as well as members of the broader public. For those using community-engaged pedagogies or Students-as-Partners approaches, the terms "translation" and "mobilization" may not even make sense, because their audiences are already directly engaged in their work. Also, knowledge mobilization models emphasize "impact," which of course, as many have written about, is very difficult to prove in the complex environment of higher education (e.g., Kezar, 2018; Verwoord & Poole, 2016; Miller-Young & Poth, 2021). As Janice and a colleague wrote in the context of a CTL self-study, positivistic assumptions of linear cause and effect cannot be applied in complex systems which "conceptualize learning as occurring within constantly changing and embedded contexts as diverse as the individuals themselves … In such a complex context, where many factors and variables interact, the outcomes of activities are not only unpredictable but often unknown" (Miller-Young & Poth, 2021, p. 2). What mobilization logic models do have in common, though, is the necessity of building relationships with additional audiences beyond those directly involved in your work, and of course responding and engaging with those who are interested in your work, in order to facilitate uptake (Figure 14.1).

Because of the importance and interrelatedness of audience and message, it can be helpful to start by thinking about the questions listed below (adapted from Kreber, 2007b; Mollet et al., 2017; Chick & Friberg, 2022; Moore et al., 2022):

- What topics and foci within the SoTL landscape do I want to focus on and be known for? What positionality do I choose to adopt?
- What new knowledge, applications, relationships, and/or questions do I want my SoTL work to generate?
- Who are the audiences or "stakeholders" who would benefit?
- How or why might they benefit? How does this move the field forward?
- How can I make my content usable, adaptable, actionable, and shareable by others, given the contextual nature of teaching and learning?
- What venues can I use to make my SoTL work visible and useful for them? How do I know I've made a difference?

Thinking about these questions is useful at the beginning and throughout the entire research process in order to engage with broader and multiple audiences, as appropriate. According to Mollet et al. (2017), the biggest questions to focus on, and the easiest to ignore, are the questions about who your audience is and what you'd like them to do with the content you provide.

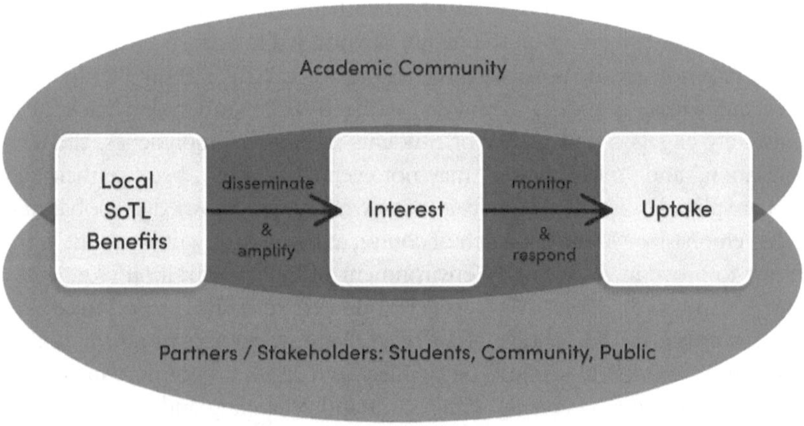

FIGURE 14.1 A logic model for amplifying SoTL, adapted from Phipps et al. (2016).

Audiences for SoTL

Students as a Primary Audience

SoTL is somewhat unique in the academy in the sense that students are the primary participants and hopefully beneficiaries of the work. Yet without some careful planning, it would be possible for students to be largely unaware of the results of the scholarship and the changes to the design of their learning experience that may have resulted. A research assistant, traveling with one of us to a SoTL conference, was astonished to see hundreds of professors gathering to discuss teaching and learning. When we thought about this astonishment, we realized that unless a professor goes out of their way to be transparent about the scholarly aspects of their pedagogy and any SoTL work they may engage in, students have no way of knowing about it. Professors may mention that they attend conferences, whether it is a SoTL conference or a disciplinary based one, but may not think to describe what they learned.

A number of scholars such as Kreber (2007a) and McKinney (2012) have argued that students should be explicitly included as part of the audience for SoTL. McKinney suggests that in so doing, we might support students in finding ways of improving their own learning, thus increasing their agency. Like Felten, Kreber says that SoTL should be disseminated in venues "that reach those audiences that are most likely to appreciate and build on it" (p. 6), but adds that students should be considered essential to this audience. Maurer et al. (2021) argue that intentionally sharing findings with students is a critical form of knowledge mobilization for SoTL. They suggest that first and foremost, sharing SoTL with students is a means of demonstrating care for students and their learning, which, they point out, "is an ethical imperative for teachers" (p. 337).

Maurer et al. (2021) put forward a framework for thinking about sharing SoTL with students in three ways: "sharing as *dissemination*, sharing as *translation*, and sharing as *co-creation*" (pp. 335–336). In their formulation, dissemination means sharing results of SoTL work (both your own and the work of others) with students, "positioning students as recipients of knowledge or, in knowledge mobilization terms, as the 'end user'" (p. 336). Translation takes the important step of intentionally translating these results into practice, ideally involving students in this redesign. Finally, in co-creation, a transformative Students-as-Partners approach is undertaken (as described in Chapter 11), where students become co-inquirers throughout the life of the project, where "students influence the process of generating as well as sharing and co-owning the outcome" (p. 336). Congruent with this transformative paradigm, the intent here is to disrupt "traditional hierarchies and power structures between teachers and students" (p. 337). Students become knowledge generators rather than mere consumers.

Even for work that is not co-created, consider what students might want to know about you if you were recruiting them for a study or hiring them as a research assistant. What previous work have you done and what impact did it have? What is the goal of your current work? You might mention this work in class as a means of sharing why your course is designed the way it is, or you might consider telling this story through the content on your academic website, as a few examples.

Academic Community

As SoTL researchers, relying on our colleagues to simply find us at conferences or in the literature is not sufficient, and we must consider ways we can amplify our findings through other strategies. There are multiple groups comprising your academic audience, and while certain strategies such as social media might reach multiple audiences at the same time (more on that below), for others you may need to tailor your approach for reaching each one. This can feel overwhelming, but remember that you may want to focus on a different audience at different stages in the research process.

In the special issue of *New Directions in Teaching and Learning, The Scholarship of Teaching and Learning: Institutional Impact* (Simmons, 2016), several articles attempted to frame different ways of thinking about levels of influence or "impact" in SoTL (see, for example, Kenny et al., 2016; Wutherick & Yu, 2016). We now try to avoid a focus on using the term impact, for reasons explained above in relation to knowledge mobilization—a simplistic cause-and-effect relationship is difficult to measure (Miller-Young & Poth, 2021; Verwoord & Poole, 2016). In their article in this special issue, Verwoord and Poole (2016) brought together Roxå and Mårtensson's previous work (2009, 2012) on small significant networks in teaching environments, and Williams et al.'s (2013) article describing interactions between the micro, meso, and macro levels of the institution (see also Poole & Simmons, 2013).

In a well-known 2016 blog post, Friberg added a fourth level, the mega, which is at multi-institutional level. This is now referred to ubiquitously in SoTL as the 4M framework (and also demonstrates how non-traditional dissemination of ideas, such as in a blog, can sometimes have enormous influence). In our view, this conceptualization bears a relationship to and is informed by systems theory, which considers open systems as hierarchical and defined by relationships between components (or levels), and are therefore also emergent, in that they can only be described by the system as a whole, not by any of its components independently. One example of systems thinking is Bronfenbrenner's ecological model (1977, 1981), which is heavily drawn upon in K–12 educational theory to understand influences from the opposite direction—of the surrounding contexts on the individual child as they develop. Bronfenbrenner (1981) in his seminal work on the topic considers "how development is to be conceived in the framework of an ecological theory" (p. 27), including the microsystem, macrosystem, exosystem, and megasystem.

In our 'SoTL^2' article (Miller-Young et al., 2016), we also note that what level individuals seemed to describe their potential reach seemed to depend, at least in part, in how long they had been at the institution. We suggest "length of time may indicate career stage, level of security as represented through tenure, and institutional or disciplinary networks outside of the SoTL context". In our subsequent work with developing SoTL scholars we have continued to observe this pattern—that career stage seems to have an important influence on what aspect is of most interest. A recently completed PhD and new faculty member is likely to be focused at the classroom level, while a SoTL engaged chair of department might turn their attention to curriculum. We want to emphasize that one level is not "better" or more desirable than another, and we ourselves travel fluidly between them depending on the nature of the SoTL work we are doing at any given time.

SoTL is different from narrow specializations, where the key new work will be published in a handful of well-known venues—instead, it can disperse across SoTL, DBER, higher education, and faculty development publications. At an individual (micro) level, you might be transforming your own classroom practice. Think about how you can get your good work into the hands of practitioners, like the instructors in the classroom who might want to try the pedagogies you have been studying, or might benefit from the insights you have provided about student learning—this is more at a meso level, especially if we are talking about groups at your own institution. You may want to think about venues, such as asking to present a workshop through your institutional teaching and learning center, or attending local conferences aimed at higher education instructors. One SoTL collaborative writing group called this "leading up," and provide additional strategies to consider, taking into account your own micro level and institutional cultures (Miller-Young et al., 2017).

A further audience is at the institutional level (macro), where your research might influence policy, for example. You might send out relevant findings to leaders in your institution, ask to present at an appropriate committee, or simply seek out informal conversations with colleagues and leaders that might have a stake in the work you have been doing. You might be interested in conducting multi-institutional work, which is what Friberg (2016) describes as the mega level. But we also note the importance of thinking of SoTL contributions to the discipline. This can be your home discipline (thinking of DBER) or it can be SoTL, where you might reach instructors from many different disciplines who might find your research applicable. For this audience, social media can be particularly useful and influential (see below).

Depending on the home academic discipline, many of us as academics carry a feeling that only a small number of other experts will be interested in our highly specialized, niche research. If this describes you, work to challenge this position in yourself when it comes to SoTL. Like other applied research, the point of the work is to bring it out into the light for a broad audience where it can improve practice, provide insight, and encourage others to inquire into teaching and learning.

Public Scholarship

In a recent book *Going Public Reconsidered: Engaging With the World Beyond Academe Through the Scholarship of Teaching and Learning*, Friberg and Chick (2022) note the limits of even the mega level: "the 4M framework positions academia as the outer edge of SoTL's impact" and argue, "we have work to do with how we reach audiences beyond ourselves" (p. 3). Therefore, they suggest a further extension of the 4M framework to include what they call the "ultra" level, by which they mean an audience of the general public beyond higher education. They note the challenge of conceptualizing SoTL as overlapping with public scholarship; after all, scholarship of teaching and learning definitionally is thought of as something applied within the post-secondary context. Making an argument that there is potential for broader application, Friberg and Chick go on to suggest two avenues to pursue for those who wish to step into this arena: engaging in public SoTL to amplify SoTL-generated knowledge, and to inform societal dialogues. Thus, the impetus behind SoTL as public scholarship might be seen in this light to lend itself to the pursuit of social justice and a better world, and educators such as Mays Imad, who explores the role of compassion and trauma-informed pedagogy (e.g., 2022, 2021), but also reclaiming beauty and wonder in education (2019), demonstrating how teaching and learning inquiry can consider larger questions of interest to those outside the academy. This is a current and emerging discussion in SoTL; however, we might think of theorists such as bell hooks, who wrote about educational theory and influenced public discourse (see, for example, *Teaching to Transgress*, 1994).

Chick and Friberg's edited volume (2022) brings together chapters from active and experienced SoTL scholars finding their way towards broader audiences, and includes big idea topics such as social justice, activism, and global knowledge democracy, but also includes practical pieces on leveraging traditional media, social media, and writing blogs. For most SoTL researchers, especially those starting out, reaching a "whole public" is unrealistic and probably not relevant or desirable. However, it is realistic to focus on particular groups, for example, a professional organization, or a school board, or a government agency, or voters in a particular district. Thinking in the terms of knowledge mobilization can be helpful, as discussed earlier in the chapter.

Reaching Multiple Audiences Simultaneously

In the previous sections we have discussed some ways to target specific audiences, such as through conversations with colleagues or by talking about research with students, or leveraging traditional media to reach the broader public. Of course, scholars today are also using a variety of digital tools and social media for research and communication. Social media is another way to get content to a broad audience, which as Mollet et al. (2017) point out "can also include your desired audience—though they are not always one and the same" (p. 14).

One way to think of social media is in terms of content, networks, and tools, with different levels of shareability (Mollet et al., 2017). Content is comprised of your thoughts, reflections, and insights and can be formatted and shared on websites and blog posts, podcasts, infographics and data visualizations, slides, images, and videos. Social networks are the connections that get your content to a broad audience. Some tools, such as Twitter, YouTube, and LinkedIn have content and connectivity built in, whereas content platforms, such as blog posts and websites, require the leveraging of network platforms to share the content. So if sharing your work publicly, you will have to consider students, colleagues, and the broader public as potential audiences simultaneously, although depending on the content you share and the networks you use, one may be more likely than the others. This brings both opportunity and challenge.

Many resources exist for using social media and especially for writing blog posts, and making podcasts and videos (see for example, Moore et al. 2022, Healey et al. 2020, and Mollet et al. 2017). Moore et al.'s chapter in Friberg & Chick (2022) provides concrete details of how to use social media platforms not only for amplifying your work but also tracking interest and uptake through alt-metrics such as number of paper downloads, number of retweets, diversity of social media followers, and more. Sharing visual elements related to your scholarly interests, such as those described in Chapter 13, can help increase the visibility of your communications. As Moore et al. (2022) also emphasize, engaging in social media is not only about amplifying your own work; it is also an effective and flexible way to engage in a broader academic and public conversation about teaching and learning. For example, at most SoTL conferences there is a lively "backchannel" real-time discussion happening (on platforms such as Twitter) during and surrounding presentations. Outside of conferences, social media can be a way to connect with others working in similar interests, seek and provide mentorship, amplify the work of others, and indeed to contribute to the public discourse, as an academic engaged in serious thinking about teaching and learning. There are important professional caveats to consider, as well as your own personal comfort level around privacy, but you will notice that academics who build a strong community and following online often share small glimpses of their personal life (often their pets, for example), which can help increase interest and make connections.

Be aware, also, that building an online network requires a fairly significant investment of time. It requires regular engagement in order to make and sustain the connections. It is also important to stay informed on up-to-date recommendations for making your communications as inclusive as possible, for example by providing transcripts for videos and "alt-text" for images. As a SoTL researcher, you will have to decide who is the best audience for your work, how much additional time you want to invest, and how much of your personal life you want to share. While none of us would claim to be exemplary at building a social media profile, some relatively simple strategies that we ourselves have used include:

- putting a link to our website and our most recent work in our email signature file;
- making small, digestible pieces of already disseminated work (posters, visual representations, images, rubrics, questionnaires, interview protocols, and other supporting files) available (and citable) in easy-to-find, open, and online places;
- creating a Google scholar profile;
- posting pre-prints of a paper in a repository if it is not published open access;
- posting slides before a conference and letting attendees know the link is available; and
- making an image file of an interesting finding or idea, or a visual abstract of a paper, and posting on our website and/or sharing through our networks.

Data from SoTL research could even be shared openly, if appropriate, although this would need to be part of your ethics application.

There are, of course, other cautions to consider. Anything that is co-created, disseminated publicly, and/or leaves a digital footprint should be shared with sensitivity to both the researchers and the researched, and with the awareness that publicly disseminated artifacts could also potentially be used as a source of data for additional research. Further, disseminating publicly can make us vulnerable to attack or at least misrepresentation of our work. Discomfort with who owns social media tools and what their business models are may also give us pause for thought, even platforms that are academically focused such as Academica.edu and ResearchGate. And then there's the possibility of creating echo chambers due to network platforms' algorithms. These complexities present many new challenges for ethical SoTL work and scholarship more broadly. The digital landscape will continue to evolve, but in the meantime some researchers may want to stick to tools provided by not-for-profit organizations and their own institutions. At a minimum, we recommend you get an ORCiD ID, develop your institutionally supported website with key content, including visuals, as well as links to useful resources posted in your institutional repository where they will get a doi and be both searchable and permanently citable.

There are many options available to us as scholars who want our work to have a broad impact. As you begin to share your SoTL work, it can be useful to return to those two important questions: first, what audiences are you intending to reach? And second, how can you make your work easily used, adapted, and shared by others? While traditional modes are still important for those of us working in the academy, there is much to be gained from reaching your colleagues through nimble and non-traditional means, by considering students as not only a potential but a primary audience for your work, and by thinking about what your work might have to contribute to the public sphere beyond academia.

Key Concepts

- Audiences for SoTL include students, colleagues, academic staff, community partners, and the public.
- Consider what audiences might benefit the most from your work, and who you would like it to reach when determining what avenues to pursue in addition to peer-reviewed dissemination.
- Think about how you can make your content usable, adaptable, actionable, and shareable by others, given the contextual nature of teaching and learning.
- Social media is a powerful and versatile tool to reach multiple audiences quickly and in a way that can not only generate interest in your work but provide opportunities for connection.
- The 4M framework (micro, meso, macro, mega) is a useful heuristic for thinking about potential audiences for your work. The ultra level encourages us to think about going beyond academia into public scholarship.

Further Reading

Chick, N. L., & Friberg, J. C. (Eds.). (2022). *Going public reconsidered: Engaging with the world beyond academe through the scholarship of teaching and learning.* Stylus.

Maurer, T. W., Woolmer, C., Powell, N. L., Sisson, C., Snelling, C., Stalheim, O. R., & Turner, I. J. (2021). Sharing SoTL findings with students: An intentional knowledge mobilization strategy. *Teaching and Learning Inquiry*, 9(1), 333–348. https://doi.org/10.20343/teachlearninqu.9.1.22.

McKinney, K. (2012). Increasing the impact of SoTL: Two sometimes neglected opportunities. *International Journal for the Scholarship of Teaching and Learning*, 6(1), Article 3.

McKinney, K. (2007). *Enhancing learning through the scholarship of teaching and learning: The challenges and joys of juggling*. Anker.

Miller-Young, J. E., Anderson, C., Kiceniuk, D., Mooney, J., Riddell, J., Schmidt Hanbidge, A., Ward, V., Wideman, M.A., & Chick, N. (2017). Leading up in the Scholarship of Teaching and Learning. *Canadian Journal for the Scholarship of Teaching and Learning*, 8(2). https://doi-org/10.5206/cjsotl-rcacea.2017.2.4

Mollett, A., Brumley, C., Gilson, C., & Williams, S. (2017). *Communicating your research with social media: A practical guide to using blogs, podcasts, data visualisations and video*. Sage.

Schwier, R. (2020). *SoTL Chat* [Audio podcast]. University of Saskatchewan. https://sotl-uofs.libsyn.com/.

Simmons, N. (Ed.). (2016). *The scholarship of teaching and learning in Canada: Institutional impact. New directions for teaching and learning, 146*. Jossey-Bass.

FINAL THOUGHTS

We hope this book has been useful for both novice and experienced SoTL researchers in conceptualizing, conducting, and communicating their work. We hope that those who have read it will have a greater understanding of the field, the research methodologies available to them, and how that fits with their own discipline. We hope for some, it gives them a start in designing and conducting a SoTL project, while for others it has furthered and deepened their knowledge, and that all have ideas of things they would like to read more about and where to look for such reading. It should be clearer how research methodologies connect to different values, worldviews, and ideas of how the world can be known. We have discussed throughout the importance of solid research ethics—both formal processes but also an informal and continuous orientation, as we recognize the inherent power relationships embedded into the student–instructor relationship.

Early in the book, we explored criteria for judging good SoTL (Felten, 2013) and talked about where good studies begin and how to ground this in a theoretical framework. Towards the end, we explored the importance of sharing results of research and different ways to go about that. However, this book has a particular focus on Felten's (2013) third principle: that SoTL should be methodologically sound. We wanted to provide some high-level theoretical framing of research methodologies and designs on the one hand, as well as practical advice on collecting and analyzing data on the other. All of this, as will be a familiar concept by now, should be considered within a research paradigm framework that takes into account the worldview of the chosen methodology. This choice is based on many considerations: the home discipline of the SoTL researcher, their own comfort level, expertise,

DOI: 10.4324/9781003447054-19

and commitments, and importantly, the research question under investigation. We saw a need for a comprehensive text, which represented the full spectrum of research methodologies represented currently in the field, but also some of the possible directions the field has only begun to explore.

We have attempted to trace definition and developments in the landscape of SoTL, which like any field continues to evolve in real time. However, unlike many disciplines, SoTL is relatively new, with three short decades since what is usually considered its inception in 1990 (Boyer), and out of a growing intensity of interest in post-secondary contexts in scholarly teaching. Because of its newness, it continues to change quite rapidly, so what we have written here is really just a snapshot in time. However, we do not see SoTL as an island, evolving in isolation. Through broad referencing in this book we have tried to make many connections to other disciplines and fields, in particular, educational research and DBER. As explained, we hope that this relationship will continue and strengthen its ties over time, each benefiting from the dialogue. As authors, our own intense dialogue through the process of writing has expanded and enriched our thinking, and thus we know first-hand the value of such conversation. In SoTL, we have the opportunity to work most often in multidisciplinary teams, but this also may extend into truly interdisciplinary work.

We wanted to include as many voices as possible that are active participants in the SoTL landscape, but we need to also go beyond those familiar voices. In the current historical moment, both in SoTL and in the broader society, we are all considering how to be more inclusive, respectful, and porous in our communities, and to seriously think about power, positionality, social justice, and decolonization. If we are serious about this in SoTL, it means taking both a broader and deeper approach to our research methodologies, to the questions we ask, and to who has a place at the table. SoTL is, at its very heart, about students, and engaging with students as equal partners is a critical turn in the SoTL movement. Relinquishing power and our position of expertise does not necessarily come easily to most of us trained in academic disciplines: as Indigenous perspectives teach us, at universities we tend to be disciplined into Western knowledge systems that reproduce power rather than emancipate. Most of us have participated in these systems, as the interpretivists would say, beyond our wanting and doing. But we do have choices; as SoTL researchers we can carefully craft our questions, choose our methodologies wisely, partner with students where possible, take a social justice perspective where needed, question our own positionality, and do rigorous work as asked of us by the methods we choose. We can creatively get our good work and insights into the hands of those who need them. We can think deeply about how our work can contribute to better teaching and learning in classrooms, to better programs, better universities, and if we're very lucky, a more just society and better world.

GLOSSARY

Analysis	The process of examining something complex by breaking it into smaller parts.
Analytic memo	Notes recorded by researchers during the entire research process from project conception through analysis and dissemination. These notes document thoughts, questions, and decisions.
Artifact	An object or performance created by an individual or group.
A priori codes	Labels that were developed before examining the current data set.
Attribute codes	Labels giving essential demographic information.
Basic Qualitative Research	Also called generic qualitative research. An interpretive approach that uses reflexive thematic analysis to understand how people interpret their experiences and the meaning they make of them in relation to a phenomenon.
Bias	A systematic error in data, typically due to a measurement or sampling error in quantitative research. In qualitative research, bias refers to a perceptive lens that colors the data analysis.
Category	A group of codes sharing particular characteristics.
Code	A label applied to a segment of data. Codes can either be data-derived or researcher-derived.

DOI: 10.4324/9781003447054-20

Coding	A process of organizing, labeling, identifying patterns, and finding relationships within a data set. In first cycle coding methods, the researcher is working with data directly; in second cycle coding methods, the researcher is working with the codes that have already been generated.
Coherence	A criteria for judging qualitative research, the different elements of the research process (question, methodology, data analysis) are aligned and connect to the literature.
Concept	A theoretical idea which is used to explain and predict a phenomenon (e.g., the behavior of individuals or groups, such as attitude, motivation, etc.).
Consistency	The findings are consistent with the data collected.
Constant comparison	A method of coding where the first participant's data is collected and coded before moving on to the next, which is compared to the first, and so on. The codes evolve and change as the analysis proceeds.
Content analysis	An empirical qualitative method that identifies recurring content in the data set.
Correlation	A linear relationship between variables.
Credibility	The findings are seen as believable by participants and audience
Critical	A worldview that examines and interprets the world in terms of power relationships; we experience multiple subjective realities depending on our social location.
Critical realism	A worldview that integrates subjectivist and objectivist perspectives, a theory driven approach interested in context, stratified explanations of phenomena.
Data	Pieces of information.
Deduction	using general principles or theory to make inferences about specific instances.
Disciplinary-based educational research	Research on teaching and learning using discipline-based perspectives.
Empirical	based on observations, viewed through a relatively transparent lens.

Epistemology	System of knowledge, reflecting an understanding of the nature of knowledge and how the world can be known.
Ethics	Moral principles that regulate behavior. For research involving human participants, common ethical principles are respect, concern for well-being, and justice.
Ethnography	A qualitative research methodology that uses thick description to make meaning of culture.
Focus group	A type of group interview involving a small number of participants.
Generalizability	The extent to which the research findings apply beyond the sample or study from which the findings were generated. Analytical generalizability – the generalizability of findings or theory to settings outside of a particular study (also see external validity). Statistical generalizability – generalizability of measurements or observations of a sample to the rest of the population from which a sample is intended to represent (also see internal validity).
Genre	A category of communication with agreed-upon parameters.
Grounded theory	An approach to research that uses theoretical sampling and the constant comparison method to inductively build theory from data.
Hegemony	Societal structures that legitimate inequitable power relationships.
Hermeneutics	A research methodology focused on the art of interpretation and the role of insight and language, often conducts conversational interviews, interested in dialogues and the relationship of experience to texts. Also, a philosophical tradition and related to phenomenology.
Heuristic	A conceptual structure to aid thinking, based on experience.
Idiographic	Relates to the unique, concrete, specific, and contingent.
In vivo codes	Labels using the participants' own words.
Indicator	an observable behavior that is assumed to be related to the concept of interest.

Indigenous research methodologies	Based on Indigenous knowledge that is holistic and resists categorization by Western knowledge systems, based on relational ethics and a worldview that prioritizes interconnectedness.
Induction	Using specific instances to make inferences about a general principle or theory.
Inference	An opinion or interpretation based upon data or accepted premises.
Instrument	A measurement tool such as a rubric or questionnaire.
Interpretive	Worldview that sees the world as multiple contextual realities interpreted by individuals who then co-construct knowledge.
Internal consistency	A measure of how well items on a quantitative instrument relate to the concept being measured (usually using Cronbach's alpha).
Interdisciplinary	Combining two or more disciplines.
Interrater reliability	The extent to which two or more individuals would assign the same code or score to an item.
Interview	A conversation between two or more individuals designed to elicit qualitative data about the research topic. Interviews can be categorized as structured, semi-structured, or unstructured depending on the amount of freedom interviewer and interviewee(s) have in shaping the conversation.
Item-total-correlation	A measure of how well a single item correlates with the total score of a concept being measured.
Intrarater reliability	The extent to which a rater is consistent with their decisions over time.
Knowledge mobilization	Making research results accessible to stakeholders who can use them in practice (more commonly used term in social science).
Knowledge translation	Making research results understandable to a public audience (more commonly used in health science and science).
Latent content	Underlying meaning that must be inferred from the content.
Manifest content	Easily identifiable content or meaning.
Method	description of how the participants were selected and how the data was collected and analyzed.

Methodology	Underlying design or approach used, rooted in the research paradigm. It articulates the world view of the researcher for the purposes of the study.
Mixed methods	A research approach that integrates both quantitative and qualitative methodologies, either concurrently or sequentially.
Multidiscipinary	Involving multiple disciplines.
Narrative inquiry	A research methodology that gathers participant stories to make sense of a phenomenon, focused on how the participant makes meaning of their experiences through narrating them.
Normal distribution	The theoretical distribution of mean scores for a variable, with the mean, median and mode at the centre.
Objectivity	The research process and findings are intended to be independent of the researcher.
Observation	The process of gathering information through the senses
Ontology	Understanding of the nature of reality.
Open access	Work that is published online with reduced barriers to access.
Paradigm	A systematic perspective on the nature of knowledge and the world shared by a research community, including beliefs, values, and practices.
Parametric tests	Statistical tests that assume a normal distribution of data.
Peer review	A quality assurance process for academic publishing where work is sent to experts in the field for their comments about whether it should be published.
Phenomenography	An empirical qualitative method that tries to map variation.
Phenomenology	An interpretive research methodology that typically conducts interviews and attempts to understand some essence of lived human experience in relation to a phenomenon. Interested in the senses and embodiment. Also a philosophical tradition.
Photo-voice	A data gathering technique that involves participants taking pictures of and then explaining the significance of particular objects or scenes.

Population (types)	See below examples Sample population – the group of individuals studied. Target population – a group of individuals, with the defining characteristics of the population of interest, that the researcher can identify and recruit from. Population (of interest) – the population that the researcher would like to be able to generalize their findings to.
Positionality	Articulation of the researcher's identity, role, context, and relationship to the research question.
Positivism	Worldview that there is a single, knowable, observable reality that is independent of the context or observer.
Postmodernism	A deconstructive worldview that there are multiple realities and attempts to disrupt grand narratives, rejecting unifying theories.
Post-positivism	Worldview that there is a single observable reality that can only be imperfectly known.
Problem statement	A statement that defines the issue attempting to be addressed through research.
Public scholarship	Reaching an audience beyond academia, the general public.
Purpose statement	A statement defining what the research project sets out to accomplish.
Qualitative	Research that is interested in qualities and complexity.
Quantitative	Research that is interested in reducing complexity in order to find patterns amongst variables and populations.
Questionnaire	An instrument for collecting self-report data from participants, consisting of a series of closed and/or open-ended questions.
Reflection	The process of and ideas resulting from careful consideration.
Reflexive thematic analysis	A qualitative method of coding that values researcher subjectivity, transparency, and self-reflection throughout the process.
Reliability	The extent to which an instrument produces the same result if used multiple times (precision).
Replicability	The extent to which, if the same study is repeated, the findings will be the same.

Research question	A question that directs the research inquiry; it should be specific about context and phrased in such a way that the question is answerable and not a yes/no question.
Research design	A plan for how the research will be carried out.
Research process	articulation of all phases of the research, from design to dissemination.
Resonance	A criteria for judging qualitative research, the research is seen as evocative and connects to the reader's experience, potentially transferable.
Sampling (types)	See below examples Probability sampling – the researcher randomly selects participants from the target population in order to minimize the possibility of bias. Convenience sampling – the researcher selects participants because they are available and agree to participate (a form of non-probability sampling). Snowball sampling – the researcher asks participants to identify others, or pass along to others the invitation, to participate in the study (a form of non-probability sampling).
Sampling error	Error that occurs due to the sample population having different characteristics than the target population.
Saturation	The point at which additional data will not provide additional information or insight.
Scale	Type of measurement *or* a validated instrument that measures a specific construct. Categorical scale – a scale used for one or more category of description. Nominal scale – a categorical scale with no order to the categories, e.g., gender. Ordinal scale – a categorical scale that has an order but ranks do not correspond to a consistent magnitude of difference. Continuous scale – see below examples Interval scale – a scale with equal distance between scores but no meaningful zero. Ratio scale – a scale with equal distance between scores and a zero score.

Scholarly teaching	Critical reflection on experiences and published literature with the goal of improving one's teaching and learning practices.
Scholarship of Teaching and Learning	Research on elements of teaching and learning contexts. It can be grounded in a particular discipline but may be relevant to multiple disciplines.
Score	The value assigned to an artifact, which turns it into quantitative data.
Secondary use of data	Using data that was originally collected or created for a different purpose.
Sincerity	A criterion for judging qualitative research, the research is seen as self-reflexive on the part of the researcher.
Statistical significance	The likelihood that a relationship between variables is not due to chance.
Students-as-Partners	A research and pedagogical movement to destabilize hierarchies in higher education by having faculty and students work together to improve teaching and learning.
Subjectivity	The perspective that the research cannot be separated from the researcher.
Survey	A research approach/design intended to collect enough data from a sample in order to make inferences about a population, usually involves a questionnaire.
Systematic	Structured and intentional, not random or spontaneous.
Template analysis	A qualitative method that compares an existing framework with specific data.
Thematic analysis	A popular qualitative method with several variations depending upon the methodology of the researcher. In all versions, data is examined for recurring themes.
Theme	An abstraction derived from the codes and categories of the data set. Theme development requires the researcher to move beyond description to interpretation.
Theoretical framework	Based on theory, the lens through which to design the study, interpret the data, and analyze the results.
Theory	Cohesive articulation and understanding of complex contexts or ideas in a coherent

	framework, developed by individuals and/or within disciplines, utilized differently in qualitative and quantitative research.
Think-aloud	A data-gathering technique where participants describe their thought processes as they do an activity.
Transferability	Research that is relevant to other contexts, results can be usefully adapted and applied but not expected to be replicable.
Triangulation	A technique used in qualitative research when more than one data collection method or type of data is used to answer a research question, in order to enhance credibility.
Validity (types)	See below examples Construct validity – how well an instrument measures what it is supposed to measure (instrument accuracy). External validity – the extent to which the research findings are generalizable to contexts beyond that of the study. Internal validity – how well the research findings match reality within the context of the study.
Variability	A measure of how spread out a data set is.
Variable (types)	See below examples Independent variable – a variable that is manipulated or controlled in order to measure its effects. Dependent variable – the outcome variable that is being measured in an experimental design.

REFERENCES

Absolon, K. (2011). *Kaandossiwin: how we come to know*. Fernwood Publishing.

Acai, A., Akesson, B., Allen, M., Chen, V., Mathany, C., McCollum, B., Spencer, J., & Verwoord, R. E. M. (2017). Success in student-faculty/staff SoTL partnerships: Motivations, challenges, power, and definitions. *The Canadian Journal for the Scholarship of Teaching and Learning*, 8(2). https://doi.org/10.5206/cjsotl-rcacea.2017.2.8.

Adams, S., Bekker, S., Fan, Y., Gordon, T., Shepherd, L. J., Slavich, E., & Waters, D. (2022). Gender bias in student evaluations of teaching: 'Punish [ing] those who fail to do their gender right'. *Higher Education*, 83(4), 787–807. https://doi.org/10.1016/j.jpubeco.2016.11.006.

Ahern, K. J. (1999). Ten tips for reflexive bracketing. *Qualitative Health Research*, 9 (3), 407–411. https://doi.org/10.1177/104973239900900309.

AHRECS. (2014). SoTL resource books. https://ahrecs.com/previous-projects/sotl-resource-booklets/.

Åkerlind, G. S. (2005). Variation and commonality in phenomenographic research methods. *Higher Education Research and Development*, 24(4), 321–334. https://doi.org/10.1080/07294360500284672.

Åkerlind, G. S. (2015). From phenomenography to variation theory: A review of the development of the variation theory of learning and implications for pedagogical design in higher education. *Higher Education Research and Development*, 2(July), 5–26. https://www.herdsa.org.au/herdsa-review-higher-education-vol-2/5-26.

Albudaiwi, D. (2017). Survey: Open-ended questions. In M. Allen (Ed.), *The Sage encyclopedia of communication research methods* (Vol. 4, pp. 1716–1717). Sage.

Allen, S., & Knight, J. (2009). A method for collaboratively developing and validating a rubric. *International Journal for the Scholarship of Teaching and Learning*, 3 (2), n2. https://doi.org/10.20429/ijsotl.2009.030210.

Ambady, N., & Rosenthal, R. (1993). Half a minute: Predicting teacher evaluations from thin slices of nonverbal behavior and physical attractiveness. *Journal of*

Personality and Social Psychology, 64(3), 431. https://doi.org/10.1037/0022-3514.64.3.431.

Ambrose, S. A., Bridges, M. W., DiPietro, M., Lovett, M. C., & Norman, M. K. (2010). *How learning works: Seven research-based principles for smart teaching.* John Wiley & Sons.

American Educational Research Association. (2014). *Standards for educational and psychological testing.* American Educational Research Association. https://www.aera.net/Publications/Books/Standards-for-Educational-Psychologica l-Testing-2014-Edition.

Angelo, T., & Cross, K. (1993). *Classroom assessment techniques: A handbook for college teachers* (2nd ed.). Jossey-Bass.

Anyon, J. (1981). Social class and school knowledge. *Curriculum Inquiry*, 11(1), 3–42.

Archer, M., Bhaskar, R., Collier, A., Lawson, T., & Norrie, A. (Eds.) (1998). *Critical realism: Essential readings.* Routledge.

Artino Jr., A. R., La Rochelle, J. S., Dezee, K. J., & Gehlbach, H. (2014). Developing questionnaires for educational research: AMEE Guide No. 87. *Medical Teacher*, 36(6), 463–474. https://doi.org/10.3109/0142159X.2014.889814.

Association of Research Libraries. (2022). ARL positions on open access principles and practices. https://www.arl.org/principles-and-practices/.

Atkins, L., & Wallace, S. (2012). *Qualitative research in education.* Sage. https://dx.doi.org/10.4135/9781473957602.

Austin Center for Design. (2019). *Wicked problems: Problems worth solving.* https://www.wickedproblems.com/.

Baddeley, A. (1999). *Essentials of human memory.* Psychology Press.

Badyl, D. K, & Singh, T. (2017). Learning theories: The basics to learn in medical education. *International Journal of Applied Basic Medical Research*, 7, S1–3. http s://doi.org/10.4103/ijabmr.IJABMR_385_17.

Bailey, S. (2014). *Academic writing: A handbook for international students* (4th ed.). Routledge.

Barr, R. B., & Tagg, J. (1995). From teaching to learning: A new paradigm in undergraduate education. *Change*, 27(6), 13–25. https://doi.org/10.1080/00091383.1995.10544672.

Barrett, M., Hershock, C., McCarthy, M., Melville, M., & Mertz, J. (2021). What type of debrief is best for learning during think-pair-shares? *Teaching & Learning Inquiry*, 9(1), 45–60. https://doi.org/10.20343/teachlearninqu.9.1.5.

Bartsch, R. A. (2013a). Designing SoTL studies—Part I: Validity. *New Directions for Teaching and Learning*, 136, 17–33.

Bartsch, R. A. (2013b). Designing SoTL studies—Part II: Practicality. *New Directions for Teaching and Learning*, 136, 35–48.

Bass, R. (1999). The scholarship of teaching: What's the problem? *Inventio*, 1(1), 1–10.

Bass, R. (2020). What's the problem now? *To Improve the Academy: A Journal of Academic Development*, 39(1), 3–30. http://dx.doi.org/10.3998/tia.17063888.0039.102.

Bastien, B. (2004). *Blackfoot ways of knowing: The worldview of the Siksikaitsitapi.* University of Calgary Press.

Bastien, B. (2016). Indigenous pedagogy: A way out of dependence. In K. Burnett & G. Read (Eds.), *Aboriginal history: A reader.* Oxford University Press.

Battiste, M. (2002). Indigenous knowledge and pedagogy in First Nations education: A literature review with recommendations. Assembly of First Nations. https://

www.afn.ca/uploads/files/education/24._2002_oct_marie_battiste_indigenous knowledgeandpedagogy_lit_review_for_min_working_group.pdf.

Baudelot, C. (1994). Student rhetoric in exams. In P. Bourdieu, J. Passeron, & M. deSaint Martin (Eds.), *Academic Discourse* (pp. 80–94). Stanford University Press.

Beall, J. (2015). Criteria for determining predatory open access publishers. https://beallslist.net/wp-content/uploads/2019/12/criteria-2015.pdf.

Becker, H. S. (2007). *Writing for social scientists: How to start and finish your thesis, book, or article* (2nd ed.). University of Chicago Press.

Bennett, R., Hobson, J., Jones, A., Martin-Lynch, P., Scutt, C., Strehlow, K., & Veitch, S. (2016). Being chimaera: A monstrous identity for SoTL academics. *Higher Education Research & Development*, 35(2), 217–228. https://doi.org/10.1080/07294360.2015.1087473.

Benson, J., & Clark, F. (1982). A guide for instrument development and validation. *American Journal of Occupational Therapy*, 36(12), 789–800. https://doi.org/10.5014/ajot.36.12.789.

Berenson, C. (2018). Identifying a tradition of inquiry. In N. L. Chick (Ed.), *SoTL in action: Illuminating critical moments of practice*. Stylus.

Bergum, V. (1989). *Woman to mother: A transformation*. Bergin & Garvey Publishers.

Bernstein, D. (2010). Finding your place in the Scholarship of Teaching and Learning. *International Journal for the Scholarship of Teaching and Learning* 4(2), Article 4. https://doi.org/10.20429/ijSOTL.2010.040204.

Bernstein, D., Burnett, A. N., Goodburn, A., & Savory, P. (2006). *Making teaching and learning visible: Course portfolios and the peer review of teaching*. Wiley.

Bernstein, J. L. (2018). Unifying SoTL methodology: Internal and external validity. *Teaching & Learning Inquiry*, 6(2), 115–126. https://doi.org/10.20343/teachlearninqu.6.2.9.

Bhaskar, R. (1975). *A realist theory of science*. Leeds Books.

Blackstock, C. (2011). The emergence of the breath of life theory. *Journal of Social Work Values and Ethics*, 8(1) 1–16.

Blair, J., Czaja, R. F., & Blair, E. A. (2013). *Designing surveys: A guide to decisions and procedures*. Sage.

Bloch-Schulman, S., Conkling, S. W., Linkon, S. L., Manarin, K., & Perkins, K. (2016). Asking bigger questions: An invitation to further conversation. *Teaching and Learning Inquiry*, 4(1), 108–114. https://doi.org/10.20343/teachlearninqu.4.1.12.

Bloom, B. S. (1956). *Taxonomy of educational objectives: The classification of educational goals. Handbook I: Cognitive domain*. David McKay Company.

Bohn-Gettler, C. (2018). The complexities of comprehension: Conducting think-aloud studies with multiple interacting variables. In *SAGE Research Methods Cases Part 2*. https://dx.doi.org/10.4135/9781526439550.

Boice, R. (1990). *Professors as writers: A self-help guide to productive writing*. New Forums.

Boling, W., Berlin, K., Rahn, R., Vogelzang, J., & Walter, G. (2018). Institutional review board basics for pedagogy research. *Pedagogy in Health Promotion*, 4(3), 172–177. https://doi.org/10.1177/2373379918793400.

Boman, J., & Yeo, M. (2020). Exploring and learning from failure in facilitation. *International Journal of Academic Development*, 25(1), 19–30. https://doi.org/10.1080/1360144X.2019.1700120.

Booth, S., & Woollacott, L. C. (2018). On the constitution of SoTL: Its domains and contexts. *Higher Education*, 75(3), 537–551. https://doi.org/10.1007/s10734-017-0156-7.

Borton, T. (1970) *Reach, touch and teach*. Hutchinson.

Boyer, E. L. (1990). *Scholarship reconsidered: Priorities of the professoriate*. Jossey-Bass.

Braun, V., & Clarke, V. (2006). Using thematic analysis in psychology. *Qualitative Research in Psychology*, 3(2), 77–101. https://doi.org/10.1191/1478088706qp063oa.

Braun, V., & Clarke, V. (2013). *Successful qualitative research: A practical guide for beginners*. Sage.

Braun, V., & Clarke, V. (2019). Reflecting on reflexive thematic analysis. *Qualitative Research in Sport, Exercise and Health*, 11(4), 589–597. https://doi.org/10.1080/2159676X.2019.1628806.

Braun, V., Clarke, V., Hayfield, N., & Terry, G. (2019) Thematic analysis. In P. Liamputtong (Ed.), *Handbook of research methods in health social sciences*. Springer. https://doi.org/10.1007/978-981-10-5251-4_103.

Brett, J. (1991). The bureaucratization of writing. *Meanjin*, 50(4), 513–522.

Brockmeier, J., & Carbaugh, D. (2001). *Narrative and identity: Studies in autobiography, self and culture*. John Benjamins Publishing Company.

Bronfenbrenner, U. (1977). Toward an experimental ecology of human development. *American Psychologist*, 32(7), 513.

Bronfenbrenner, U. (1981). *The ecology of human development: Experiments by nature and design*. Harvard University Press.

Bronnimann, J., West, D., Huijser, H., & Heath, D. (2018). Applying learning analytics to the Scholarship of Teaching and Learning. *Innovative Higher Education*, 43(5), 353–367. https://doi.org/10.1007/s10755-018-9431-5.

Brookfield, S. (1995). *Becoming a critically reflective teacher*. Jossey-Bass.

Brookfield, S. (1998). Critically reflective practice. *The Journal of Continuing Education in the Health Professions*, 18(4), 197–205. https://doi.org/10.1002/chp.1340180402.

Brooks, J., & King, N. (2017). *Template analysis for business and management students*. Sage. https://doi.org/10.4135/9781473983304.

Brooks, J., McCluskey, S., Turley, E., & King, N. (2015). The utility of template analysis in qualitative psychology research. *Qualitative Research in Psychology*, 12 (2), 202–222. https://doi.org/10.1080/14780887.2014.955224.

Burke, K. (1941). *The philosophy of literary form*. University of California Press.

Burke Johnson, R., & Stefurak, T. (2013). Considering the evidence and credibility discussion in evaluation through the lens of dialectical pluralism. *New Directions for Evaluation*, 2013(138), 37–48.

Burton, L. (2002). Methodology and methods in mathematics education research: Where is "The Why?" In S. Goodchild & L. English (Eds.), *Researching mathematics classrooms: A critical examination of methodology* (pp. 1–10). Praeger.

Byrne, D. (2022) A worked example of Braun and Clarke's approach to reflexive thematic analysis. *Quality and Quantity*, 56, 1391–1412. https://doi.org/10.1007/s11135-021-01182-y.

Caelli, K., Ray, L., & Mill, J. (2003). 'Clear as mud': Toward greater clarity in generic qualitative research. *International Journal of Qualitative Methods*, 2(2),1–13. https://doi.org/10.1177/160940690300200201.

Calder, L. (2018). Student think-alouds: Making thinking and learning visible. In N. L. Chick (Ed.), *SoTL in action: Illuminating critical moments of practice* (pp. 109–116). Stylus.

Calderon, D. (2014). Speaking back to manifest destinies: A land education-based approach to critical curriculum inquiry. *Environmental Education Research*, 20(1), 24–36. doi:10.1080/13504622.2013.865114.

Cappello, A., & Miller-Young, J. (2020). Who are we citing and how? A SoTL citation analysis. *Teaching and Learning Inquiry*, 8(2), 3–16. https://doi.org/10.20343/teachlearninqu.8.2.2.

Caputo, J. D. (1987). *Radical hermeneutics*. Indiana University Press.

Caputo, J. D. (2000). *More radical hermeneutics*. Indiana University Press.

Carter, M. J., & Fuller, C. (2016). Symbols, meaning, and action: The past, present, and future of symbolic interactionism. *Current Sociology*, 64(6), 931–961. https://doi.org/10.1177/0011392116638396.

Cartmel, J., Macfarlane, K., & Nolan, A. (2013). Looking to the future: Producing transdisciplinary professionals for leadership in early childhood settings. *Early Years (London, England)*, 33(4), 398–412. https://doi.org/10.1080/09575146.2013.852522.

Cerbin, B. (2011). *Lesson study using classroom inquiry to improve teaching and learning in higher education*. Stylus.

Cerbin, B. (2018). Classroom observations: Exploring how learning works. In N. L. Chick (Ed.), *SoTL in action: Illuminating critical moments of practice* (pp. 82–91). Stylus.

Chan, E. R., & Miller-Young, J. (2022). Interview protocol for understanding experiences of students from underrepresented groups in undergraduate engineering education. Education and Research Archive, University of Alberta Library. https://doi.org/10.7939/r3-5a6g-9696.

Chapnick, A., & Kukucha, C. (2016, May 10). The pros and cons of editing a collection of essays. *University Affairs*. https://www.universityaffairs.ca/career-advice/the-scholarly-edition/the-pros-and-cons-of-editing-a-collection-of-essays/.

Charmez, K., Thornberg, R., Keane, E. (2018). Evolving grounded theory and social justice inquiry. In N. K. Denzin & Y.S. Lincoln (Eds.), *The Sage handbook of qualitative research* (5th ed.) (pp. 411–433). Sage.

Chick, N. L. (2017). Does reading SOTL matter? Difficult questions of impact. *InSight: A Journal of Scholarly Teaching*, 12, 9–13. https://doi.org/10.46504/12201700ch.

Chick, N. L. (Ed.) (2018). *SoTL in action: Illuminating critical moments of practice*. Stylus.

Chick, N. L. (2022). Public SoTL: Amplifying the purposes, audiences, and products of the scholarship of teaching and learning. In Chick, N. L. & Friberg, J. C. (Eds.), *Going public reconsidered: Engaging with the world beyond academe through the Scholarship of Teaching and Learning*. Stylus.

Chick, N. L., Bunnell, S., Felten, P., Higgs, B., Long, A., Manarin, K., Marquis, B., Mårtensson, K., Matthews, K., Moore, J. L., & Scharff, L. (2017). ISSOTL conference pedagogy. https://issotl.com/issotl-conference-pedagogy/.

Chick, N. L., & Friberg, J. C. (Eds.) (2022). *Going public reconsidered: Engaging with the world beyond academe through the Scholarship of Teaching and Learning*. Stylus.

Chilisa, B. (2020). *Indigenous research methodologies* (2nd ed.). Sage.
Ciccone, A. (2018). Learning matters: Asking meaningful questions. In N. L. Chick (Ed.), *SoTL in action: Illuminating critical moments of practice* (pp. 15–22). Stylus.
Clandinin, D. J., & Connolly, M. (2000). *Experience and story in qualitative research.* Jossey-Bass.
Clandinin, D. J., & Huber, J. (2002). Narrative inquiry: Toward understanding life's artistry. *Curriculum Inquiry*, 32(2), 161–169.
Clandinin, D. J., & Rosiek, J. (2007). Mapping a landscape of narrative inquiry: Borderland spaces and tensions. In D. J. Clandinin (Ed.), *Handbook of narrative inquiry: Mapping a methodology* (pp. 35–76). Sage.
Clarke, V. (2022). Navigating the messy swamp of qualitative research: Are generic reporting standards the answer? *Qualitative Research in Psychology*, 19(4), 1004–1012. https://doi.org/10.1080/14780887.2021.1995555.
Cohen, J. (1992). A power primer. *Psychological Bulletin*, 112, 155–159.
Cook-Sather, A. (2018). Tracing the evolution of student voice in educational research. In R. Bourke & J. Loveridge (Eds.), *Radical collegiality through student voice: Educational experience, policy, and practice.* Springer.
Cook-Sather, A., & Abbot, S. (2016). Translating partnerships: How faculty-student collaboration in explorations of teaching and learning can transform perceptions, terms, and selves. *Teaching and Learning Inquiry*, 4(2), 36–49. https://doi.org/10.20343/teachlearninqu.4.2.5.
Cook-Sather, A., Abbot, S., & Felten, P. (2019). Legitimating reflective writing in SoTL: "Dysfunctional illusions of rigor" revisited. *Teaching and Learning Inquiry*, 7(2), 14–27. http://dx.doi.org/10.20343/teachlearninqu.7.2.2.
Cook-Sather, A., Bovill, C., & Felten, P. (2014). *Engaging students as partners in learning and teaching: A guide for faculty.* Jossey-Bass.
Cormier, P., & Ray, L. (2018). A tale of two drums: *Kinoo'amaadawaad Megwaa Doodamawaad*—"They are learning with each other while they are doing." In D. McGregor, J. P. Restoule, & R. Johnston (Eds.), *Indigenous research: Theories, practices, and relationships* (pp. 112–125). Canadian Scholars.
Creamer, E. G. (2018). *An introduction to fully integrated mixed methods research* (1st ed.). Sage.
Creswell, J. W. (2007). *Qualitative inquiry and research design: Choosing among five approaches* (2nd ed.). Sage.
Creswell, J. W., & Guetterman, T. C. (2019). *Educational research: planning, conducting, and evaluating quantitative and qualitative research* (6th ed.). Pearson.
Creswell, J. W., & Plano Clark, V. L. (2017). *Designing and conducting mixed methods research.* Sage.
Creswell, J. W. & Poth, C. N. (2018). *Qualitative inquiry and research design: Choosing among five approaches* (4th ed.). Sage.
Currie, G. (2017). Conscious connections: Phenomenology and decoding the disciplines. In J. Miller-Young & J. Boman (Eds.), *Using the decoding the disciplines framework for learning across disciplines* (pp. 37–48). Jossey-Bass.
Dastur, F. (2000). Phenomenology of the event: Waiting and surprise. *Hypatia*, 15 (4), 178–189.
Dawson, P. (2017). Assessment rubrics: Towards clearer and more replicable design, research and practice. *Assessment & Evaluation in Higher Education*, 42(3), 347–360. https://doi.org/10.1080/02602938.2015.1111294.

de Bie, A., Prasad, S. K., Nguyen, E., & Marquis, E. (2022). Considerations for seeking equity and justice through pedagogical partnership: Four partners in conversation. *Imagining SoTL: Selections From the Banff Symposium*, 2(1), 19–38.

Deci, E. L., & Ryan, R. M. (2012). Self-determination theory. In P. A. M. Van Lange, A. W. Kruglanski, & E. T. Higgins (Eds.), *Handbook of theories of social psychology* (pp. 416–436). Sage. https://doi.org/10.4135/9781446249215.n21.

de Leeuw, J. R. *et al.* (2022). Generalizability, transferability, and the practice-to-practice gap. *Behavioral and Brain Sciences*, 45(11). https://doi.org/10.1017/S01450525X21000406.

Deng, J. M., Streja, N., & Flynn, A. B. (2021). Response process validity evidence in chemistry education research. *Journal of Chemical Education*. https://doi.org/10.1021/acs.jchemed.1c00749.

Denzin, N. K. (2016). *Qualitative inquiry under fire: Toward a new paradigm dialogue*. Routledge. https://doi.org/10.4324/9781315421292.

Denzin, N. K., & Lincoln, Y. S. (Eds.) (2013). *Collecting and interpreting qualitative materials* (4th ed.). Sage.

Denzin, N. K., & Lincoln, Y. S. (Eds.) (2018). *The Sage handbook of qualitative research* (5th ed.). Sage.

Desimone, L. M., & Le Floch, K. C. (2004). Are we asking the right questions? Using cognitive interviews to improve surveys in education research. *Educational Evaluation and Policy Analysis*, 26(1), 1–22. https://doi.org/10.3102/01623737026001001.

Deslauriers, L., McCarty, L. S., Miller, K., Callaghan, K., & Kestin, G. (2019). Measuring actual learning versus feeling of learning in response to being actively engaged in the classroom. *Proceedings of the National Academy of Sciences*, 116 (39), 19251–19257. https://doi.org/10.1073/pnas.1821936116.

Dewey, J. (1938). *Experience and education*. Simon & Schuster.

Din, C., Alharbi, H., Maclinnis, M., Mardjetko, A., Archer-Kuhn, B., Jamniczky, H., & Jacobsen, M. (2022). Leadership, SoTL, and mentorship in a teaching scholars community of practice. *Papers on Postsecondary Learning and Teaching*, 5, 93–99.

Divan, A., Ludwig, L., Matthews, K., Motley, P., & Tomljenovic-Berube, A. (2017). Survey of research approaches utilised in the Scholarship of Teaching and Learning publications. *Teaching & Learning Inquiry*, 5(2), 16–29. https://doi.org/10.20343/teachlearninqu.5.2.3.

Dorit, A., Raichel, N., & Naamati-Schneider, L. (2021). Higher education students' reflective journal writing and lifelong learning skills: Insights from an exploratory sequential study. *Frontiers in Psychology*, 12, 707168. https://doi.org/10.3389/fpsyg.2021.707168.

Driscoll, J. (1994) Reflective practice for practise—a framework of structured reflection for clinical areas. *Senior Nurse*, 14(1): 47–50.

Eaton, S. E. (2020). Understanding academic integrity from a teaching and learning perspective: Engaging with the 4M framework. https://prism.ucalgary.ca/handle/1880/112435.

Edwards, C., Gandini, L., & Forman, G. (1998). *The hundred languages of children: The Reggio Emilia approach to early childhood education* (2nd ed.). Ablex.

Elliott, V. (2018). Thinking about the coding process in qualitative data analysis. *The Qualitative Report*, 23(11), 2850–2861. https://doi.org/10.46743/2160-3715/2018.3560.

Elliot-Johns, S. E. (2011). Reclaiming a writing voice as a new teacher educator: SoTL as portal. *IJSoTL*, 5(2), Article 22. https://doi.org/10.20429/ijsotl.2011.050222.

Ellis, L., Burke, D. M., Lomire, P., & McCormack, D. R. (2004). Student grades and average ratings of instructional quality: The need for adjustment. *Journal of Educational Research*, 9, 35–41. https://doi.org/10.1080/00220670309596626.

Ellsworth, E. (1997). *Teaching positions: Difference, pedagogy and the power of address*. Teachers College Press.

Elo, S., & Kyngäs, H. (2008). The qualitative content analysis process. *Journal of Advanced Nursing*, 62(1), 107–115. https://doi.org/10.1111/j.1365-2648.2007.04569.x.

Ericsson, K. A., & Simon, H. A. (1993). *Protocol analysis: Verbal reports as data*. MIT Press.

Ermine, W. (2007). Ethical space of engagement. *Indigenous Law Journal*, 6(1), 193–203.

Ertmer, P. A., & Newby, T. J. (2013). Article update: Behaviorism, cognitivism, and constructivism: Connecting yesterday's theories to today's contexts. *Performance Improvement Quarterly*, 6(4), 43–71. https://doi.org/10.1002/piq.21143.

Evans, M., Hole, R., Berg, L. D., Hutchinson, P., & Sookraj, D. (2009). Common insights, differing methodologies: Toward a fusion of Indigenous methodologies, Participatory Action Research, and white studies in an urban Aboriginal research agenda. *Qualitative Inquiry*, 15(5), 893–910. https://doi.org/10.1177/1077800409333392.

Fedoruk, L. (2017). *Ethics in the Scholarship of Teaching and Learning: Key principles and strategies for ethical practice*. Taylor Institute for Teaching and Learning at the University of Calgary. www.ucalgary.ca/taylorinstitute/guides.

Fedoruk, L. M. (Ed.) (2022). *Ethics and the Scholarship of Teaching and Learning* (Vol. 2). Springer Nature.

Felten, P. (2013). Principles of good practice in SoTL. *Teaching and Learning Inquiry*, 1(1), 121–125. https://doi.org/10.20343/teachlearninqu.1.1.121.

Fielding, M. (1999). Radical collegiality: Affirming teaching as an inclusive professional practice. *The Australian Education Researcher*, 26, 1–34. https://doi.org/10.1007/BF03219692.

Fleetwood, S. (2014). Bhaskar and critical realism. In P. Adler, P. du Gay, G. Morgan, & M. Reed (Eds.), *The Oxford handbook of sociology, social theory, and organizational studies: Contemporary currents* (pp. 182–219). Oxford University Press.

Fox, M. C., Ericsson, K. A., & Best, R. (2011). Do procedures for verbal reporting of thinking have to be reactive? A meta-analysis and recommendations for best reporting methods. *Psychological Bulletin*, 137(2), 316–344. https://doi.org/10.1037/a0021663.

Freeman, S., Eddy, S. L., McDonough, M., Smith, M. K., Okoroafor, N., Jordt, H., & Wenderoth, M. P. (2014). Active learning increases student performance in science, engineering, and mathematics. *Proceedings of the National Academy of Sciences*, 111(23), 8410–8415. https://doi.org/10.1073/pnas.1319030111.

Freire, P. (1970). *Pedagogy of the oppressed*. Herder & Herder.

Friberg, J. (2016, July 11). Might the 4M framework support SoTL advocacy? *The SoTL Advocate*. https://illinoisstateuniversitysotl.wordpress.com/2016/07/11/might-the-4m-framework-support-sotl-advocacy/.

Friberg, J. C., & Chick, N. L. (2022). Introduction: A framework for public SoTL. In N. L. Chick & J. C. Frieberg (Eds.), *Going public reconsidered: Engaging with the world beyond academe through SoTL* (pp. 1–14). Stylus.

Gadamer, H. G. (1999). *Truth and Method* (2nd ed.) (J. Weinsheimer & D. G. Marshall, Trans.). Continuum.

Galvan, J. L. (2012). *Writing literature reviews: A guide for students of the social and behavioral sciences* (5th ed.). Pyrczak.

Geertsema, J. (2016). Academic development, SoTL, and educational research. *International Journal for Academic Development*, 21(2), 122–134. http://dx.doi.org/10.1080/1360144X.2016.1175144.

Geertz, C. (1973). *The interpretation of culture.* Hutchinson.

Gelbman, S. M. (2011). A qualitative assessment of the learning outcomes of teaching Introductory American Politics in comparative perspective. *Journal of Political Science Education*, 7(4), 359–374. https://doi.org/10.1080/15512169.2011.615187.

George, D., & Mallery, P. (2019). *IBM SPSS statistics 26 step by step: A simple guide and reference.* Routledge.

George, L., Tauri, J., & MacDonald, L. T. T. (2020). *Indigenous research ethics: Claiming research sovereignty beyond deficit and the colonial legacy.* Emerald Publishing.

Gibbs, G. (1988). *Learning by doing: A guide to teaching and learning methods.* Further Education Unit.

Giroux, H. A. (2010). Rethinking education as the practice of freedom: Paulo Freire and the promise of critical pedagogy. *Policy Futures in Education*, 8(6), 715–721. https://doi.org/10.2304/pfie.2010.8.6.715.

Given, L. M. (Ed.) (2008). Arts-based research. In *The Sage encyclopedia of qualitative research methods* (Vol. 1, pp. 30–32). Sage. https://dx.doi.org/10.4135/9781412963909.

Glaser, B., & Strauss, A. (1967). *The discovery of grounded theory: Strategies for qualitative research.* Doubleday.

Glassick, C., Huber, M., & Maeroff, G. (1997) *Scholarship assessed: Evaluation of the professoriate.* Jossey-Bass.

Godbold, N., Irving-Bell, D., McSweeney-Flaherty, J., Torcivia, P., Schlesselman, L., & Smith, H. (2021). The Courage to SoTL. *Teaching and Learning Inquiry*, 9 (1), 380–394. https://doi.org/10.20343/teachlearninqu.9.1.25.

Goldbort, R. (2006). *Writing for science.* Yale University Press.

Grant, B. M. (2008). *Academic writing retreats: A facilitator's guide.* Higher education Research and Development Society of Australasia.

Grbich, C. (2013). *Qualitative data analysis* (2nd ed.). Sage.

Greene, A. E. (2013). *Writing science in plain English.* University of Chicago Press.

Grudniewicz, A., Moher, D., Cobey, K. D., Bryson, G. L., Cukier, S., Allen, K., Ardern, C., Balcom, L., Barros, T., Berger, M., Ciro, J. B., Cugusi, L., Donaldson, M. R., Egger, M., Graham, I. D., Hodgkinson, M., Khan, K. M., Mabizela, M., Manca, A. … Lalu, M. M. (2019). Predatory journals: No definition, no defence. *Nature*, 576, 210–212. https://doi.org/10.1038/d41586-019-03759-y.

Gubrium, J. F., Holstein, J. A., Marvasti, A. B., & McKinney, K. D. (Eds.) (2012). *The Sage handbook of interview research: The complexity of the craft.* Sage. https://dx.doi.org/10.4135/9781452218403.n14.

Guetterman, T. C., Fetters, M. D., & Creswell, J. W. (2015). Integrating quantitative and qualitative results in health science mixed methods research through joint displays. *The Annals of Family Medicine*, 13(6), 554–561.

Gunn, V., & Shopkow, L. (2007). Doing SoTL in medieval history: A cross-Atlantic dialogue. *Arts and Humanities in Higher Education*, 6(3), 255–271. https://doi.org/10.1177/1474022207080837.

Gurung, R. A. R. (2014). Getting foxy: Invoking different magesteria in the Scholarship of Teaching and Learning. *Teaching and Learning Inquiry*, 2(2), 109–114. https://doi.org/10.20343/teachlearninqu.2.2.109.

Gurung, R. A. R., & Schwartz, B. M. (2009). *Optimizing teaching and learning: Practicing pedagogical research*. John Wiley & Sons.

Gurung, R. A. R., & Schwartz, B. M. (2013). Contributions from psychology: Heuristics for interdisciplinary advancement of SoTL. In K. McKinney (Ed.), *The Scholarship of Teaching and Learning in and across the disciplines* (pp. 34–53). Indiana University Press.

Gurung, R. A. R., & Wilson, J. H. (Eds.) (2014). *Doing the Scholarship of Teaching and Learning: Measuring systematic changes to teaching and improvements in learning*. Jossey-Bass.

Halasz, J. R., & Kaufman, P. (2008). Sociology as pedagogy: How ideas from the discipline can inform teaching and learning. *Teaching Sociology*, 36(4), 301–317. https://doi.org/10.1177/0092055X0803600401.

Hamermesh, D. S., & Parker, A. (2005). Beauty in the classroom: Instructors' pulchritude and putative pedagogical productivity. *Economics of Education Review*, 24 (4), 369–376. https://doi.org/10.1016/j.econedurev.2004.07.013.

Haney, S., Dean, Y., Chronik, M., & Creig, A. (2021). Power, voice and positionality: An undergraduate student-faculty research team podcasts their experience with a Students-as-Partners framework. *Imagining SoTL*, 1, 116–121. https://doi.org/10.29173/isotl534.

Hardesty, R., Gluckman, M., & Hargis, J. (2018). The value of ethnography: A pilot study on a class on pedagogical instruction. *Transformative Dialogues: Teaching & Learning Journal*, 11(2), 1–17.

Harel, D., & Wentland, E. (2017). Survey use in academic contexts: Considerations and guidelines. In *Handbook on measurement, assessment, and evaluation in higher education* (pp. 517–528). Routledge.

Harpe, S. E. (2015). How to analyze Likert and other rating scale data. *Currents in Pharmacy Teaching and Learning*, 7(6), 836–850. https://doi.org/10.1016/j.cptl.2015.08.001.

Harris, J. (2006). *Rewriting: How to do things with texts*. Utah State University Press.

Hassel, H., & Launius, C. (2017). Crossing the threshold in introductory women's and gender studies courses: An assessment of student learning. *Teaching & Learning Inquiry*, 5(2). http://dx.doi.org/10.20343/teachlearninqu.5.2.4.

Hassel, H., Reddinger, A., & van Slooten, J. (2011). Surfacing the structures of patriarchy: Teaching and learning threshold concepts in Women's Studies. *International Journal for the Scholarship of Teaching and Learning*, 5(2). https://doi.org/10.20429/ijsotl.2011.050218.

Hayot, E. (2014). *The elements of academic style: Writing for the humanities*. Columbia University Press.

Healey, R. L., Bass, T., Caulfield, J., Hoffman, A., McGinn, M. K., Miller-Young, J., & Haigh, M. (2013). Being ethically minded: Practising the Scholarship of Teaching and Learning in an ethical manner. *Teaching and Learning Inquiry*, 1 (2), 23–33. https://doi.org/10.20343/teachlearninqu.1.2.23.

Healey, M., Flint, A., & Harrington, K. (2014). *Engagement through partnership: Students as partners in learning and teaching in higher education*. Higher Education Academy.

Healey, M., Matthews, K., & Cook-Sather, A. (2019). Writing Scholarship of Teaching and Learning articles for peer-reviewed journals. *Teaching & Learning Inquiry*, 7(2). http://dx.doi.org/10.20343/teach learn inqu.7.2.3.

Healey, M., Matthews, K., & Cook-Sather, A. (2020). *Writing about teaching and learning in higher education: Creating and contributing to scholarly conversations across a range of genres*. Elon University Center for Engaged Learning. https://doi.org/10.36284/celelon.oa3.

Held, M. B. E. (2019). Decolonizing research paradigms in the context of settler colonialism: An unsettling, mutual, and collaborative effort. *International Journal of Qualitative Methods*, 18, 1–16. https://doi.org/10.1177/1609406918821574.

Hempel, C. G. (1965). Science and human values. In *Aspects of scientific explanation and other essays in the philosophy of science* (pp. 81–96). Free Press.

Henriksson, C. & Friesen, N. (2012). Introduction: Hermeneutic phenomenology. In N. Friesen, C. Henriksson, & T. Saevi, (Eds.), *Hermeneutic phenomenology in education: Theory and methods* (pp. 1–14). Sense.

Hersch, G. (2018). Educational equipoise and the educational misconception: Lessons from bioethics. *Teaching and Learning Inquiry*, 6(2), 3–15. https://doi-org.login.ezproxy.library.ualberta.ca/10.20343/teachlearninqu.6.2.2.

Herzog, H. (2012). Interview location and its social meaning. In J. F. Gubrium, J. A. Holstein, A. B. Marvasti, & K. D. McKinney (Eds.), *The Sage handbook of interview research: The complexity of the craft* (pp. 207–218). Sage. https://dx.doi.org/10.4135/9781452218403.n14.

Hessler, M., Pöpping, D. M., Hollstein, H., Ohlenburg, H., Arnemann, P. H., Massoth, C., … Wenk, M. (2018). Availability of cookies during an academic course session affects evaluation of teaching. *Medical Education*, 52(10), 1064–1072. https://doi.org/10.1111/medu.13627.

Hewson, K., & Easton, L. (2022). Packing up the big tent: Que(e)rying and decolonizing SoTL. *Imagining SoTL: Selections from the Banff Symposium*, 2(1), 63–78.

hooks, b. (2014). *Teaching to transgress*. Routledge.

Hsieh, H.-F., & Shannon, S. E. (2005). Three approaches to qualitative content analysis. *Qualitative Health Research*, 15(9), 1277–1288. https://doi.org/10.1177/1049732305276687.

Hubball, H., & Clarke, A. (2010). Diverse methodological approaches and considerations for SoTL in higher education. *The Canadian Journal for the Scholarship of Teaching and Learning*, 1(1). http://dx.doi.org/10.5206/cjsotl-rcacea.2010.1.2.

Hubball, H., Clarke, A., & Poole, G. (2010) Ten-year reflections on mentoring SoTL research in a research-intensive university. *International Journal for Academic Development*, 15(2), 117–129. https://doi.org/10.1080/13601441003737758.

Huber, M. T., & Hutchings, P. (2005). *The advancement of learning: Building the teaching commons*. Jossey-Bass.

Huber, M. T., & Morreale, S. P. (Eds.) (2002). *Disciplinary styles in the Scholarship of Teaching and Learning: Exploring common ground.* AAHE & Carnegie Foundation for the Advancement of Teaching.

Hutchings, P. (Ed). (2000). *Opening lines: Approaches to the Scholarship of Teaching and Learning.* Carnegie Foundation for the Advancement of Teaching.

Hutchings, P. (Ed.) (2002). *Ethics of inquiry: Issues in the Scholarship of Teaching and Learning.* Carnegie Foundation for the Advancement of Teaching.

Hutchings, P., Huber, M., & Ciccone, A. (2011). *The Scholarship of Teaching and Learning reconsidered: Institutional integration and impact.* Jossey-Bass.

Hutchings, P., & Shulman, L. S. (1999). The scholarship of teaching: New elaborations, new developments. *Change: The Magazine of Higher Learning*, 31(5), 10–15. https://doi.org/10.1080/00091389909604218.

Imad, M. (2019). Reimagining STEM education: Beauty, wonder, and connection. *Liberal Education*, 105(2), n2.

Imad, M. (2021). Transcending adversity: Trauma-informed educational development. *To Improve the Academy: A Journal of Educational Development*, 39(3). https://doi.org/10.3998/tia.17063888.0039.301.

Imad, M. (2022). Trauma-informed education for wholeness: Strategies for faculty & advisors. *New Directions for Student Services*, 2022(177), 39–47. https://doi.org/10.1002/ss.20413.

Jaakkola, E. (2020). Designing conceptual articles: Four approaches. *AMS Review*, 10(1–2), 18–26. https://doi.org/10.1007/s13162-020-00161-0.

Jaarsma, A., Kinaschuk, K., & Xing, L. (2016). Kierkegaard, despair and the possibility of education: Teaching existentialism existentially. *Studies in Philosophy and Education*, 35, 445–461.

Jackson, A. Y., & Mazzei, L. A. (2011). *Thinking with theory in qualitative research: Viewing data across multiple perspectives.* Routledge.

James, A. (2001). Ethnography in the study of children and childhood. In P. Atkinson, A. Coffey, S. Delamont, J. Lofland, & L. Lofland (Eds.), *Handbook of ethnography* (pp. 246–257). Sage.

Jardine, D. W. (1998). *To dwell with a boundless heart.* Peter Lang Publishing.

Jarldorn, M. (2019). *Photovoice handbook for social workers: Method, practicalities and possibilities for social change.* Springer. https://doi.org/10.1007/978-3-319-94511-8.

Jasper, M. A. (2005). Using reflective writing within research. *Journal of Research in Nursing*, 10(3), 247–260. https://doi.org/10.1177/174498710501000303.

Jhangiani, R. S., Troisi, J. D., Fleck, B., Legg, A. M., & Hussey, H. D. (Eds.) (2015). *A compendium of scales for the Scholarship of Teaching and Learning.* https://teachpsych.org/ebooks/compscalessotp.

Johns, C. (1995). Framing learning through reflection within Carper's fundamental ways of knowing in nursing. *Journal of Advanced Nursing*, 22(2), 226–234. https://doi.org/10.1046/j.1365-2648.1995.22020226.x.

Johnston, R, McGregor, D., & Restoule, J. P. (2018). Relationships, respect, and responsibility: Taking up Indigenous research approaches. In D. McGregor & J. P Restoule, (Eds.), *Indigenous research: Theories, practices, and relationships* (pp. 1–21). Canadian Scholars.

Joseph-Richard, P., & Jessop, T. (2020). A phenomenographic study of research informed teaching through the eyes of Masters' students. *Studies in Higher Education*, 45(4), 847–861. https://doi.org/10.1080/03075079.2018.1554640.

Jossan, K. S., Gauthier, A., & Jenkinson, J. (2021). Cultural implications in the acceptability of game-based learning. *Computers & Education*, 174, 104305. https://doi.org/10.1016/j.compedu.2021.104305.

Julien, H. (2008). Survey research. In L. M. Given (Ed.), *The Sage encyclopedia of qualitative research methods* (pp. 847–848). Sage.

Jung, I. (2019). Connectivism and networked learning. In I. Jung (Ed.), *Open and distance education theory revisited* (pp. 47–55). Springer. https://doi.org/10.1007/978-981-13-7740-2_6.

Kanuka, H. (2011). Keeping the scholarship in the Scholarship of Teaching and Learning. *International Journal for the Scholarship of Teaching and Learning*, 5(1), Article 3. https://doi.org/10.20429/ijsotl.2011.050103.

Kara, H. (2022). *Qualitative research for quantitative researchers.* Sage.

Kelsky, K. (2012, July 24). Should I do an edited collection?https://theprofessorisin.com/2012/07/24/should-i-do-an-edited-collection/.

Kenny, N., Watson, G. P., & Desmarais, S. (2016). Building sustained action: Supporting an institutional practice of SoTL at the University of Guelph. *New Directions for Teaching and Learning*, 146, 87–94.

Kezar, A. (2018). *How colleges change: Understanding, leading, and enacting change.* Routledge.

Kilgore, D. W. (2001). Critical and postmodern perspectives on adult learning. *New directions for adult and continuing education*, 89, 53–61.

Kim, J. H. (2016). *Understanding narrative inquiry.* Sage.

Kincheloe, J. L., McLaren, P., Steinberg, S. R., & Monzó, L. D. (2018). Critical pedagogy and qualitative research: Advancing the bricolage. In N. K. Denzin & Y. S. Lincoln (Eds.), *The Sage handbook of qualitative research* (5th ed.) (pp. 235–260). Sage.

Kinchin, I. M., Streatfield, D., & Hay, D. B. (2010). Using Concept Mapping to Enhance the Research Interview. *International Institute for Qualitative Methodology*, 9(1), 52–68.

Kinchin, I. (2017). SoTL and biological education. *Journal of Biological Education*, 51(3), 213–214. https://doi.org/10.1080/00219266.2017.1332714.

Knaflic, C. (2015). *Storytelling with data: A data visualization guide for business professionals.* John Wiley & Sons.

Knoblauch, H. (2005). Focused ethnography. *Forum: Qualitative Social Research*, 6 (3), Article 44.

Kolb, D. A. (1984). *Experiential learning: Experience as the source of learning and development.* Prentice Hall.

Kovach, M. (2009). *Indigenous methodologies: Characteristics, conversations and contexts.* University of Toronto Press.

Kovach, M. (2018). Doing Indigenous methodologies: A letter to a research class. In N. K. Denzin & Y. S. Lincoln (Eds.), *The Sage handbook of qualitative research* (5th ed.) (pp. 214–234). Sage.

Kozhevnikov, A., & Vincent, S., (2019). Critical realism, In P. Atkinson, S. Delamont, A. Cernat, J. W. Sakshaug, & R. A. Williams (Eds.), *Sage Research Methods Foundations.* Sage. https://dx.doi.org/10.4135/9781526421036782465.

Kreber, C. (2004). An analysis of two models of reflection and their implications for educational development. *International Journal for Academic Development*, 9(1), 29–49. https://doi.org/10.1080/1360144042000296044.

Kreber, C. (2007a). The Scholarship of Teaching and Learning: No one way. *Interchange: Newsletter of the Centre for Teaching, Learning and Assessment at the University of Edinburgh*, 1–6.

Kreber, C. (2007b). What's it really all about? The Scholarship of Teaching and Learning as an authentic practice. *International Journal for the Scholarship of Teaching & Learning*, 1(1). https://doi.org/10.20429/ijsotl.2007.010103.

Kreber, C. (2013). The transformative potential of the scholarship of teaching. *Teaching and Learning Inquiry: The ISSOTL Journal*, 1(1), 5–18. https://doi.org/10.20343/teachlearninqu.1.1.5.

Krueger, R. A., & Casey, M. A. (2015). *Focus groups: A practical guide for applied research*. Sage.

Kuhn, T. S. (1962). *The structure of scientific revolution*. The University of Chicago Press.

Kuhn, T. S. (1977). Objectivity, value judgment, and theory choice. In *The essential tension: Selected studies in scientific tradition and change*. The University of Chicago Press.

Kyd, J. (2010). What is the difference between research and scholarship? [Video] YouTube. https://www.youtube.com/watch?v=JIrUWOfEy7w.

Larsson, M., Mårtensson, K., Price, L., & Roxå, T. (2020). Constructive friction? Charting the relation between educational research and the Scholarship of Teaching and Learning. *Teaching and Learning Inquiry*, 8(1), 61–75. https://doi.org/10.20343/teachlearninqu.8.1.5.

Lauer, C. (2012). A comparison of faculty and student perspectives on course evaluation terminology. *To Improve the Academy*, 31(1), 194–211. https://doi.org/10.1002/j.2334-4822.2012.tb00682.x.

Lave, J., & Wenger, E. (1991). *Situated learning: Legitimate peripheral participation*. Cambridge University Press.

Leavy, P. (Ed.) (2018). *Handbook of arts-based research*. The Guilford Press.

Lemieux, C., & Roettger, E. (2019). Students' reasoning during a calculus two-stage exam. https://directorymathsed.net/public/Ireland/IrelandPapersPDF&Docx/Lemieux%20&%20Roettger%20(6).pdf.

LeVasseur, J. J. (2003). The problem of bracketing in phenomenology. *Qualitative Health Research*, 13(3), 408–420. https://doi.org/10.1177/1049732302250337.

Levitt, H. M., Bamberg, M., Creswell, J. W., Frost, D. M., Josselson, R., & Suárez-Orozco, C. (2018). Journal article reporting standards for qualitative primary, qualitative meta-analytic, and mixed methods research in psychology: The APA Publications and Communications Board task force report. *American Psychologist*, 73(1), 26–46. http://dx.doi.org/10.1037/amp0000151.

Lincoln, Y. S., Lynham, S. A., & Guba, E. G. (2018). Paradigmatic controversies, contradictions, and emerging confluences, revisited. In N. K. Denzin & Y. S. Lincoln (Eds.), *The Sage handbook of qualitative research* (5th ed.) (pp. 108–150). Sage.

Lindstrom, G., Baptiste, S. K., & Shade, S. (2021). "Mokakit Iyikakimaat": Autoethnographic reflections as a movement toward a pedagogy of resilience. In J. Macdonald & J. Markides (Eds.), *Brave work in Indigenous education* (pp. 29–40). Dio Press.

MacLean, M., & Poole, G. (2010). An introduction to ethical considerations for novices to research in teaching and learning in Canada. *The Canadian Journal for the Scholarship of Teaching and Learning*, 1(2), Article 7. http://dx.doi.org/10.5206/cjsotl-rcacea.2010.2.7.

MacMillan, M. (2014). Student connections with academic texts: A phenomenographic study of teaching. *Teaching in Higher Education*, 19(8), 943–954. https://doi.org/10.1080/13562517.2014.934345.

MacMillan, M. (2018). The SoTL literature review: Exploring new territory. In N. L. Chick (Ed.), *SoTL in action: Illuminating critical moments of practice* (pp. 23–31). Stylus.

MacNell, L., Driscoll, A., & Hunt, A. N. (2015). What's in a name: Exposing gender bias in student ratings of teaching. *Innovative Higher Education*, 40(4), 291–303. https://doi.org/10.1007/s10755-014-9313-4.

Maguire, M., & Delahunt, B. (2017). Doing a thematic analysis: A practical, step-by-step guide for learning and teaching scholars. *All Ireland Journal of Higher Education*, 9(3).

Manarin, K. (2012). Reading value: Student choice in reading strategies. *Pedagogy*, 12(2), 281–297. https://doi.org/10.1215/15314200-1503595.

Manarin, K. (2016). Interpreting undergraduate research posters in the literature classroom. *Teaching & Learning Inquiry*, 4(1). http://dx.doi.org/10.20343/teachlearninqu.4.1.8.

Manarin, K. (2017). Reading the stories of teaching and learning—ISSOTL 2016 opening keynote. *Teaching & Learning Inquiry*, 5(1), 1–8. https://doi.org/10.20343/teachlearninqu.5.1.13.

Manarin, K. (2018). Close reading: Paying attention to student artifacts. In N. L. Chick (Ed.), *SoTL in action: Illuminating critical moments of practice* (pp. 100–108). Stylus.

Manarin, K., & Abrahamson, E. (2016) Troublesome knowledge of SoTL. *International Journal for the Scholarship of Teaching and Learning*, 10(2), Article 2. https://doi.org/10.20429/ijsotl.2016.100202.

Manarin, K., Adams, C., Fendler, R., Marsh, H., Pohl, E., Porath, S., & Thomas, A. (2021). Examining the focus of SoTL literature—teaching and learning? *Teaching and Learning Inquiry*, 9(1), 349–364. https://doi.org/10.20343/teachlearninqu.9.1.23.

Manarin, K., Carey, M., Rathburn, M., & Ryland, G. (2015). *Critical reading in higher education: Academic goals and social engagement.* Indiana University Press.

Marchand, H. (2012). Contributions of Piagetian and post-Piagetian theories to education. *Educational Research Review*, 7(3), 165–176. https://doi.org/10.1016/j.edurev.2012.04.002.

Margolis, E., & Zunjarwad, R. (2018). Visual research. In N. K. Denzin & Y. S. Lincoln (Eds.), *The Sage handbook of qualitative research* (5th ed.) (pp. 600–626). Sage.

Marquis, E., Guitman, R., Nguyen, E. & Woolmer, C. (2021). "It's a little complicated for me": Faculty social location and experiences of pedagogical partnership. *Higher Education Research & Development*, 40(6), 1191–1204. https://doi.org/10.1080/07294360.2020.1806789.

Marsh, H. W., & Roche, L. A. (2000). Effects of grading leniency and low workload of students' evaluations of teaching: Popular myth, bias, validity, or innocent bystanders? *Journal of Educational Psychology*, 92, 202–228. https://doi.org/10.1037/0022-0663.92.1.202.

Martin, E., & Ramsden, P. (2000). The scholarship of teaching [Special issue]. *Higher Education Research and Development*, 19(2).

Martin, R. C. (2013). Navigating the IRB: The ethics of SoTL. *New Directions in Teaching and Learning*, 136, 59–71. https://doi.org/10.1002/tl.20076.

Marton, F. (1986). Phenomenography—a research approach to investigating different understandings of reality. *Journal of Thought*, 21(3), 28–49. https://www.jstor.org/stable/42589189.

Maslow, A. (1970). *Motivation and personality* (2nd ed.). Harper and Row.

Maurer, T. W. (2018). Methods and measures matter: Meaningful questionnaires. In N. L. Chick (Ed.), *SoTL in action: Illuminating critical moments of practice* (pp. 71–81). Stylus.

Maurer, T. W., Woolmer, C., Powell, N. L., Sisson, C., Snelling, C., Stalheim, O. R., & Turner, I. J. (2021). Sharing SoTL findings with students: An intentional knowledge mobilization strategy. *Teaching and Learning Inquiry*, 9(1), 333–348. https://doi.org/10.20343/teachlearninqu.9.1.22.

Mayers, M. (2001). *Street kids & streetscapes: Panhandling, politics, and prophecies.* Peter Lang Publishers.

Mayring, P. (2000). Qualitative content analysis. *FQS Forum*, 1(2), Article 20. https://doi.org/10.17169/fqs-1.2.1089.

McCarthy, K. S., & McNamara, D. S. (2021). The multidimensional knowledge in text comprehension framework. *Educational Psychologist*, 56(3), 196–214. https://doi.org/10.1080/00461520.2021.1872379.

McCollum, B., Sepulveda, A., & Moreno, Y. (2016). Representational technologies and learner problem-solving strategies in chemistry. *Teaching and Learning Inquiry*, 4(2), 105–121. https://doi.org/10.20343/teachlearninqu.4.2.10.

McConnell, C., Marquis, E., & Mercer-Mapstone, L. (2017, November 6). #Collaborative auto-ethnography: SoTL methods series #2. https://illinoisstateuniversitysotl.wordpress.com/2017/11/06/collaborative-auto-ethnography-sotl-methods-series-2/.

McGrath, A. (2014). Just checking in: The effect of an office hour meeting and learning reflection in an introductory statistics course. *Teaching Psychology*, 41(1), 83–87. https://doi.org/10.1177/0098628313514186.

McGregor, D., Restoule, J. P., & Johnston, R. (Eds.) (2018). *Indigenous research: Theories, practices, and relationships.* Canadian Scholars.

McKinney, K. (2004). The Scholarship of Teaching and Learning: Past lessons, current challenges, and future visions. *To Improve the Academy*, 22(1), 3–19. https://doi.org/10.1002/j.2334-4822.2004.tb00399.x.

McKinney, K. (2007). *Enhancing learning through the Scholarship of Teaching and Learning: The challenges and joys of juggling.* Jossey-Bass

McKinney, K. (2012). Increasing the impact of SoTL: Two sometimes neglected opportunities. *International Journal for the Scholarship of Teaching and Learning*, 6(1), Article 3.

McKinney, K. (Ed.) (2013). *The Scholarship of Teaching and Learning in and across the disciplines.* Indiana University Press.

McKinney, K. (2014, November 3). The "big tent": Benefits and limitations. *The SoTL Advocate.* https://illinoisstateuniversitysotl.wordpress.com/2014/11/03/the-big-tent-benefits-and-limitation/.

McLeod, A., Savage, A., & Simkin, M. G. (2018). The ethics of predatory journals. *Journal of Business Ethics*, 153(1), 121–131. https://doi.org/10.1007/s10551-016-3419-9.

Meade, A. W., & Craig, S. B. (2012). Identifying careless responses in survey data. *Psychological Methods*, 17(3), 437. https://doi.org/10.1037/a0028085.

Merleau-Ponty, M. (1945). *The phenomenology of perception*. Routledge and Kegan Paul.

Merriam, S. B., Caffarella, R. S., & Baumgartner, L. M. (2006). *Learning in adulthood: A comprehensive guide*. John Wiley & Sons.

Merriam, S. B., & Tisdell, E. J. (2016). *Qualitative research: A guide to design and implementation*. Jossey-Bass.

Meyer, J. H. F., & Land, R. (2005). Threshold concepts and troublesome knowledge (2): Epistemological considerations and a conceptual framework for teaching and learning. *Higher Education*, 49(3), 373–388. https://doi.org/10.1007/s10734-004-6779-5.

Mezirow, J. (1991). *Transformative dimensions of adult learning*. Jossey-Bass.

Middendorf, J., & Pace, D. (2004). Decoding the disciplines: A model for helping students learn disciplinary ways of thinking. In D. Pace & J. Middendorf (Eds.), *New directions of teaching and learning, 98. Decoding the disciplines: A model for helping students learn disciplinary ways of thinking* (pp. 1–12). Jossey-Bass.

Middendorf, J., & Shopkow, L. (2018). *Overcoming student learning bottlenecks: Decode the critical thinking of your discipline*. Stylus.

Miles, M. B., Huberman, A. M., & Saldaña, J. (2014). *Qualitative data analysis: A methods sourcebook*. Sage.

Miller-Young, J. (2013). Calculations and expectations: How engineering students describe three-dimensional forces. *The Canadian Journal for the Scholarship of Teaching and Learning*, 4(1), Article 4. http://dx.doi.org/10.5206/cjsotl-rcacea.2013.1.4.

Miller-Young, J. (2018). Conducting interviews: Capturing what is unobserved. In N. L. Chick (Ed.), *SoTL in action: Illuminating critical moments of practice* (pp. 92–99). Stylus.

Miller-Young, J. E., Anderson, C., Kiceniuk, D., Mooney, J., Riddell, J., Schmidt Hanbidge, A., Ward, V., Wideman, M. A., & Chick, N. L. (2017). Leading up in the Scholarship of Teaching and Learning. *Canadian Journal for the Scholarship of Teaching and Learning*, 8(2). https://doi-org/10.5206/cjsotl-rcacea.2017.2.4.

Miller-Young, J., Beck, S., & Jamieson, M. (2021a). Gamifying and evaluating first-year design: Development of a questionnaire to assess student experience and motivation in a large, online course. *Proceedings of the Canadian Engineering Education Association (CEEA)*. https://doi.org/10.24908/pceea.vi0.14828.

Miller-Young, J., Jamieson, M., & Beck, S. (2023). Diverse experiences and belonging in an online, first-year, team-based engineering design course. *Teaching in Higher Education*, 1–17. https://doi.org/10.1080/13562517.2022.2162816.

Miller-Young, J., Marin, L. F., Poth, C., Vargas-Madriz, L. F., & Xiao, J. (2021b). The development and psychometric properties of an educational development impact questionnaire. *Studies in Educational Evaluation*, 70, 101058. https://doi.org/10.1016/j.stueduc.2021.101058.

Miller-Young, J., & Poth, C. N. (2021). "Complexifying" our approach to evaluating educational development outcomes: Bridging theoretical innovations with frontline practice. *International Journal for Academic Development*, 1–14. https://doi.org/10.1080/1360144X.2021.1887876.

Miller-Young, J., & Yeo, M. (2015). Conceptualizing and communicating SoTL: A framework for the field. *Teaching & Learning Inquiry*, 3(2), 37–53. https://doi.org/10.20343/teachlearninqu.3.2.37.

Miller-Young, J., Yeo, M., & Manarin, K. (2018). Challenges to disciplinary knowing and identity: Experiences of scholars in a SoTL development program. *International Journal for the Scholarship of Teaching and Learning*, 12(1), Article 3. https://doi.org/10.20429/ijsotl.2018.120103.

Miller-Young, J., Yeo, M., & Manarin, K. (2023). Navigating boundary experiences in SoTL: Pinch points, paradigms and perspectives. In J. Miller-Young & N. L. Chick (Eds.), *Becoming a SoTL Scholar*. Elon University Press.

Miller-Young, J., Yeo, M., Manarin, K., Carey, M., & Zimmer, J. (2016). $SoTL^2$: Inquiring into the impact of inquiry. *The Scholarship of Teaching and Learning in Canada: Institutional Impact. New Directions for Teaching and Learning*, 146, 55–62. https://doi.org/10.1002/tl.20187.

Mingers, J. (2014). *Systems thinking, critical realism and philosophy: A confluence of ideas*. Routledge.

Molesworth, M., Nixon, E., & Scullion, R. (2009). Having, being and higher education: The marketisation of the university and the transformation of the student into consumer. *Teaching in Higher Education*, 14(3), 277–287. doi:10.1080/13562510902898841.

Mollett, A., Brumley, C., Gilson, C., & Williams, S. (2017). *Communicating your research with social media: A practical guide to using blogs, podcasts, data visualisations and video*. Sage.

Montgomery, D. (2012). *Helping teachers develop through classroom observation* (2nd ed.). Routledge.

Moore, J. L. (2018). Writing SoTL: Going public for an extended audience. In N. L. Chick & J. Rhem (Eds.), *SoTL in action: Illuminating critical moments of practice* (pp. 119–126). Stylus.

Moore, J., Hamshire, C., & Felten, P. (2022). *Social media and public SoTL*. In N. L. Chick & J. C. Friberg (Eds.), *Going public reconsidered: Engaging with the world beyond academe through the scholarship of teaching and learning*. Stylus.

Moran, D. (2000). *Introduction to phenomenology*. Routledge.

Moran, D. (2002). Editor's introduction. In D. Moran & T. Mooney (Eds.), *The phenomenology reader* (pp. 1–26). Routledge.

Moreton-Robinson, E. (2013). Towards an Australian Indigenous women's standpoint theory: A methodological tool. *Australian Feminist Studies*, 28(78), 331–347. https://doi.org/10.1080/08164649.2013.876664.

Morgan, D. L. (1997). *Focus groups as qualitative research*. Sage. https://dx.doi.org/10.4135/9781412984287.

Morgan, D. L. (2007). Paradigms lost and pragmatism regained. Methodological implications of combining qualitative and quantitative methods. *Journal of Mixed Methods Research*, 1, 48–76. https://doi.org/10.1177/2345678906292462.

Morrison, C. D. (2014). From "sage on the stage" to "guide on the side": A good start. *International Journal for the Scholarship of Teaching and Learning*, 8(1), Article4. https://doi.org/10.20429/ijsotl.2014.080104.

Muecke, M. A. (1994). *On the evaluation of ethnographies.* In J. M. Morse (Ed.), *Critical issues in qualitative research methods* (pp. 187–209). Sage.

Naested, I., Potvin, B., & Waldron, P. (2004). *Understanding the landscape of teaching.* Pearson Prentice Hall.

Nash, R. (2019) *Liberating scholarly writing: The power of personal narrative.* Information Age Publishing.

Nathan, R. [Small, C.]. (2005). *My freshman year: What a professor learned by becoming a student.* Cornell University Press.

Neuendorf, K. (2017). *The content analysis guidebook* (2nd ed.). Sage. https://dx.doi.org/10.4135/9781071802878.

Ng, L., & Carney, M. (2017). Scholarly personal narrative in the SoTL tent. *Teaching and Learning Inquiry*, 5(1), 133–145. https://doi.org/10.20343/teachlearninqu.5.1.10.

NIH. (2014). Frequently asked questions about the NIH public access policy. https://publicaccess.nih.gov/faq.htm#753.

Norton, L. S. (2009). *Action research in teaching and learning: A practical guide to conducting pedagogical research in universities.* Routledge.

Nowell, L., & Friberg, J. C. (2022). *SoTL and knowledge translation.* In N. L. Chick & J. C. Friberg (Eds.), *Going public reconsidered: Engaging with the world beyond academe through the scholarship of teaching and learning.* Stylus.

Nowell, L. S., Norris, J. M., White, D. E., & Moules, N. J. (2017). Thematic analysis: Striving to meet the trustworthiness criteria. *International Journal of Qualitative Methods*, 16(1). https://doi.org/10.1177/1609406917733847.

O'Connor, C. (2015). A practice-led approach to aligning learning theories with learning and teaching strategies in third level chemistry education. *Irish Journal of Academic Practice.* 4(1), Article 7. https://doi.org/doi:10.21427/D7B42F.

O'Meara, K., Terosky, A. L., & Neumann, A. (2008). Faculty careers and work lives: A professional growth perspective. *ASHE Higher Education Report*, 34(3), 1–221.

Onwuegbuzie, A. J., & Daniel, L. G. (2003). Typology of analytical and interpretational errors in quantitative and qualitative educational research. *Current issues in Education*, 6.

Ossa Parra, M., Gutiérrez, R., & Aldana, M. F. (2015). Engaging in critically reflective teaching: From theory to practice in pursuit of transformative learning. *Reflective Practice*, 16(1), 16–30. https://doi.org/10.1080/14623943.2014.944141.

Padilla, J. L., & Benítez, I. (2014). Validity evidence based on response processes. *Psicothema*, 26(1), 136–144. https://doi.org/10.7334/psicothema2013.259.

Pathak, A. A. (2010). Opening my voice, claiming my space: Theorizing the possibilities of postcolonial approaches to autoethnography. *Journal of Research Practice*, 6(1).

Patton, M. Q. (2002). *Qualitative research & evaluation methods* (3rd ed.). Sage.

Pecorari, D. (2021). Predatory conferences: What are the signs? *Journal of Academic Ethics*, 19, 343–361. https://doi.org/10.1007/s10805-021-09406-4.

Percy, W. H., Kostere, K., & Kostere, S. (2015). Generic qualitative research in psychology. *The Qualitative Report*, 20(2), 76–85. https://doi.org/10.46743/2160-3715/2015.2097.

Pete, S., Schneider, B., & O'Reilly, K. (2013). Decolonizing our practice—indigenizing our teaching. *First Nations Perspectives*, 5(1), 99–115.

Philips, D. (1990). Positivistic science: Myths and realities. In E. Guba (Ed.), *The paradigm dialog* (pp. 81–96). Free Press.

Phipps, D. J., Cummings, J., Pepler, D., Craig, W., & Cardinal, S. (2016). The co-produced pathway to impact describes knowledge mobilization processes. *Journal of Community Engagement and Scholarship*, 9(1), 31–40.

Pinnegar, S. & Daynes, J. G. (2007). Locating narrative inquiry historically: Thematics in the turn to narrative. In D. J. Clandinin (Ed.), *Handbook of narrative inquiry: Mapping a methodology* (pp. 3–34). Sage.

Piwowar, H., Priem, J., Larivière, V., Alperin, J. P., Matthias, L., Norlander, B., Farley, A., West, J., & Haustein, S. (2018). The state of OA: A large-scale analysis of the prevalence and impact of Open Access articles. *Peer J*, 6, e4375. https://doi.org/10.7717/peerj.4375.

Plano Clark, V. L., Garrett, A. L., & Leslie-Pelecky, D. L. (2010). Applying three strategies for integrating quantitative and qualitative databases in a mixed methods study of a nontraditional graduate education program. *Field Methods*, 22(2), 154–174. https://doi.org/10.1177/1525822X09357174.

Podsakoff, P. M., MacKenzie, S. B., Lee, J. Y., & Podsakoff, N. P. (2003). Common method biases in behavioral research: A critical review of the literature and recommended remedies. *Journal of Applied Psychology*, 88(5), 879. https://doi.org/10.1037/0021-9010.88.5.879.

Poole, G. (2013). Square one: What is research? In K. McKinney (Ed.), *The Scholarship of Teaching and Learning in and across the disciplines* (pp.135–151). Indiana University Press.

Poole, G. (2018). Using intuition, anecdote, and observation. In N. L. Chick (Ed.), *SoTL in action: Illuminating critical moments of practice* (pp. 7–14). Stylus.

Poole, G., & Simmons, N. (2013). Contributions of the scholarship of teaching and learning to quality enhancement in Canada. *Enhancing Quality in Higher Education* (pp. 118–128). Routledge.

Poth, C. (2014). What constitutes effective learning experiences in a mixed methods research course? An examination from the student perspective. *International Journal of Multiple Research Approaches*, 8(1), 74–86. https://doi.org/10.5172/mra.2014.8.1.74.

Potter, M. K., & Kustra, E. D. H. (2011). The relationship between scholarly teaching and SoTL: Models, distinctions, and clarifications. *International Journal for the Scholarship of Teaching and Learning*, 5(1), Article 23. https://doi.org/10.20429/ijsotl.2011.050123.

Qu, S. Q., & Dumay, J. (2011). The qualitative research interview. *Qualitative Research in Accounting and Management*, 8(3), 238–264. https://doi.org/10.1108/11766091111162070.

Reed-Danahay, D. (2009). Anthropologists, education, and autoethnography. *Reviews in Anthropology*, 38(1), 28–47. https://doi.org/10.1080/00938150802672931.

Reichard, D. A., & Takayama, K. (2013). Exploring student learning in unfamiliar territory: A humanist and a scientist compare notes. In K. McKinney (Ed.), *The Scholarship of Teaching and Learning in and across the disciplines* (pp. 169–185). Indiana University Press.

Resnik, D. B. (2022) Research ethics timeline. https://www.niehs.nih.gov/research/resources/bioethics/timeline/index.cfm.

Richlin, L., & Cox, M. D. (2004). Developing scholarly teaching and the Scholarship of Teaching and Learning through faculty learning communities. *New Directions for Teaching and Learning*, 97, 127–135. https://doi.org/10.1002/tl.139.

Robbins, C. K. (2016). White women, racial identity, and learning about racism in graduate preparation programs. *Journal of Student Affairs Research and Practice*, 53(2), 256–268. http://dx.doi:10.1080/19496591.2016.1143834.

Roberts, C., & Hyatt, L. (2018). *Dissertation journey: A practical comprehensive guide to planning, writing, and defending your dissertation* (3rd ed.). Corwin.

Robinson, J. M. (2018). *The SoTL conference: Learning while professing.* In N. L. Chick (Ed.), *SoTL in action: Illuminating critical moments of practice* (pp. 143–150). Stylus.

Rock, P. (2001). Symbolic interactionism and ethnography. In P. Atkinson, A. Coffey, S. Delamont, J. Lofland, & L. Lofland (Eds.), *Handbook of ethnography* (pp. 26–38). Sage.

Rolfe, G. (2014). Reach, touch and teach: Terry Borton. *Nurse Education Today*, 34 (4), 488–489. https://doi.org/10.1016/j.nedt.2013.11.003.

Rolfe, G., Freshwater, D., & Jasper, M. (2001) *Critical reflection for nurses and the caring professions: A user's guide.* Palgrave.

Roxå, T., & Mårtensson, K. (2009). Significant conversations and significant networks—exploring the backstage of the teaching arena. *Studies in Higher Education*, 34(5), 547–559. https://doi.org/10.1080/03075070802597200.

Roxå, T., & Mårtensson, K. (2012). How effects from teacher training of academic teachers propagate into the meso level and beyond. In E. Simon & G. Pleschova (Eds.), *Teacher development in higher education: Existing programs, program impact, and future trends* (pp. 213–233). Routledge.

Russell-Mundine, G. (2012). Reflexivity in Indigenous research: Reframing and decolonising research. *Journal of Hospitality and Tourism Management*, 19, 44–49. https://doi.org/10.3316/informit.891335054846604.

Ryan, R. M., & Deci, E. L. (2000). Self-determination theory and the facilitation of intrinsic motivation, social development, and well-being. *American Psychologist*, 55 (1), 68. https://doi.org/10.1037/0003-066X.55.1.68.

Ryan, R. M., & Deci, E. L. (2020). Intrinsic and extrinsic motivation from a self-determination theory perspective: Definitions, theory, practices, and future directions. *Contemporary Educational Psychology*, 61, 101860.

Saldana, J. (2011). *Fundamentals of qualitative research.* Oxford University Press.

Saldana, J. (2016). *The coding manual for qualitative researchers.* Sage.

Salmons, J. (2016). *Doing qualitative research online.* Sage.

Samaras, A. P., & Freese, A. R. (2009). Looking back and looking forward: An historical overview of the self-study school. In C. A. Lassonde, S. Galman, & C. Kosnik (Eds.), *Self-study research methodologies for teacher educators* (pp. 3–20). Sense Publishers.

Santos, L., & Cheeseman, J. (2019). *The active learning initiative: Supporting teaching in the ALC and beyond.* Presented at the International Forum on Active Learning Classrooms. August 7–9, 2019, Minneapolis, USA.

Saunders, B., Sim, J., Kingstone, T., Baker, S., Waterfield, J., Bartlam, B., Burroughs, H., & Jinks, C. (2018). Saturation in qualitative research: Exploring its conceptualization and operationalization. *Quality & quantity*, 52(4), 1893–1907. https://doi.org/10.1007/s11135-017-0574-8.

Schön, D. (1984). *The reflective practitioner: How professionals think in action.* Basic.

Schönwetter, D. J., Gareau-Wilson, N., Sanches, R., Cunha, D. D. S., & Mello, I. (2016). Assessing the impact of voice-over screen-captured presentations delivered online on dental students' learning. *Journal of Dental Education*, 80(2). https://doi.org/10.1002/j.0022-0337.2016.80.2.tb06069.x.

Schwandt, T. A. (1998). The interpretive review of educational matters: Is there any other kind? *Review of Educational Research*, 68, 409–412.

Schwier, R. (Host). (2020, May 19). Situating SoTL research in the 4M Framework with Nicola Simmons [Audio podcast episode]. In *SoTL Chat*. University of Saskatchewan. https://sotl-uofs.libsyn.com/situating-sotl-research-in-the-4m-framework-with-nicola-simmons.

Secolsky, C., & Denison, D. B. (Eds.) (2017). *Handbook on measurement, assessment, and evaluation in higher education*. Routledge.

Shabot, S. C., & Landry, C. (Eds.) (2018). *Rethinking feminist phenomenology: Theoretical and applied perspectives*. Rowman & Littlefield.

Shulman, L. S. (1993). Teaching as community property. *Change*, 25(6), 6–7. https://doi.org/10.1080/00091383.1993.9938465.

Shulman, L. S. (2000). From Minsk to Pinsk: Why a scholarship of teaching and learning? *Journal of Scholarship in Teaching and Learning*, 1(1), 48–53. https://scholarworks.iu.edu/journals/index.php/josotl/article/view/1582.

Shulman, L. S. (2005). Signature pedagogies in the professions. *Daedalus*, 134(3), 52–59. https://doi.org/10.1162/0011526054622015.

Simmons, N. (Ed.). (2016). *The scholarship of teaching and learning in Canada: Institutional impact. New directions for teaching and learning, 146*. Jossey-Bass.

Simpson, L. (2014). Land as pedagogy: Nishnabeeg intelligence and rebellious transformation. *Decolonization: Indigeneity, Education & Society*, 3(3), 1–25.

Smith, D. (1991). Hermeneutic inquiry: The hermeneutic imagination and the pedagogic text. In E. C. Short (Ed.), *Forms of curriculum inquiry* (pp. 187–207). State University of New York Press.

Smith, S. J. (1993). Physically remembering childhood. In B. Levering, S. Miedema, & A. Oberg (Eds.), *Reflections on pedagogy and method* (Volume III, pp. 161–182). Uriah Heep.

Snijders, I., Wijnia, L., Dekker, H. J. J., Rikers, R. M. J. P., & Loyens, S. M. M. (2021). What is in a student-faculty relationship? A template analysis of students' positive and negative critical incidents with faculty and staff in higher education. *European Journal of Psychology of Education*. https://doi.org/10.1007/s10212-021-00549-x.

Sollaci, L. B., & Pereira, M. G. (2004). The introduction, methods, results, and discussion (IMRAD) structure: A fifty-year survey. *Journal of the Medical Library Association: JMLA*, 92(3), 364–367.

St. Pierre, E., & Jackson, A. Y. (2014). Qualitative data analysis after coding. *Qualitative Inquiry*, 20(6), 715–719. https://doi.org/10.1177/1077800414532435.

Stanlick, S. (2011, October 12). Debating the question question. Qualitative Research Series. Research Salad. https://researchsalad.wordpress.com/2011/10/12/qualitative-research-series-debating-the-question-question/.

Steiner, H. H., & Hakala, C. M. (2021). What do SoTL practitioners need to know about learning? *Teaching and Learning Inquiry*, 9(1), 79–85. https://doi.org/10.20343/teachlearninqu.9.1.7.

Stewart, M. (2021). Understanding learning: Theories and critique. In L. Hunt & D. Chalmers (Eds.), *University teaching in focus: A learning-centred approach* (2nd ed.) (pp. 3–28). Taylor & Francis Group.

Stockley, D., & Balkwill, L. (2013). Raising awareness of research ethics in SoTL: The role of educational developers. *The Canadian Journal for the Scholarship of Teaching and Learning*, 4(1). https://doi.org/10.5206/cjsotl-rcacea.2013.1.7.

Strawser, M. (2009). Assessing assessment: Toward a hermeneutic-phenomenological perspective. *InSight: A Journal of Scholarly Teaching*, 4, 56–68.

Streveler, R. A., Litzinger, T. A., Miller, R. L., & Steif, P. S. (2008). Learning conceptual knowledge in the engineering sciences: Overview and future research directions. *Journal of Engineering Education*, 97(3), 279–294. https://doi.org/10.1002/j.2168-9830.2008.tb00979.x.

Suber, P. (2012). *Open access*. The MIT Press. https://library.oapen.org/handle/20.500.12657/26065.

Suskie, L. (2018). *Assessing student learning: A common sense guide*. John Wiley & Sons.

Swales, J. (1990). *Genre analysis: English in academic and research settings*. Cambridge University Press.

Swales, J. (2017). The concept of discourse community: Some recent personal history. *Composition Forum*, 37. https://compositionforum.com/issue/37/swales-retrospective.php.

Sword, H. (2012). *Stylish academic writing*. Harvard University Press.

Sword, H. (2017). *Air & light & time & space: How successful academics write*. Harvard University Press.

Sword, H. (2019). The first person. *Teaching and Learning Inquiry*, 7(1), 182–190. https://doi.org/10.20343/teachlearninqu.7.1.12.

Teaching Dimensions Observation Protocol. (2015). http://tdop.wceruw.org/.

Timans, R., Wouters, P., & Heilbron, J. (2019). Mixed methods research: What it is and what it could be. *Theory and Society*, 48(2), 193–216. https://doi.org/10.1007/s11186-019-09345-5.

Timmermans, J. A., & Ellis, D. E. (2016). Reconceptualizing the Scholarship of Teaching and Learning at the University of Waterloo: An account of influences and impact. *The Scholarship of Teaching and Learning in Canada: Institutional Impact: New Directions for Teaching and Learning*, 146, 71–78. https://doi.org/10.1002/tl.20189.

Tobin, T. (2021, September 20). How to make the most of an academic conference: Advice on navigating professional meetings in all formats—in person, virtual, and hybrid. *Chronicle of Higher Education*. https://www.chronicle.com/article/how-to-make-the-most-of-an-academic-conference.

Tourangeau, R., Rips, L. J., & Rasinski, K. (2000). *The psychology of survey response*. Cambridge University Press.

Tracy, S. J. (2010). Qualitative quality: Eight "big-tent" criteria for excellent qualitative research. *Qualitative Inquiry*, 16(10), 837–851. https://doi.org/10.1177/1077800410383121.

Tri-Agency Open Access Policy on Publications. (2016). https://www.ic.gc.ca/eic/site/063.nsf/eng/h_F6765465.html.

Tri-Council Policy Statement. (2018). Ethical conduct for research concerning humans TCPS2. https://ethics.gc.ca/eng/policy-politique_tcps2-eptc2_2018.html.

Trigwell, K. (2021). Scholarship of teaching and learning. In L. Hunt, & D. Chalmers (Eds.), *University teaching in focus: A learning-centred approach* (2nd ed.) (pp. 286–303). Taylor & Francis Group.

Truth and Reconciliation Canada. (2015) *Honouring the truth, reconciling for the future: Summary of the final report of the Truth and Reconciliation Commission of Canada*. Truth and Reconciliation Commission of Canada.

Tuck, E., McKenzie, M., & McCoy, K. (2014). Land education: Indigenous, post-colonial, and decolonizing perspectives on place and environmental education research. *Environmental Education Research*, 20(1), 1–23. https://doi.org/10.1080/13504622.2013.877708.

Vaismoradi, M., Turunen, H., & Bondas, T. (2013). Content analysis and thematic analysis: Implications for conducting a qualitative descriptive study. *Nursing & Health Sciences*, 15(3), 398–405. https://doi.org/10.1111/nhs.12048.

Vander Kloet, M., Frake-Mistak, M., McGinn, M. K., Caldecott, M., Aspenlieder, E. D., Beres, J. L., Fukuzawa, S., Cassidy, A., & Gill, A. (2017). Conditions for contingent instructors engaged in the Scholarship of Teaching and Learning. *The Canadian Journal for the Scholarship of Teaching and Learning*, 8(2). https://doi.org/10.5206/cjsotl-rcacea.2017.2.9.

Van der Zalm, J., & Bergum, V. (2000). Hermeneutic phenomenology: Providing living knowledge for nursing practice. *Journal for Advanced Nursing*, 31(1), 211–218.

Van Manen, M. (2014). *Phenomenology of practice: Meaning giving methods in phenomenological research and writing*. Left Coast Press.

Verdinelli, S., & Scagnoli, N. I. (2013). Data display in qualitative research. *International Journal of Qualitative Methods*, 12(1), 359–381. https://doi.org/10.1177/160940691301200117.

Verwoord, R., & Poole, G. (2016). The role of small significant networks and leadership in the institutional embedding of SoTL. *The Scholarship of Teaching and Learning in Canada: Institutional Impact: New Directions for Teaching and Learning*, 146, 79–86. https://doi.org/10.1002/tl.20190.

von der Heidt, T. (2015). Concept maps for assessing change in learning: A study of undergraduate business students in first-year marketing in China. *Assessment & Evaluation in Higher Education*, 40(2), 286–308.

Watson, E., Marin, L. F., White, L. N., Macciota, R., & Lefsrud, L. M. (2020). Blended learning in an upper year engineering course: The relationship between students' program year, interactions with online material, and academic performance. *Canadian Journal for the Scholarship of Teaching and Learning*, 11(3), n3. https://doi.org/10.5206/cjsotl-rcacea.2020.3.8270.

Watson, M. K., Pelkey, J., Noyes, C. R., & Rodgers, M. O. (2016). Assessing conceptual knowledge using three concept map scoring methods. *Journal of Engineering Education*, 105(1), 118–146. https://doi.org/10.1002/jee.20111.

Webb, A. (2015). Research interviews in the scholarship of teaching and learning. *Transformative Dialogues: Teaching and Learning Journal*, 8(1). https://td.journals.psu.edu/td/article/view/1181.

Webb, A. S. (2019). Navigating the lows to gain new heights: Constraints to SoTL engagement. *The Canadian Journal for the Scholarship of Teaching and Learning*, 10(2). https://doi.org/10.5206/cjsotl-rcacea.2019.2.8173.

Weimer, M. (2006). *Enhancing scholarly work on teaching and learning: Professional literature that makes a difference*. Jossey-Bass.

Weimer, M. (2008). Positioning scholarly work on teaching and learning. *International Journal for the Scholarship of Teaching and Learning*, 2(1), Article 4. https://doi.org/10.20429/ijsotl.2008.020104.

White, M., & Marsh, E. (2006). Content analysis: A flexible methodology. *Library Trends*, 55(1), 22–45. https://doi.org/10.1353/lib.2006.0053.

Williams, A. L., Verwoord, R., Beery, T. A., Dalton, H., McKinnon, J., Strickland, K., Pace, J., & Poole, G. (2013). The power of social networks: A model for weaving the Scholarship of Teaching and Learning into institutional culture. *Teaching and Learning Inquiry*, 1(2), 49–62. https://doi.org/10.20343/teachlearninqu.1.2.49.

Wilson, D. D., & Restoule, J. P. (2010). Tobacco ties: The relationship of the sacred to research. *Canadian Journal of Native Education*, 33(1), 29–45.

Wilson, S. (2008). *Research is ceremony: Indigenous research methods*. Fernwood.

Wilson, S., & Hughes, M. (2019). Why research is reconciliation. In S. Wilson, A. V. Breen, & L. Dupree (Eds.), *Research and reconciliation: Unsettling ways of knowing through Indigenous relationships* (pp. 1–19). Canadian Scholars.

Wilson, S., & Shellhammer, B. (2022). *Indigegogy: An invitation to learning in a relational way*. WBG Academic.

Wilson-doenges, G., & Gurung, R. A. R. (2013). Benchmarks for scholarly investigations of teaching and learning. *Australian Journal of Psychology*, 65(1), 63–70. https://doi.org/10.1111/ajpy.12011.

Wittgenstein, L. (1953). *Philosophical investigations*. Blackwell Publishing.

Wolfe, P. (2006). Settler colonialism and the elimination of the Native. *Journal of Genocide Research*, 8(4), 387–409. doi:10.1080/14623520601056240.

Woolmer, C. (n.d.). SoTL as co-inquiry with students: Opportunities for partnership? Worksheet on Mokakiiks Centre for SoTL website. https://drive.google.com/file/d/1XezA02b7EiMZgdMiV1mbs6G21J0gl-r8/view.

Woolmer, C., Marquis, E., Aspenlieder, E., & Goff, L. (2020). Student partnerships in higher education. In S. Marshall (Ed.), *Handbook on teaching and learning: Enhancing academic practice* (5th ed.) (pp. 81–94). Routledge.

Wuetherick, B., & Yu, S. (2016). The Canadian teaching commons: The Scholarship of Teaching and Learning in Canadian higher education. *New Directions for Teaching and Learning*, 146, 23–30.

Yeo, M., Bennett, D., McNichol, J. S., & Merkley, C. (2015). New faculty experience in times of change. *Canadian Journal of Higher Education*, 45(4), 283–297. https://doi.org/10.47678/cjhe.v45i4.184576.

Yeo, M., & Boman, J. (2017). Disciplinary approaches to assessment. *Journal of Further and Higher Education*, 43(4), 482–493. https://doi.org/10.1080/0309877X.2017.1367371.

Yeo, M., Manarin, K., & Miller-Young, J. (2018). Phenomenology of surprise in a SoTL scholars' program. *Teaching and Learning Inquiry*, 6(2), 16–28. https://doi.org/10.20343/teachlearninqu.6.2.3.

Yeo, M. & Woolmer, C. (2022). Wrestling the monster: Novice SoTL researchers, ethics, and the dual role. In L. Fedoruck (Ed.), *Ethics and the Scholarship of Teaching and Learning*. Springer, pp. 29–42.

Yin, R. (1994). *Case study research, design and methods* (2nd ed.). Sage.

INDEX

Note: **Bold** indicates a table and *italic* indicates a figure.

Made in United States
Troutdale, OR
06/12/2024

20507285R00166